BATMAN

ARKHAM UNHINGED

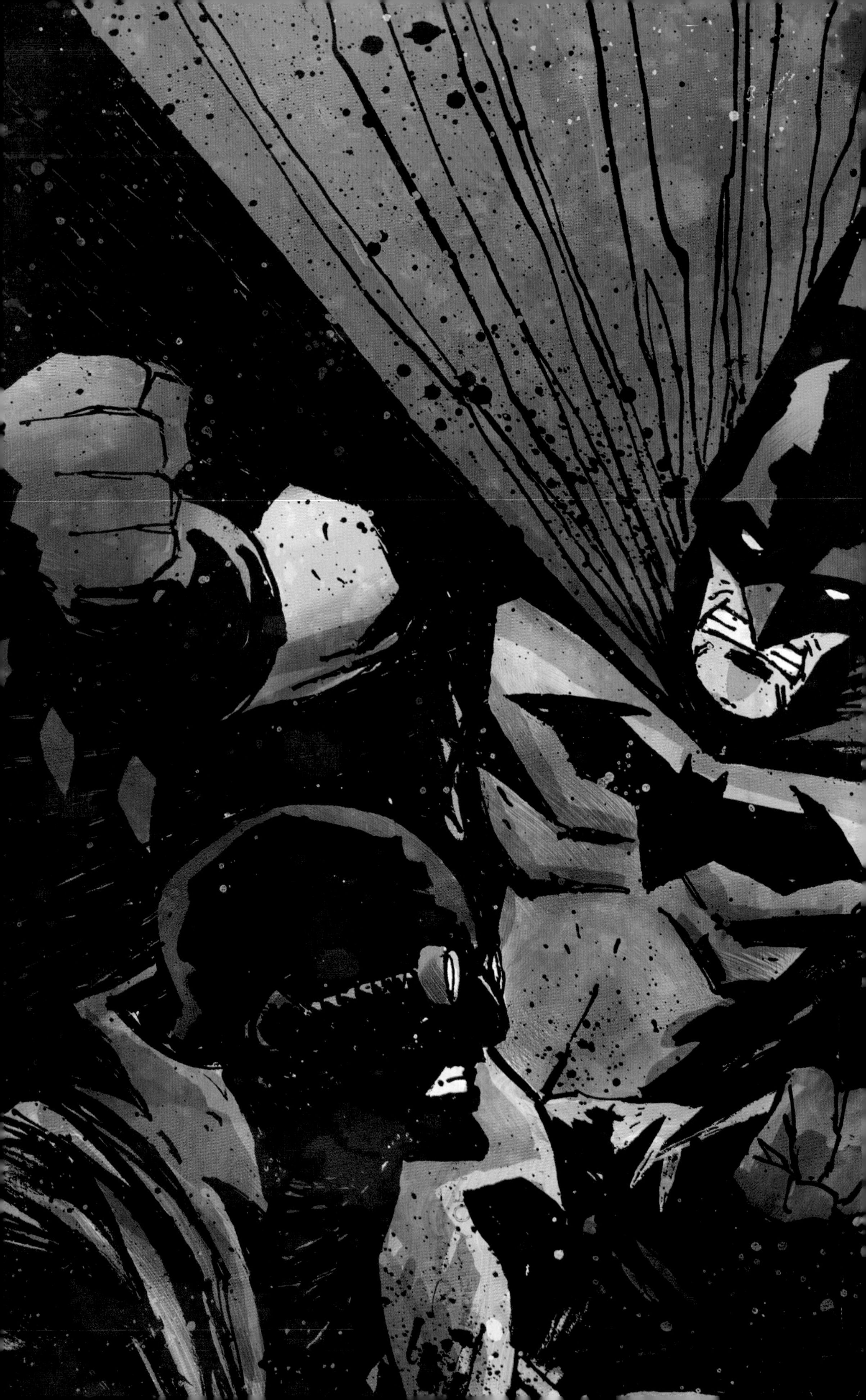

KAREN TRAVISS writer

CHRISTIAN DUCE RICCARDO BURCHIELLI
FEDERICO DALLOCCHIO TONY SHASTEEN
BEN LOBEL artists

ALEJANDRO SANCHEZ
ALLEN PASSALAQUA colorists

TRAVIS LANHAM letterer

CHRIS MITTEN collection cover artist

BATMAN CREATED BY BOB KANE

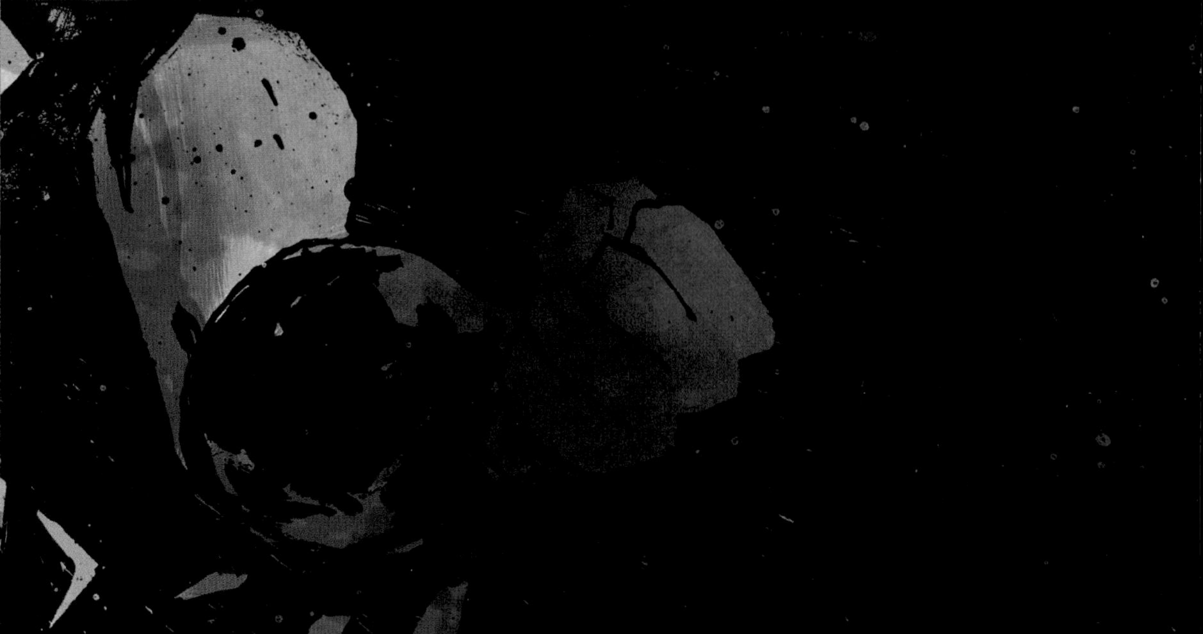

Jim Chadwick Editor – Original Series
Sarah Gaydos Assistant Editor – Original Series
Robin Wildman Editor
Robbin Brosterman Design Director – Books
Louis Prandi Publication Design

Hank Kanalz Senior VP – Vertigo & Integrated Publishing

Diane Nelson President
Dan DiDio and Jim Lee Co-Publishers
Geoff Johns Chief Creative Officer
Amit Desai Senior VP – Marketing & Franchise Management
Amy Genkins Senior VP – Business & Legal Affairs
Nairi Gardiner Senior VP – Finance
Jeff Boison VP – Publishing Planning
Mark Chiarello VP – Art Direction & Design
John Cunningham VP – Marketing
Terri Cunningham VP – Editorial Administration
Larry Ganem VP – Talent Relations & Services
Alison Gill Senior VP – Manufacturing & Operations
Jay Kogan VP – Business & Legal Affairs, Publishing
Jack Mahan VP – Business Affairs, Talent
Nick Napolitano VP – Manufacturing Administration
Sue Pohja VP – Book Sales
Fred Ruiz VP – Manufacturing Operations
Courtney Simmons Senior VP – Publicity
Bob Wayne Senior VP – Sales

BATMAN: ARKHAM UNHINGED VOLUME 4

DC Comics, 1700 Broadway, New York, NY 10019
A Warner Bros. Entertainment Company.
Printed by RR Donnelley, Salem, VA, USA. 7/18/14. First Printing.
ISBN: 978-1-4012-4681-5

Library of Congress Cataloging-in-Publication Data

Traviss, Karen.
Batman : Arkham Unhinged, Volume 4 / Karen Traviss,
pages cm
ISBN 978-1-4012-4681-5 (hardback)
1. Graphic novels. I. Title.
PN6728.B36T73 2014
741.5'973—dc23
2014011628

SUSTAINABLE FORESTRY INITIATIVE
Certified Chain of Custody
20% Certified Forest Content,
80% Certified Sourcing
www.sfiprogram.org
SFI-01042
APPLIES TO TEXT STOCK ONLY

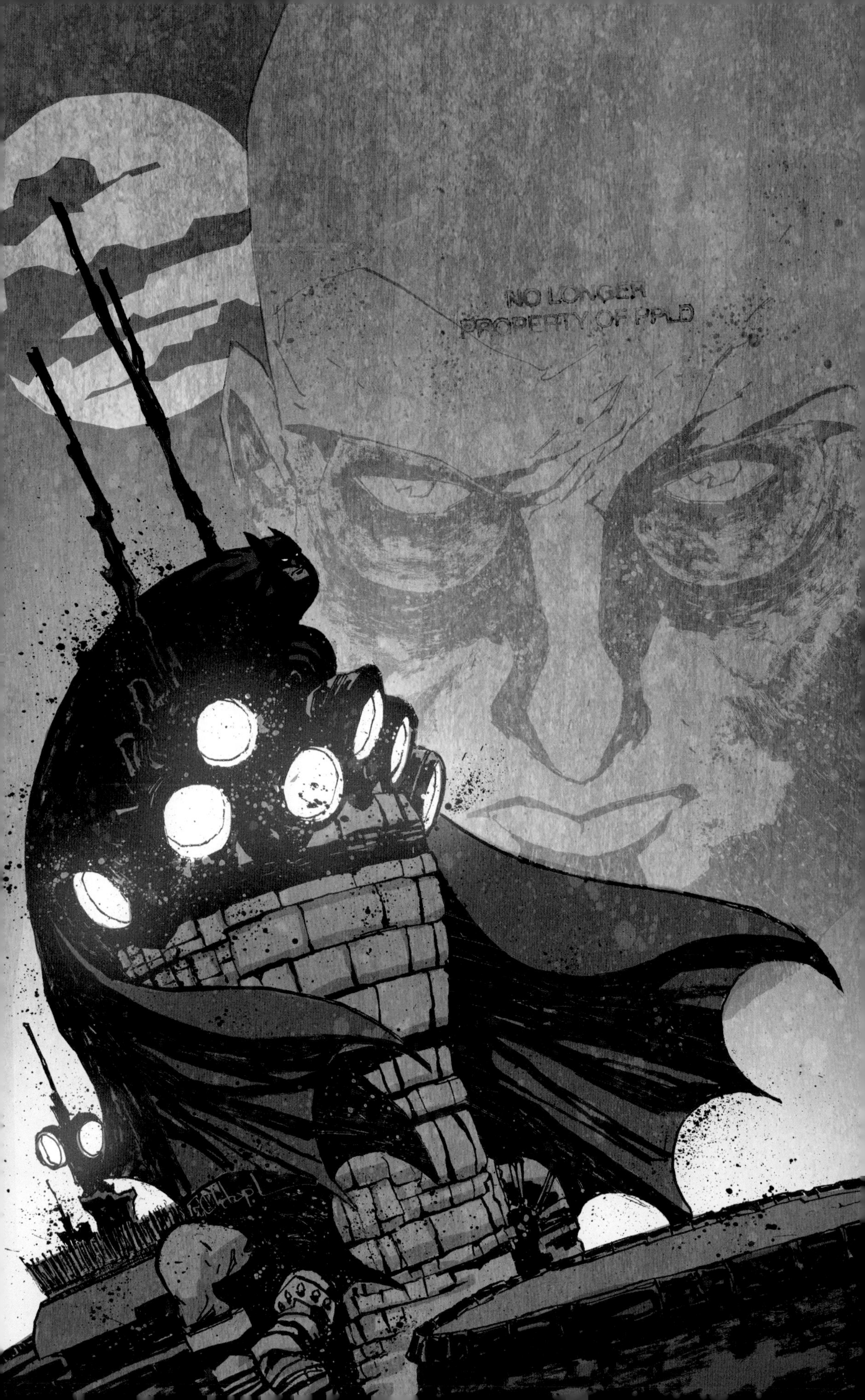

WELCOME
TO THE SLOUGH OF DESPOND
PART ONE

WRITTEN BY: KAREN TRAVISS
ART BY: RICCARDO BURCHIELLI
COLORS BY: ALEJANDRO SANCHEZ
LETTERS BY: TRAVIS LANHAM
COVER ART BY: CHRIS MITTEN

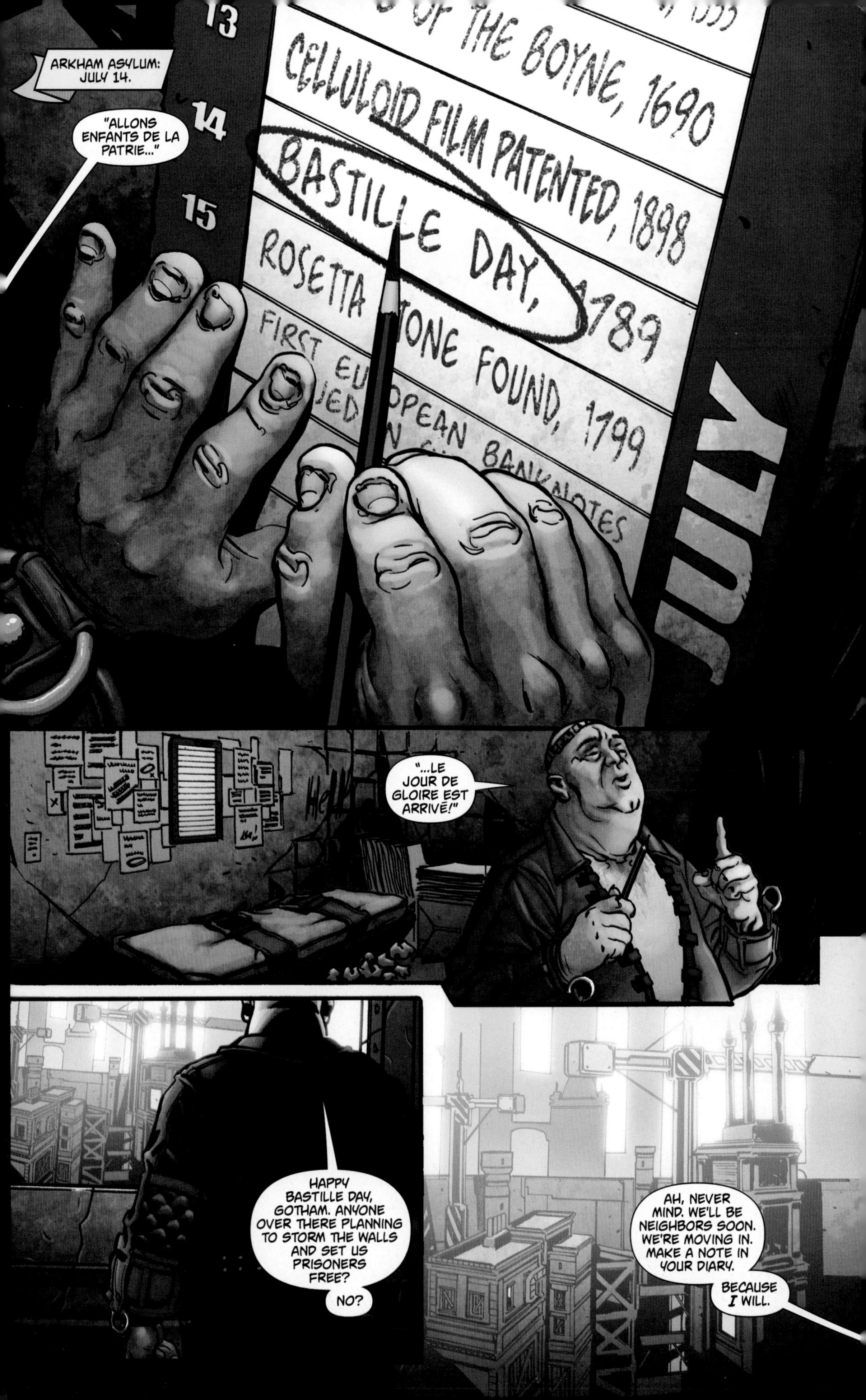

ARKHAM ASYLUM: JULY 14.
"ALLONS ENFANTS DE LA PATRIE..."
13
14
15
CELLULOID FILM PATENTED, 1898
BASTILLE DAY, 1789
JULY
"...LE JOUR DE GLOIRE EST ARRIVÉ!"
HAPPY BASTILLE DAY, GOTHAM. ANYONE OVER THERE PLANNING TO STORM THE WALLS AND SET US PRISONERS FREE?
NO?
AH, NEVER MIND. WE'LL BE NEIGHBORS SOON. WE'RE MOVING IN. MAKE A NOTE IN YOUR DIARY.
BECAUSE I WILL.

LATER THAT DAY: EN ROUTE TO THE FRENCH CONSULATE, GOTHAM.

SHOULD BE A GOOD RECEPTION, SIR. THE CONSUL GENERAL'S USUALLY MOST *HOSPITABLE* ON BASTILLE DAY.

"I'M STILL A LITTLE UNCOMFORTABLE CELEBRATING A JAIL BREAK, ALFRED. EVEN IF IT WAS IN 1789."

"LET'S DETOUR VIA THE ARKHAM SITE. I LIKE TO KEEP AN EYE ON THEIR PROGRESS."

"LOOKS SECURE ENOUGH TO ME, SIR. AS PENAL COLONIES GO, THAT IS."

"YES. AS SECURE AS THE BASTILLE..."

ARKHAM PROJECT GOTHAM CITY

SECURE SITE ALL PASSES MUST BE SHOWN

ARKHAM

ARKHAM
GOTHAM
IN PARTNER
TY

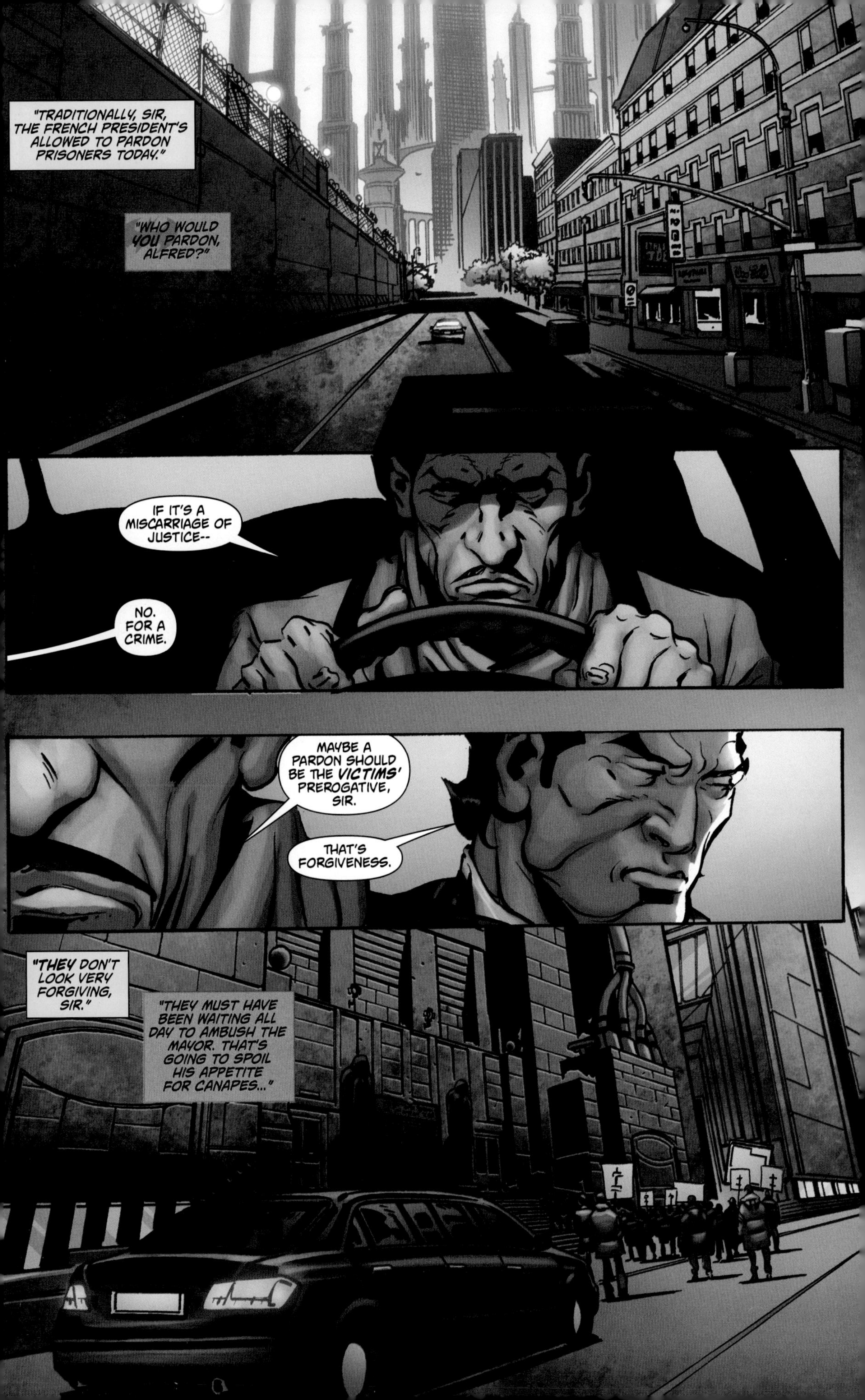
"TRADITIONALLY, SIR, THE FRENCH PRESIDENT'S ALLOWED TO PARDON PRISONERS TODAY."
"WHO WOULD YOU PARDON, ALFRED?"
IF IT'S A MISCARRIAGE OF JUSTICE--
NO. FOR A CRIME.
MAYBE A PARDON SHOULD BE THE VICTIMS' PREROGATIVE, SIR.
THAT'S FORGIVENESS.
"THEY DON'T LOOK VERY FORGIVING, SIR."
"THEY MUST HAVE BEEN WAITING ALL DAY TO AMBUSH THE MAYOR. THAT'S GOING TO SPOIL HIS APPETITE FOR CANAPES..."

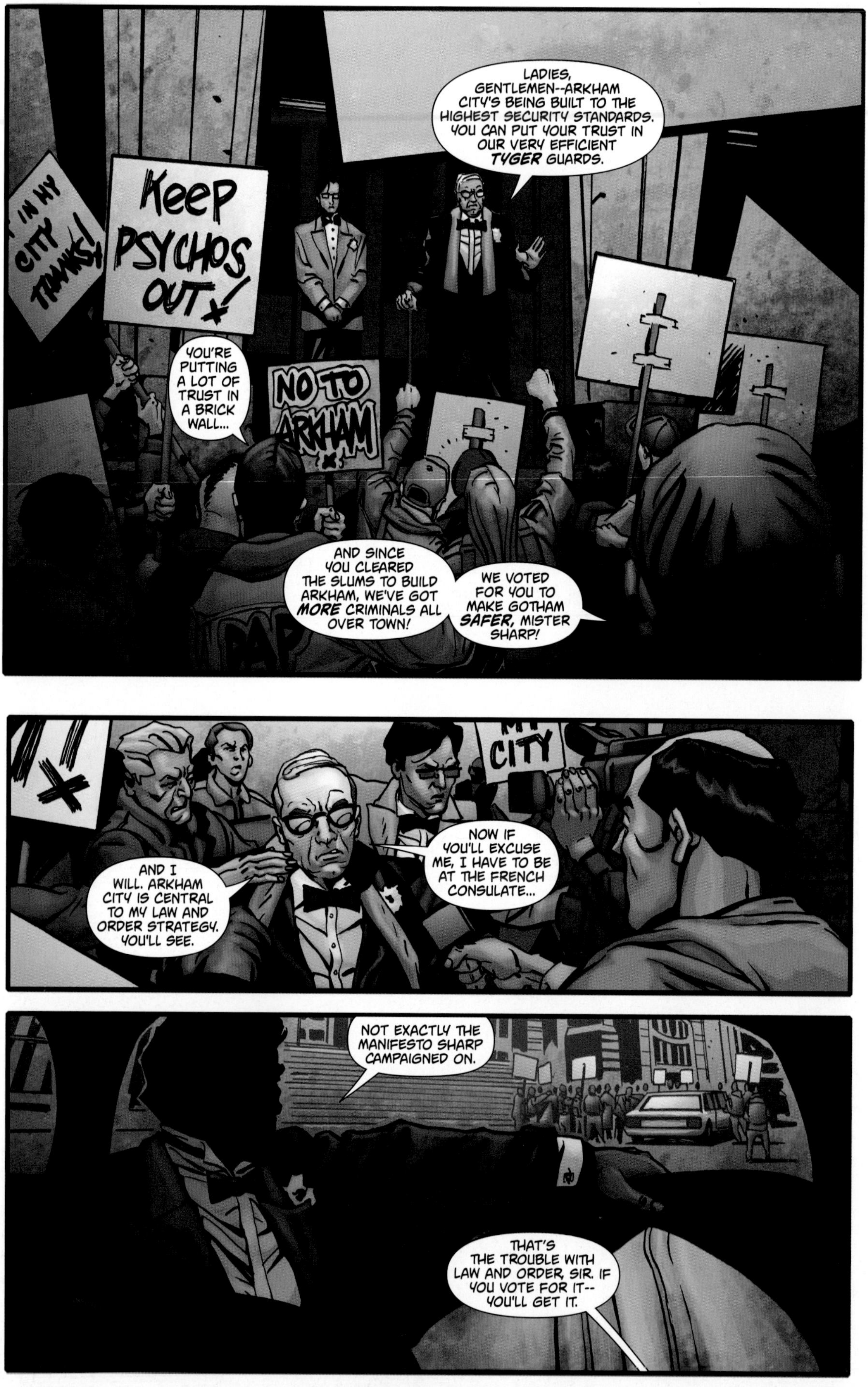

LADIES, GENTLEMEN--ARKHAM CITY'S BEING BUILT TO THE HIGHEST SECURITY STANDARDS. YOU CAN PUT YOUR TRUST IN OUR VERY EFFICIENT **TYGER** GUARDS.
KEEP PSYCHOS OUT
NO TO ARKHAM
YOU'RE PUTTING A LOT OF TRUST IN A BRICK WALL...
AND SINCE YOU CLEARED THE SLUMS TO BUILD ARKHAM, WE'VE GOT **MORE** CRIMINALS ALL OVER TOWN!
WE VOTED FOR YOU TO MAKE GOTHAM **SAFER**, MISTER SHARP!
CITY
AND I WILL. ARKHAM CITY IS CENTRAL TO MY LAW AND ORDER STRATEGY. YOU'LL SEE.
NOW IF YOU'LL EXCUSE ME, I HAVE TO BE AT THE FRENCH CONSULATE...
NOT EXACTLY THE MANIFESTO SHARP CAMPAIGNED ON.
THAT'S THE TROUBLE WITH LAW AND ORDER, SIR. IF YOU VOTE FOR IT-- YOU'LL GET IT.

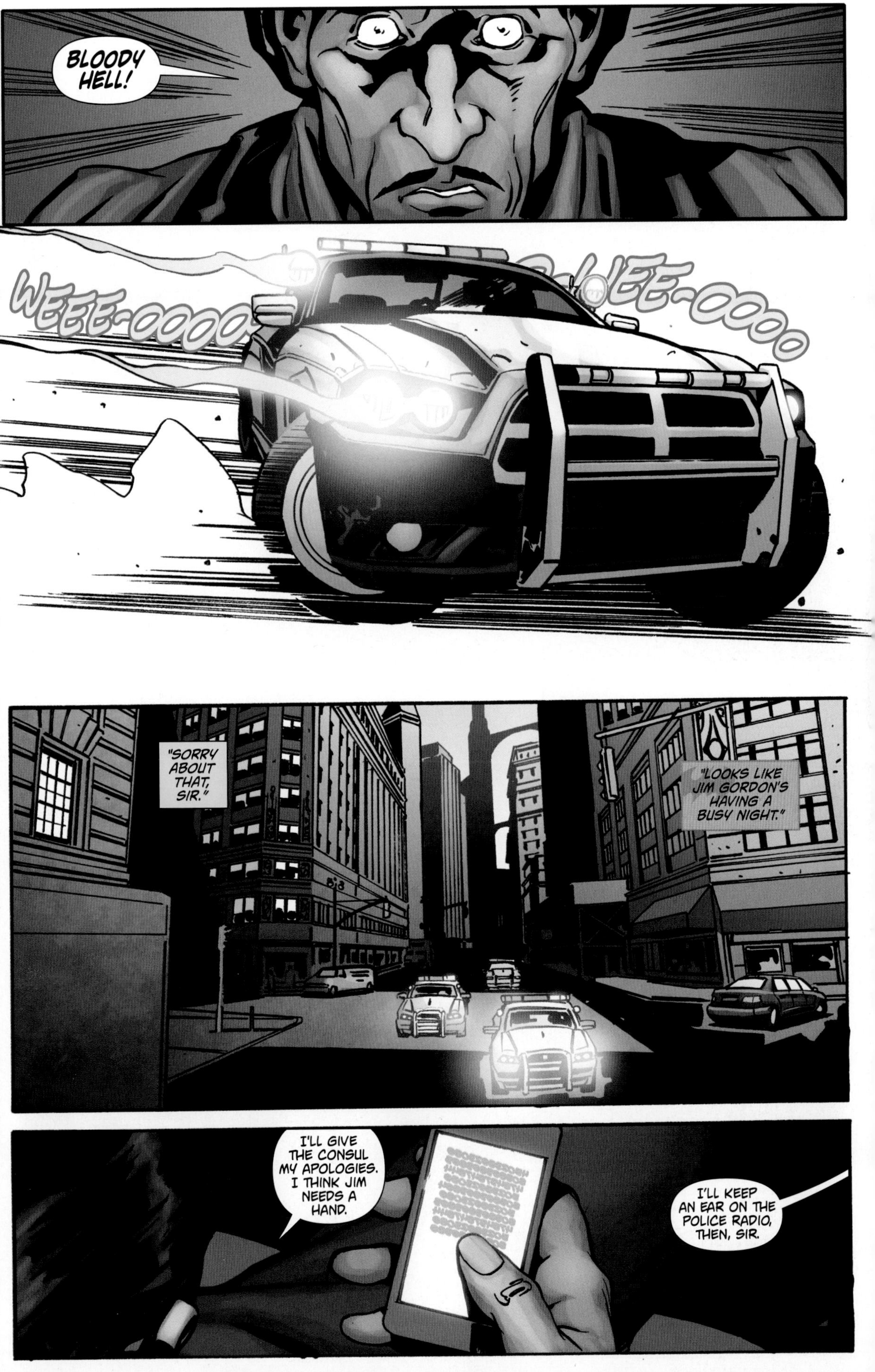
BLOODY HELL!
WEEE-OOOO
EE-OOOO
"SORRY ABOUT THAT, SIR."
"LOOKS LIKE JIM GORDON'S HAVING A BUSY NIGHT."
I'LL GIVE THE CONSUL MY APOLOGIES. I THINK JIM NEEDS A HAND.
I'LL KEEP AN EAR ON THE POLICE RADIO, THEN, SIR.

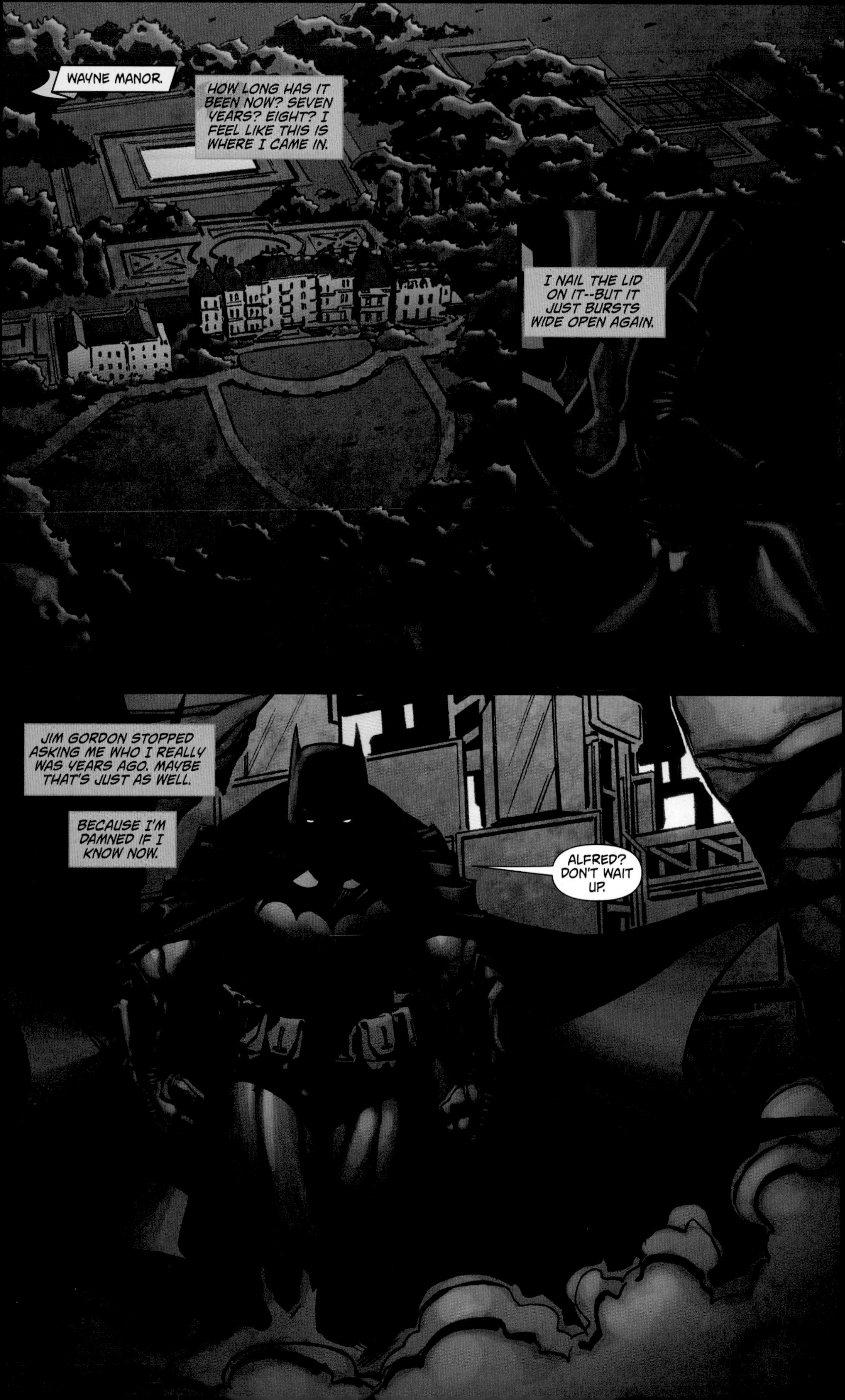
WAYNE MANOR.
HOW LONG HAS IT BEEN NOW? SEVEN YEARS? EIGHT? I FEEL LIKE THIS IS WHERE I CAME IN.
I NAIL THE LID ON IT--BUT IT JUST BURSTS WIDE OPEN AGAIN.
JIM GORDON STOPPED ASKING ME WHO I REALLY WAS YEARS AGO. MAYBE THAT'S JUST AS WELL.
BECAUSE I'M DAMNED IF I KNOW NOW.
ALFRED? DON'T WAIT UP.

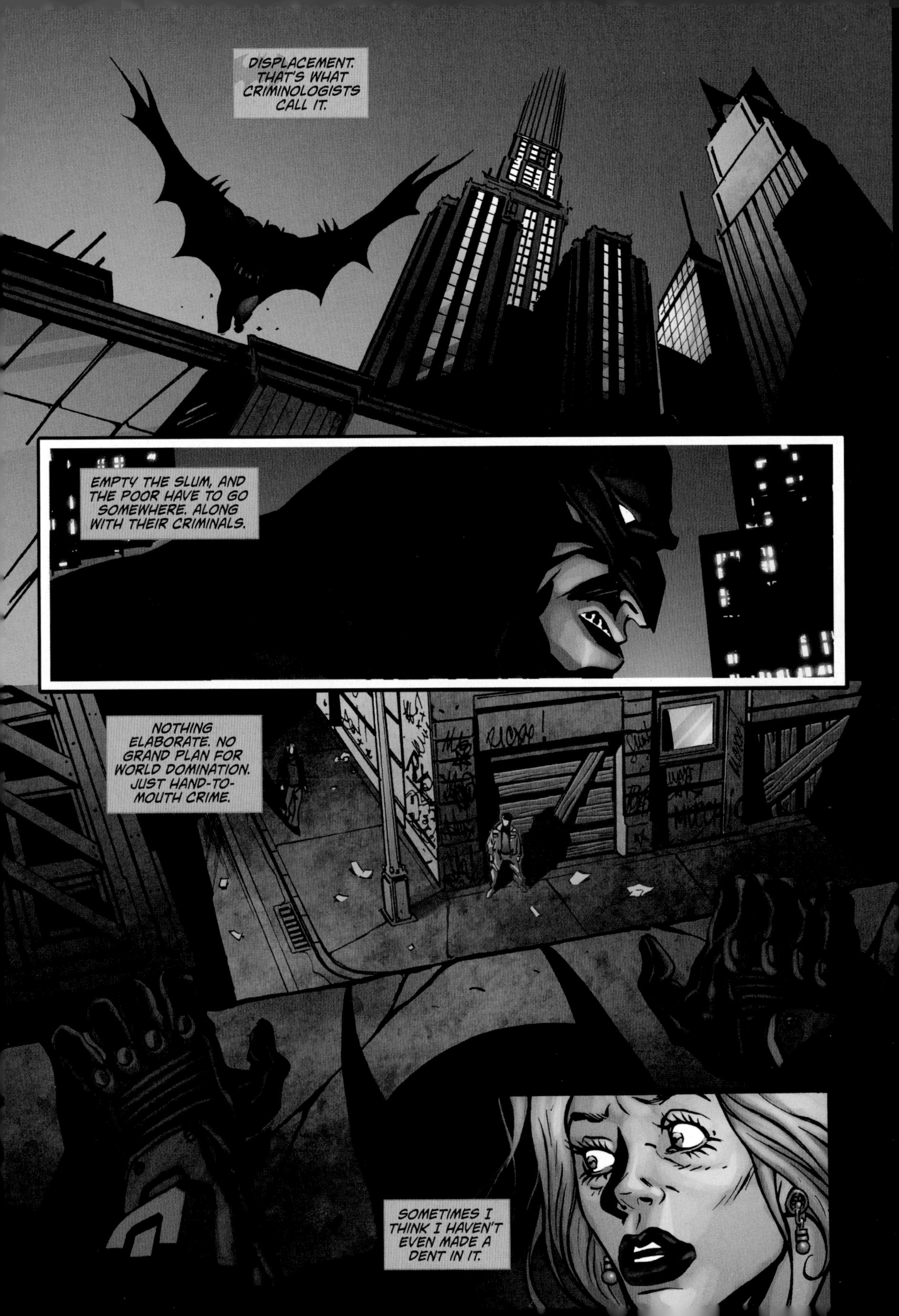
DISPLACEMENT. THAT'S WHAT CRIMINOLOGISTS CALL IT.
EMPTY THE SLUM, AND THE POOR HAVE TO GO SOMEWHERE. ALONG WITH THEIR CRIMINALS.
NOTHING ELABORATE. NO GRAND PLAN FOR WORLD DOMINATION. JUST HAND-TO-MOUTH CRIME.
SOMETIMES I THINK I HAVEN'T EVEN MADE A DENT IN IT.

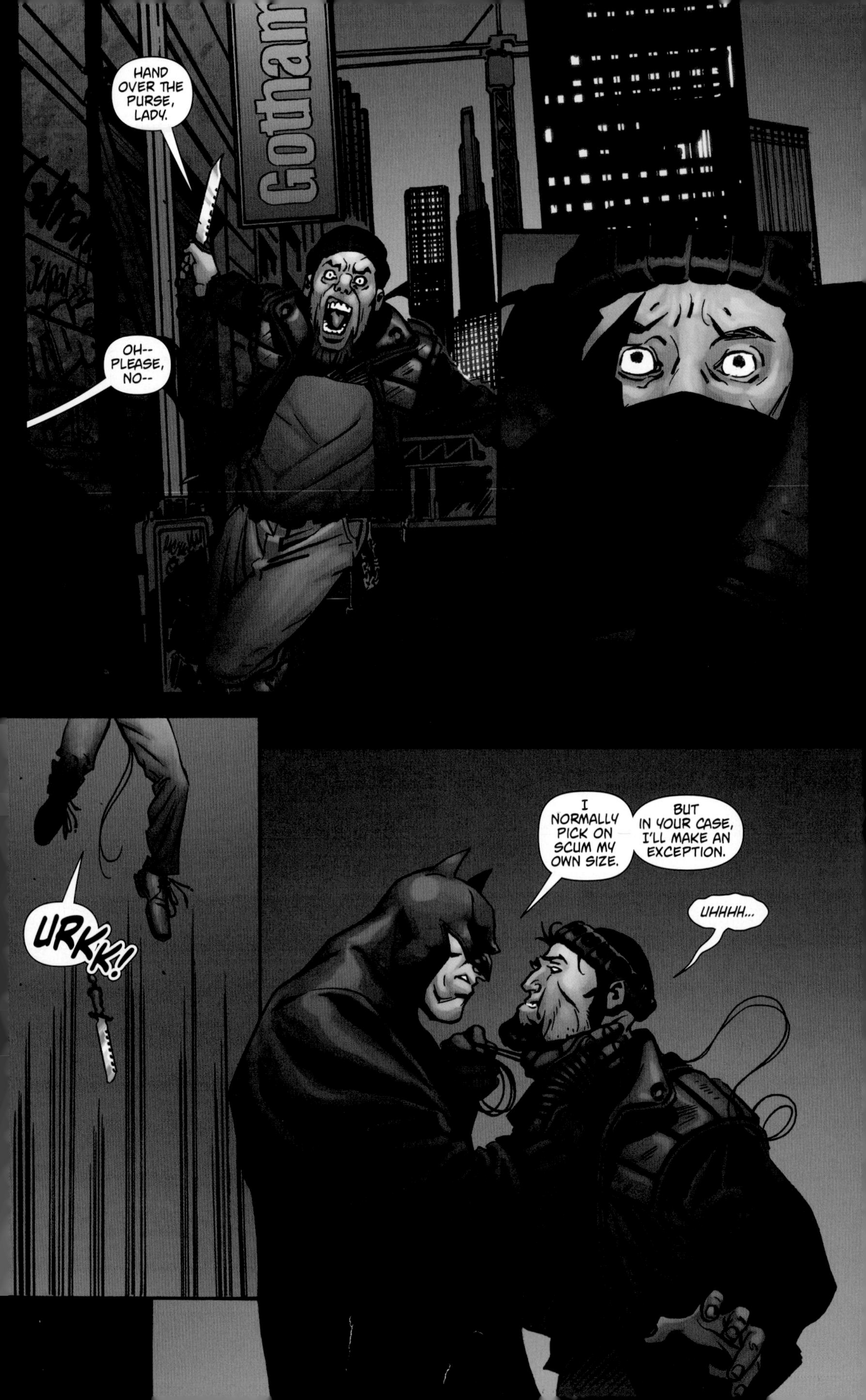
Gotham
HAND OVER THE PURSE, LADY.
OH-- PLEASE, NO--
URKK!
I NORMALLY PICK ON SCUM MY OWN SIZE.
BUT IN YOUR CASE, I'LL MAKE AN EXCEPTION.
UHHHH...

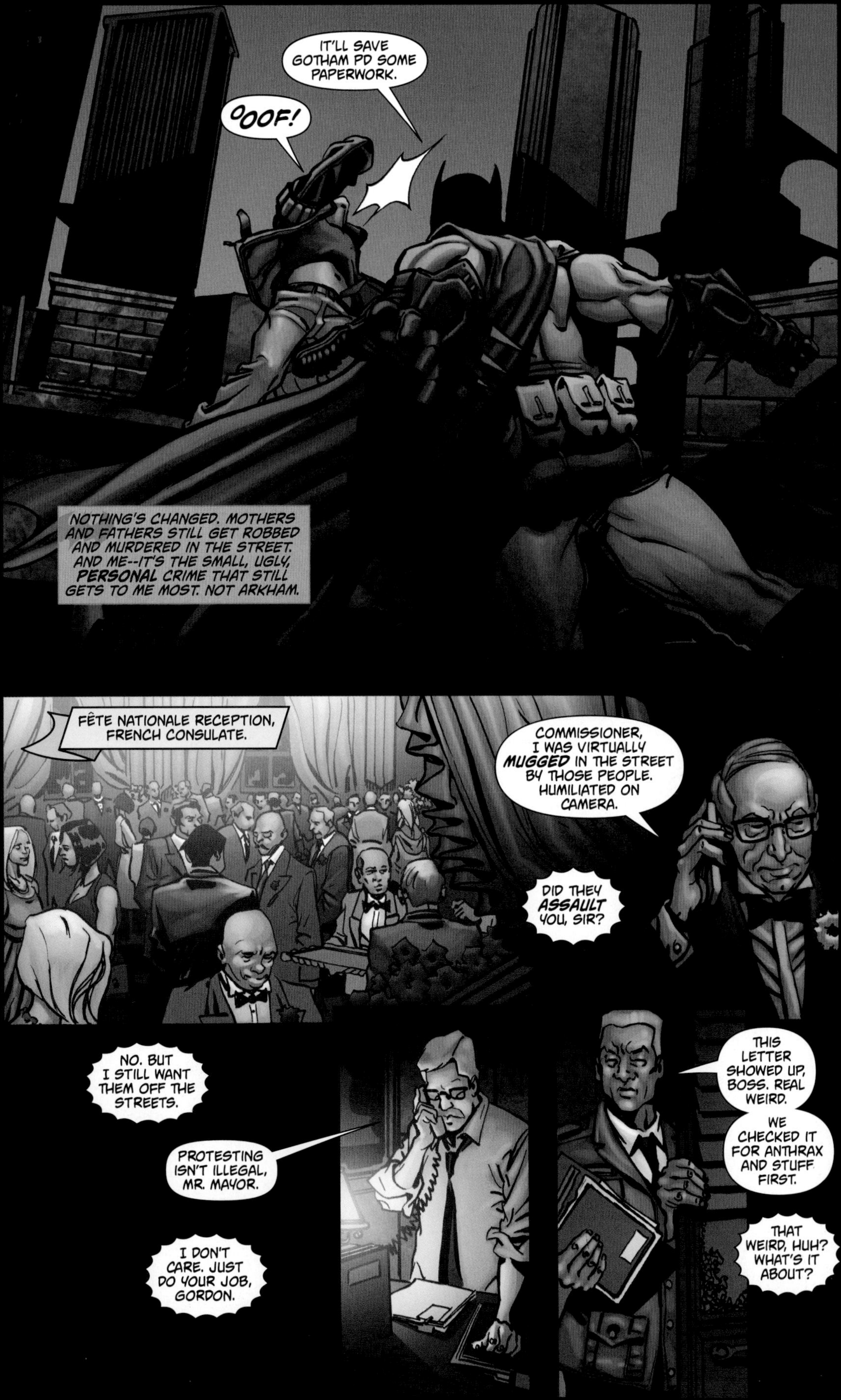

OOOF!
IT'LL SAVE GOTHAM PD SOME PAPERWORK.
NOTHING'S CHANGED. MOTHERS AND FATHERS STILL GET ROBBED AND MURDERED IN THE STREET. AND ME--IT'S THE SMALL, UGLY, PERSONAL CRIME THAT STILL GETS TO ME MOST. NOT ARKHAM.
FÊTE NATIONALE RECEPTION, FRENCH CONSULATE.
COMMISSIONER, I WAS VIRTUALLY MUGGED IN THE STREET BY THOSE PEOPLE. HUMILIATED ON CAMERA.
DID THEY ASSAULT YOU, SIR?
NO. BUT I STILL WANT THEM OFF THE STREETS.
PROTESTING ISN'T ILLEGAL, MR. MAYOR.
I DON'T CARE. JUST DO YOUR JOB, GORDON.
THIS LETTER SHOWED UP, BOSS. REAL WEIRD.
WE CHECKED IT FOR ANTHRAX AND STUFF FIRST.
THAT WEIRD, HUH? WHAT'S IT ABOUT?

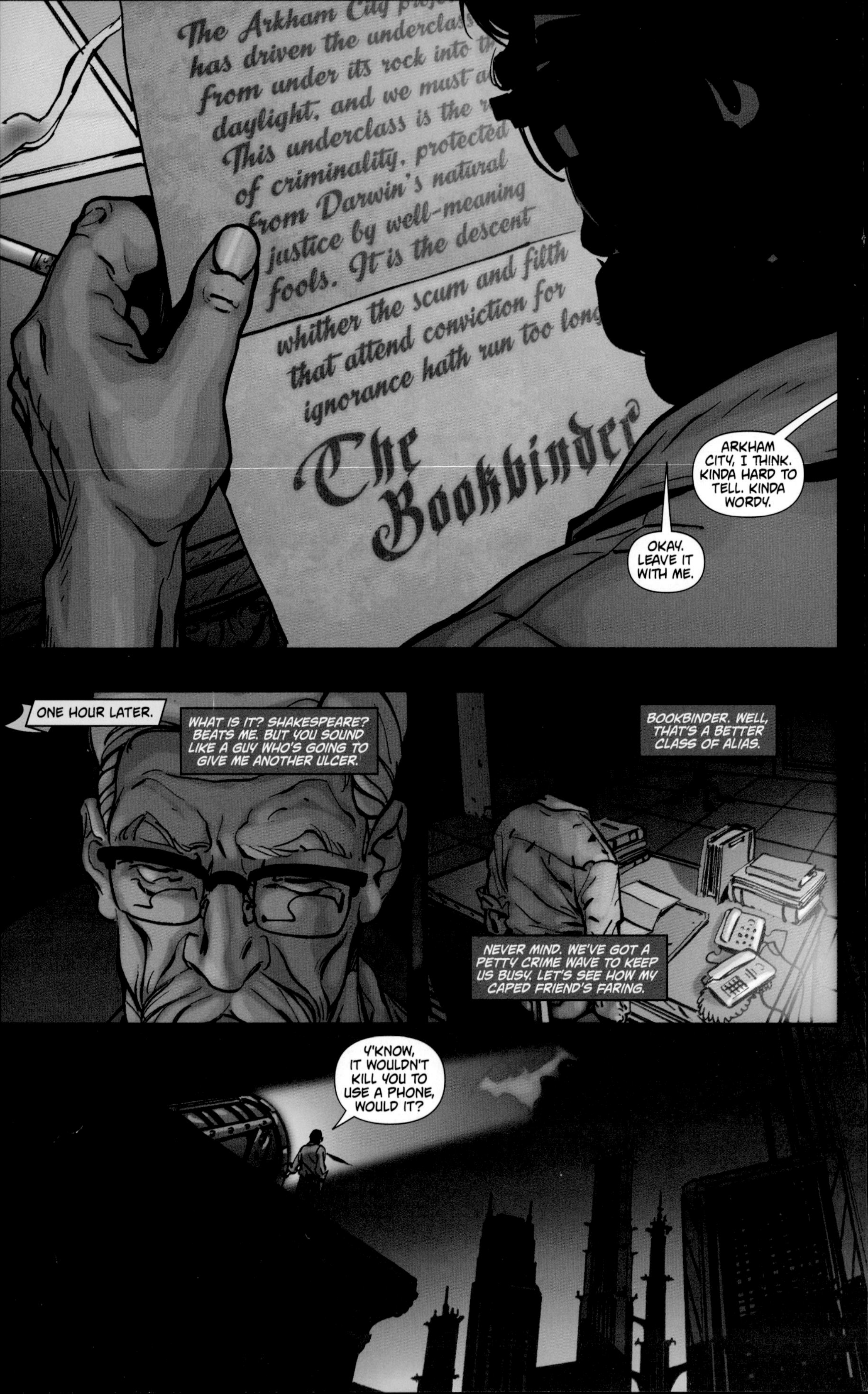
The Arkham City proje
has driven the underclass
from under its rock into th
daylight, and we must a
This underclass is the r
of criminality, protected
from Darwin's natural
justice by well-meaning
fools. It is the descent
whither the scum and filth
that attend conviction for
ignorance hath run too long
The Bookbinder
ARKHAM CITY, I THINK. KINDA HARD TO TELL. KINDA WORDY.
OKAY. LEAVE IT WITH ME.
ONE HOUR LATER.
WHAT IS IT? SHAKESPEARE? BEATS ME. BUT YOU SOUND LIKE A GUY WHO'S GOING TO GIVE ME ANOTHER ULCER.
BOOKBINDER. WELL, THAT'S A BETTER CLASS OF ALIAS.
NEVER MIND. WE'VE GOT A PETTY CRIME WAVE TO KEEP US BUSY. LET'S SEE HOW MY CAPED FRIEND'S FARING.
Y'KNOW, IT WOULDN'T KILL YOU TO USE A PHONE, WOULD IT?

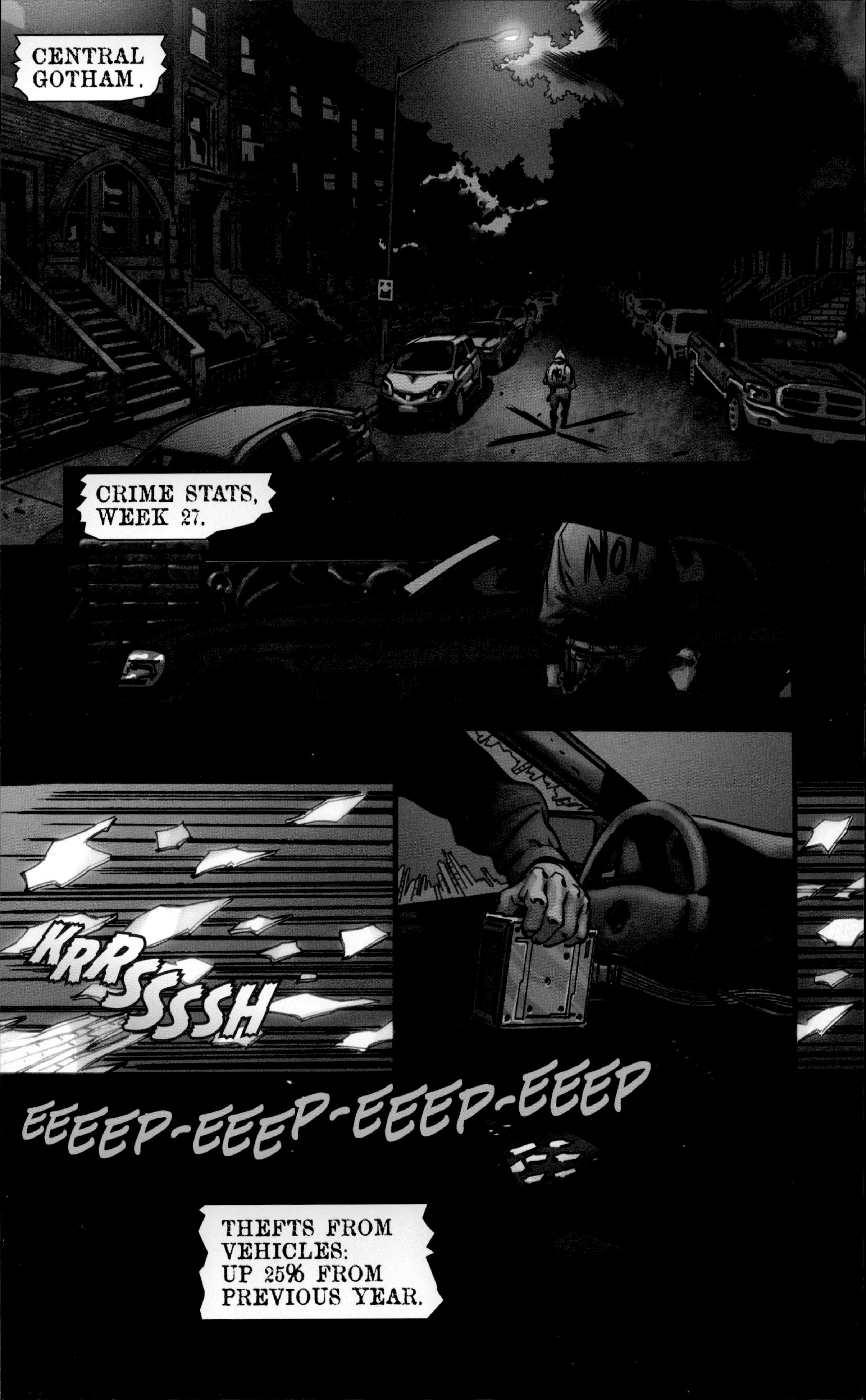
CENTRAL GOTHAM.
CRIME STATS, WEEK 27.
KRRSSSSH
EEEEEP-EEEEP-EEEEP-EEEP
THEFTS FROM VEHICLES: UP 25% FROM PREVIOUS YEAR.

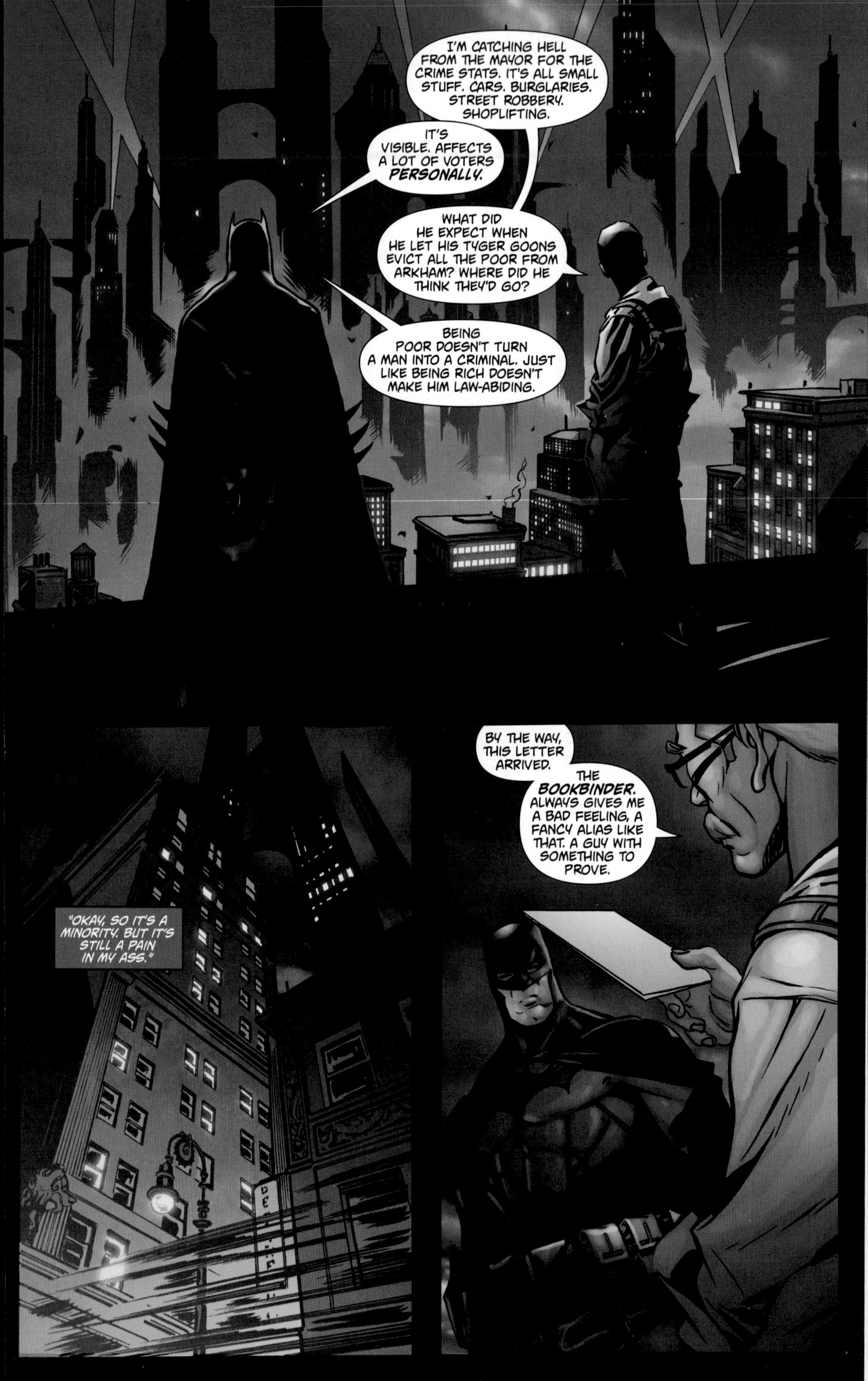
I'M CATCHING HELL FROM THE MAYOR FOR THE CRIME STATS. IT'S ALL SMALL STUFF. CARS. BURGLARIES. STREET ROBBERY. SHOPLIFTING.
IT'S VISIBLE. AFFECTS A LOT OF VOTERS PERSONALLY.
WHAT DID HE EXPECT WHEN HE LET HIS TYGER GOONS EVICT ALL THE POOR FROM ARKHAM? WHERE DID HE THINK THEY'D GO?
BEING POOR DOESN'T TURN A MAN INTO A CRIMINAL. JUST LIKE BEING RICH DOESN'T MAKE HIM LAW-ABIDING.
"OKAY, SO IT'S A MINORITY. BUT IT'S STILL A PAIN IN MY ASS."
BY THE WAY, THIS LETTER ARRIVED.
THE BOOKBINDER. ALWAYS GIVES ME A BAD FEELING, A FANCY ALIAS LIKE THAT. A GUY WITH SOMETHING TO PROVE.

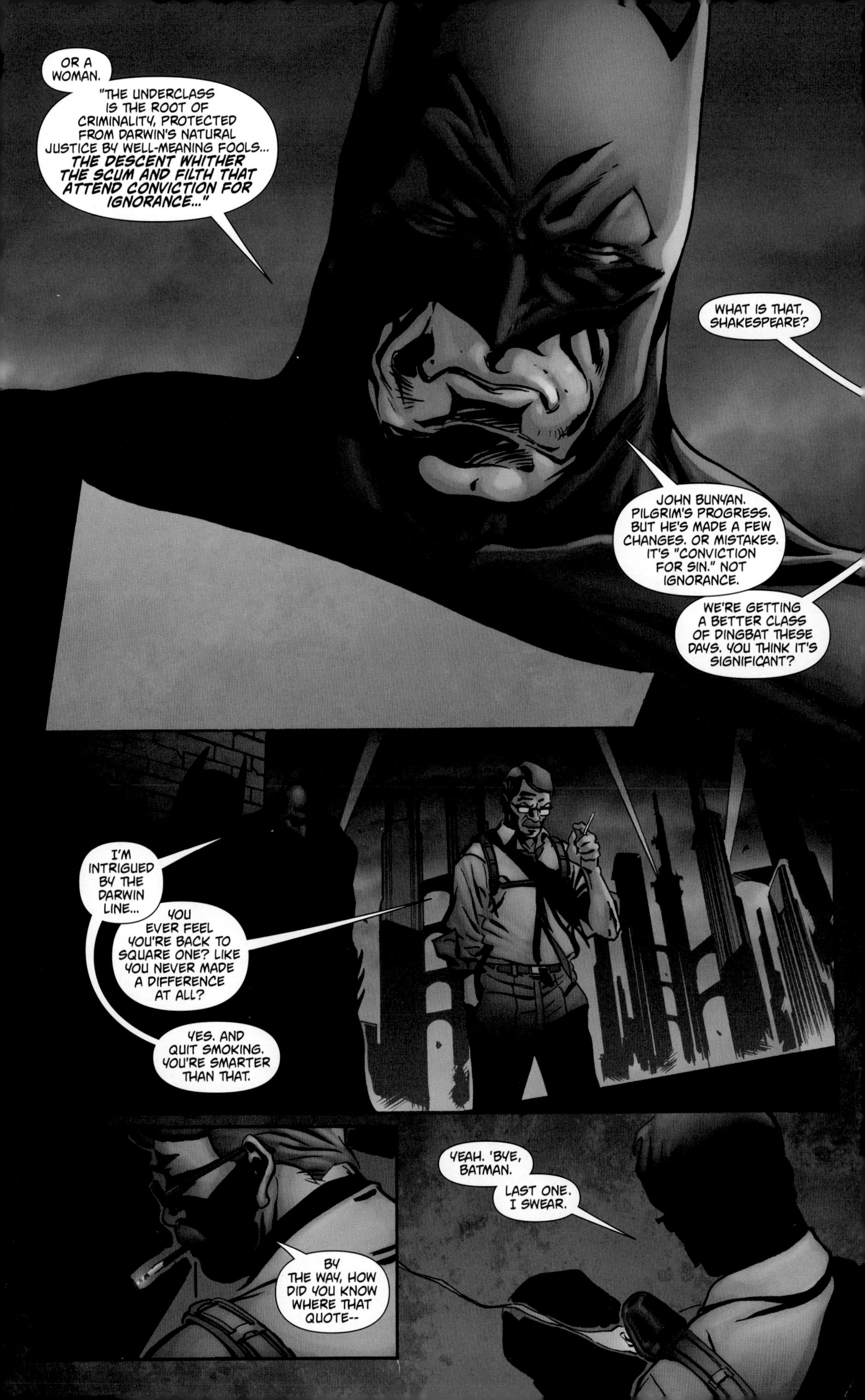
OR A WOMAN.
"THE UNDERCLASS IS THE ROOT OF CRIMINALITY, PROTECTED FROM DARWIN'S NATURAL JUSTICE BY WELL-MEANING FOOLS... THE DESCENT WHITHER THE SCUM AND FILTH THAT ATTEND CONVICTION FOR IGNORANCE..."
WHAT IS THAT, SHAKESPEARE?
JOHN BUNYAN. PILGRIM'S PROGRESS. BUT HE'S MADE A FEW CHANGES. OR MISTAKES. IT'S "CONVICTION FOR SIN." NOT IGNORANCE.
WE'RE GETTING A BETTER CLASS OF DINGBAT THESE DAYS. YOU THINK IT'S SIGNIFICANT?
I'M INTRIGUED BY THE DARWIN LINE...
YOU EVER FEEL YOU'RE BACK TO SQUARE ONE? LIKE YOU NEVER MADE A DIFFERENCE AT ALL?
YES. AND QUIT SMOKING. YOU'RE SMARTER THAN THAT.
YEAH. 'BYE, BATMAN.
LAST ONE. I SWEAR.
BY THE WAY, HOW DID YOU KNOW WHERE THAT QUOTE--

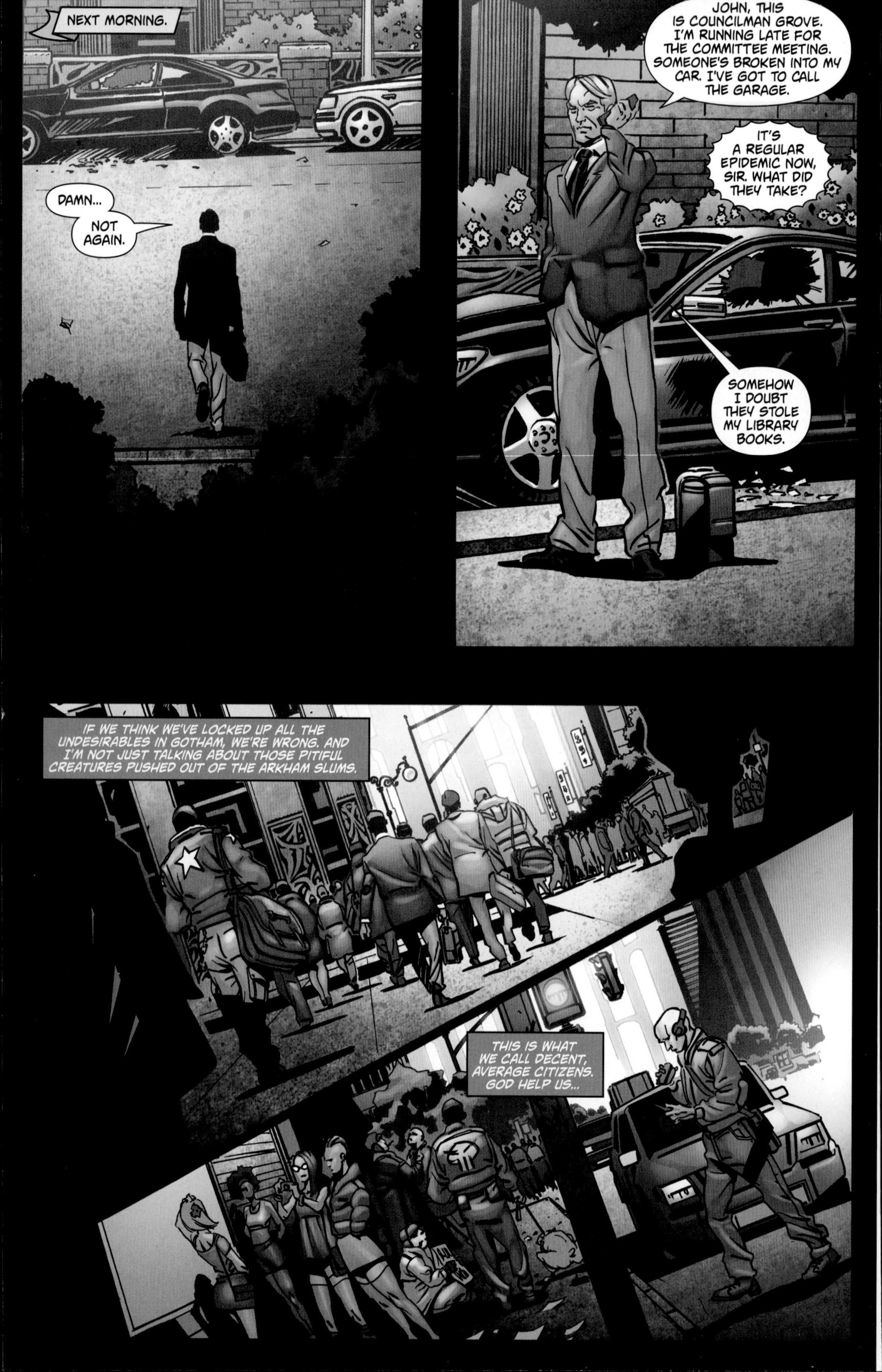
NEXT MORNING.
DAMN...
NOT AGAIN.
JOHN, THIS IS COUNCILMAN GROVE. I'M RUNNING LATE FOR THE COMMITTEE MEETING. SOMEONE'S BROKEN INTO MY CAR. I'VE GOT TO CALL THE GARAGE.
IT'S A REGULAR EPIDEMIC NOW, SIR. WHAT DID THEY TAKE?
SOMEHOW I DOUBT THEY STOLE MY LIBRARY BOOKS.
IF WE THINK WE'VE LOCKED UP ALL THE UNDESIRABLES IN GOTHAM, WE'RE WRONG. AND I'M NOT JUST TALKING ABOUT THOSE PITIFUL CREATURES PUSHED OUT OF THE ARKHAM SLUMS.
THIS IS WHAT WE CALL DECENT, AVERAGE CITIZENS. GOD HELP US...

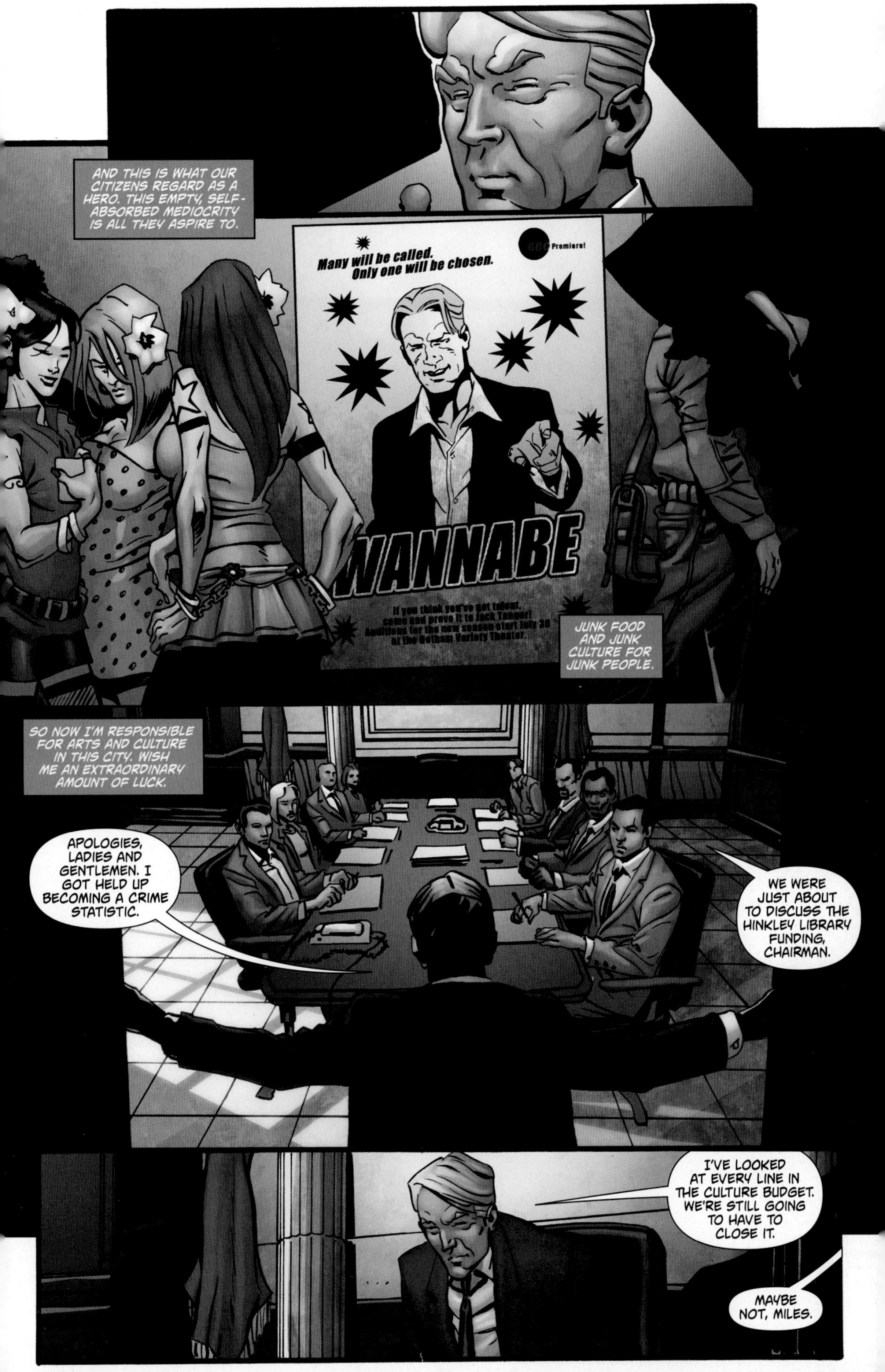

AND THIS IS WHAT OUR CITIZENS REGARD AS A HERO. THIS EMPTY, SELF-ABSORBED MEDIOCRITY IS ALL THEY ASPIRE TO.
GBC Premiere!
Many will be called. Only one will be chosen.
WANNABE
If you think you've got talent, come and prove it to Jack Tanner! Auditions for the new season start July 30 at the Gotham Variety Theater.
JUNK FOOD AND JUNK CULTURE FOR JUNK PEOPLE.
SO NOW I'M RESPONSIBLE FOR ARTS AND CULTURE IN THIS CITY. WISH ME AN EXTRAORDINARY AMOUNT OF LUCK.
APOLOGIES, LADIES AND GENTLEMEN. I GOT HELD UP BECOMING A CRIME STATISTIC.
WE WERE JUST ABOUT TO DISCUSS THE HINKLEY LIBRARY FUNDING, CHAIRMAN.
I'VE LOOKED AT EVERY LINE IN THE CULTURE BUDGET. WE'RE STILL GOING TO HAVE TO CLOSE IT.
MAYBE NOT, MILES.

THE WAYNE FOUNDATION WROTE A CHECK. ENOUGH TO KEEP THE LIBRARY OPEN FOR FIVE YEARS.

WAYNE ENTERPRISES

Dear Mayor Sharp,

Mr. Wayne was most concerne... hear of the impending cuts in ... city's libraries budget. as a ... supporter of Gotham's lite... ...tion, he has instructed ... ...tham City libraries fro... ...ed donation fro... ...ayne Foundation to ... those branches threate... closure to remain open.

IT'S HEARTENING TO KNOW THAT BRUCE WAYNE HAS SOME REGARD FOR CULTURE. I'LL SEND HIM A PERSONAL THANK-YOU.

BUT IT STILL PAINS ME THAT EVEN THIS PRINCELY SUM IS LESS THAN JACK TANNER MAKES IN A YEAR. I WON'T SAY EARNS.

ONE WEEK LATER: BIG HEARTS TELETHON NIGHT.

ENOUGH, SWEETHEART. THAT POWDER'S JUST SETTLING IN MY LINES. GOTTA LOOK YOUNG FOR THE TELETHON.

I CAN RECOMMEND A SURGEON, IF YOU LIKE...

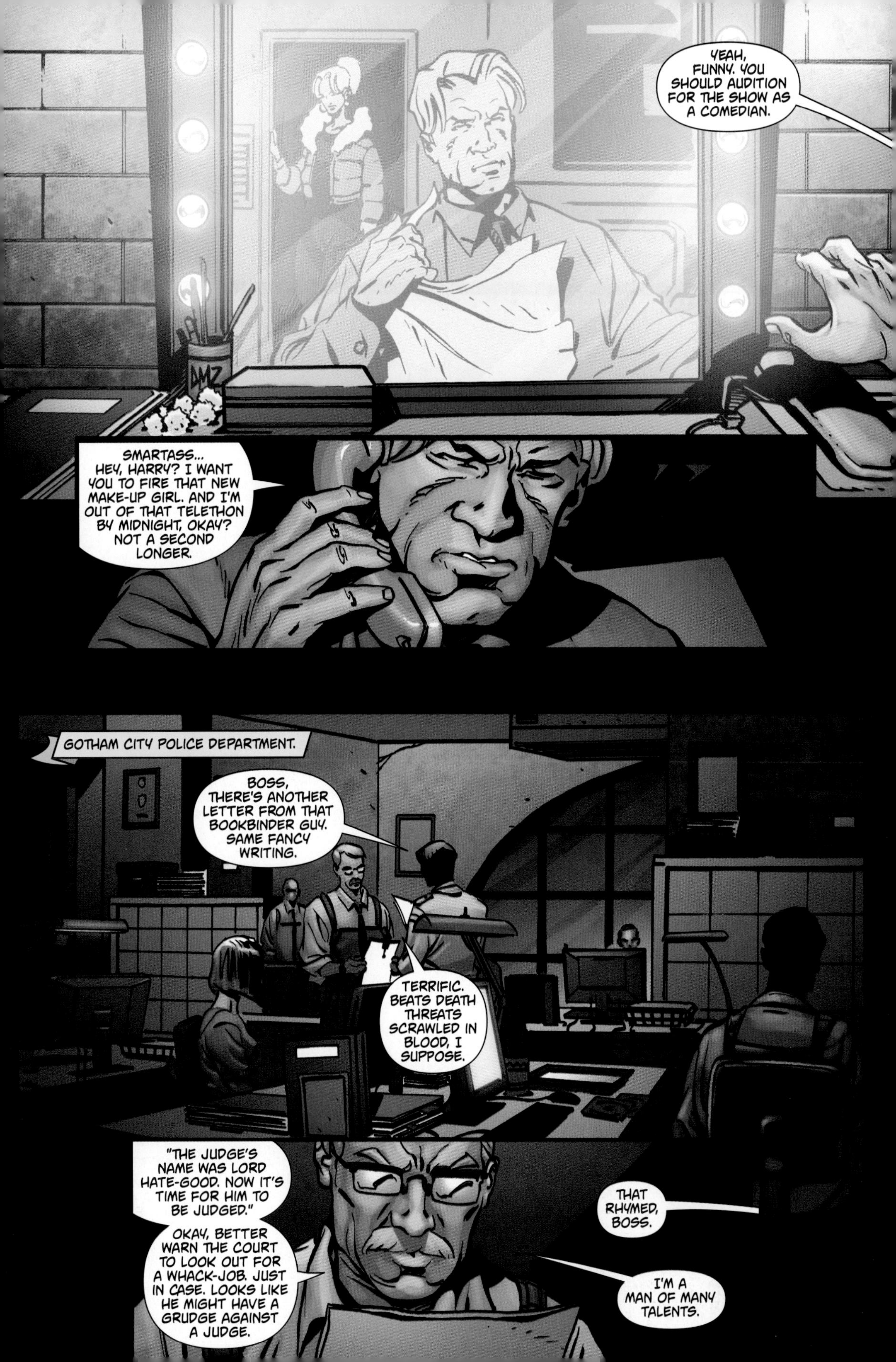
YEAH, FUNNY. YOU SHOULD AUDITION FOR THE SHOW AS A COMEDIAN.
SMARTASS... HEY, HARRY? I WANT YOU TO FIRE THAT NEW MAKE-UP GIRL. AND I'M OUT OF THAT TELETHON BY MIDNIGHT, OKAY? NOT A SECOND LONGER.
GOTHAM CITY POLICE DEPARTMENT.
BOSS, THERE'S ANOTHER LETTER FROM THAT BOOKBINDER GUY. SAME FANCY WRITING.
TERRIFIC. BEATS DEATH THREATS SCRAWLED IN BLOOD, I SUPPOSE.
"THE JUDGE'S NAME WAS LORD HATE-GOOD. NOW IT'S TIME FOR HIM TO BE JUDGED."
OKAY, BETTER WARN THE COURT TO LOOK OUT FOR A WHACK-JOB. JUST IN CASE. LOOKS LIKE HE MIGHT HAVE A GRUDGE AGAINST A JUDGE.
THAT RHYMED, BOSS.
I'M A MAN OF MANY TALENTS.

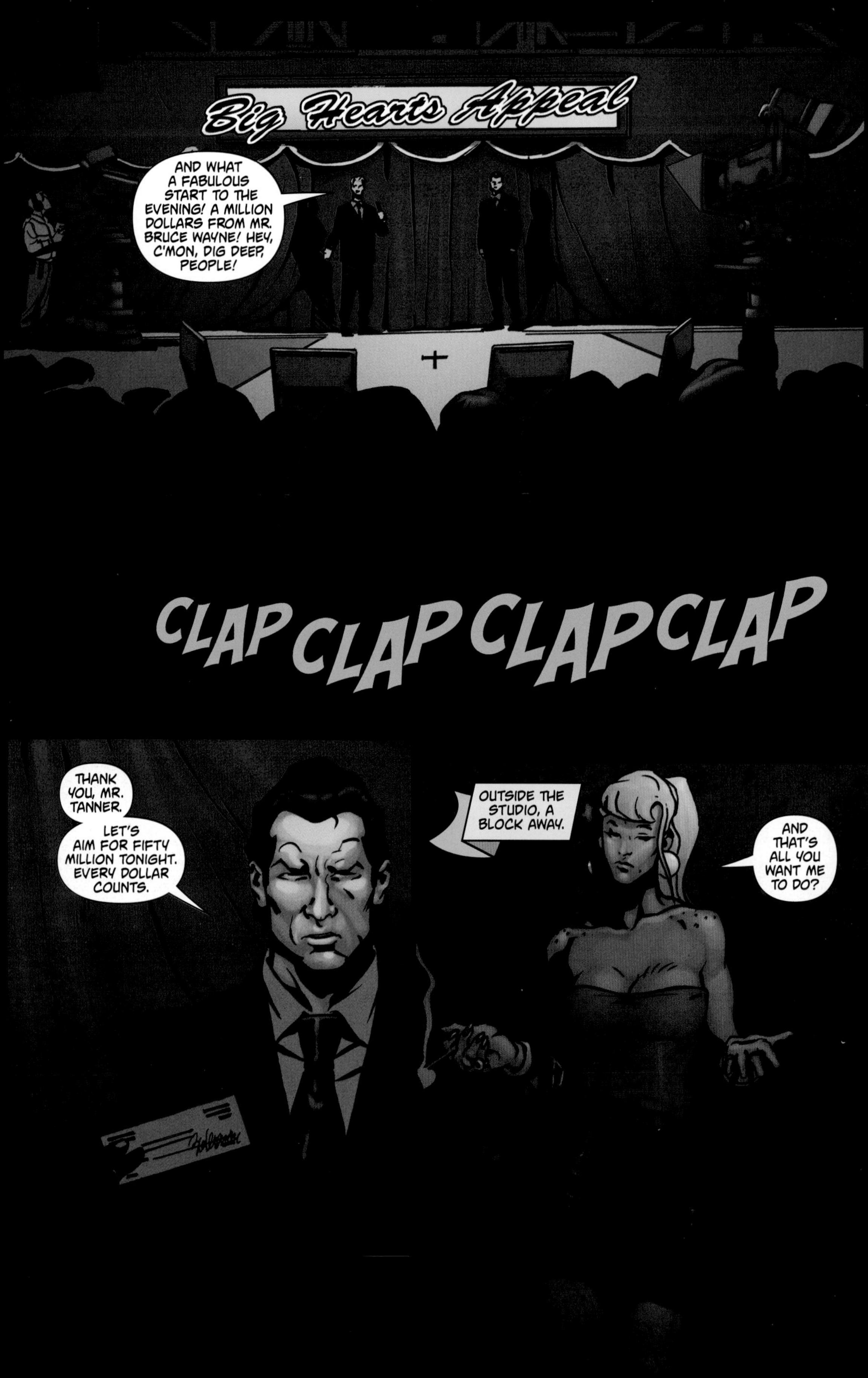
Big Hearts Appeal
AND WHAT A FABULOUS START TO THE EVENING! A MILLION DOLLARS FROM MR. BRUCE WAYNE! HEY, C'MON, DIG DEEP, PEOPLE!
CLAP CLAP CLAP CLAP
THANK YOU, MR. TANNER.
LET'S AIM FOR FIFTY MILLION TONIGHT. EVERY DOLLAR COUNTS.
OUTSIDE THE STUDIO, A BLOCK AWAY.
AND THAT'S ALL YOU WANT ME TO DO?

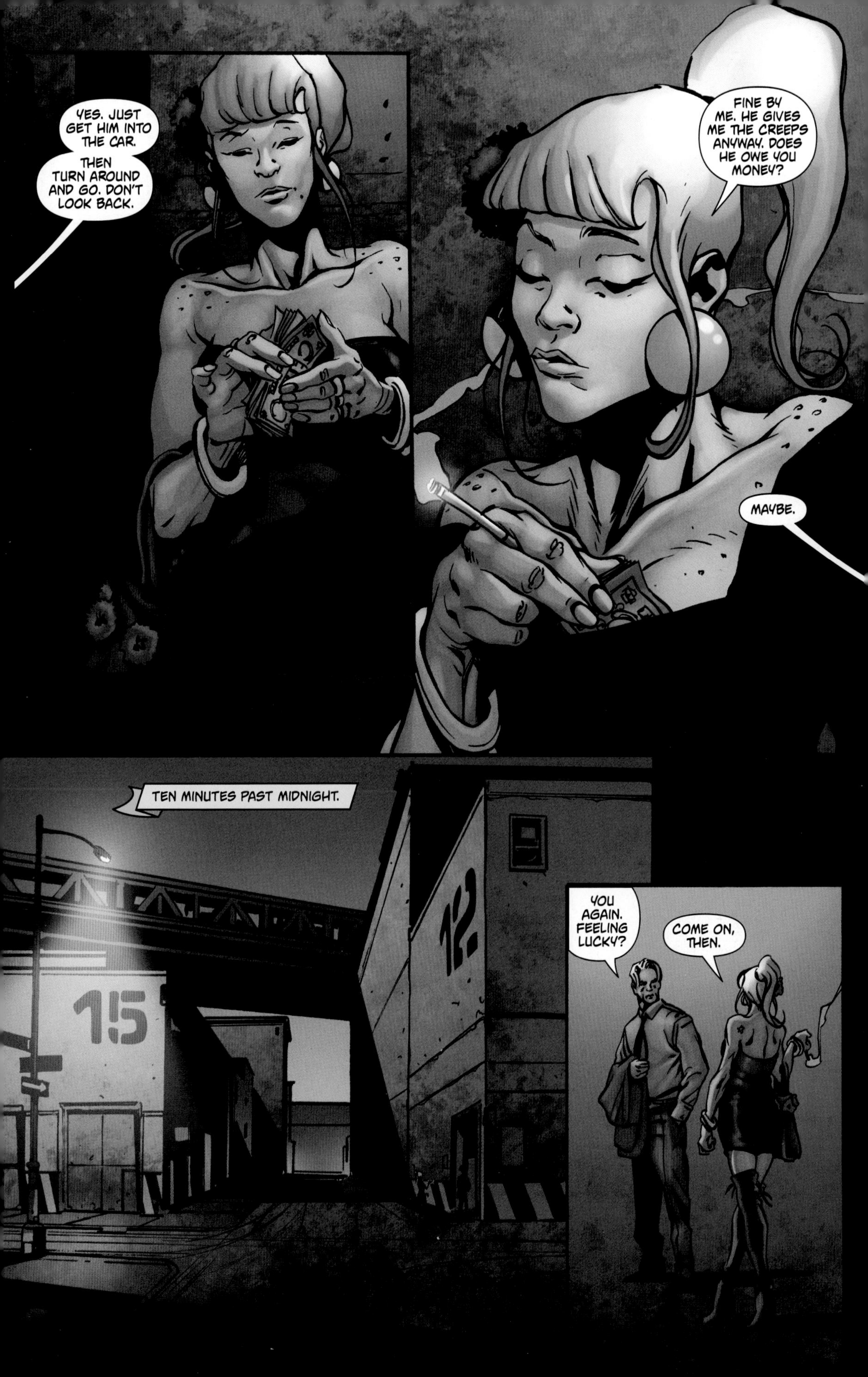
YES. JUST GET HIM INTO THE CAR.
THEN TURN AROUND AND GO. DON'T LOOK BACK.
FINE BY ME. HE GIVES ME THE CREEPS ANYWAY. DOES HE OWE YOU MONEY?
MAYBE.
TEN MINUTES PAST MIDNIGHT.
15
12
YOU AGAIN. FEELING LUCKY?
COME ON, THEN.

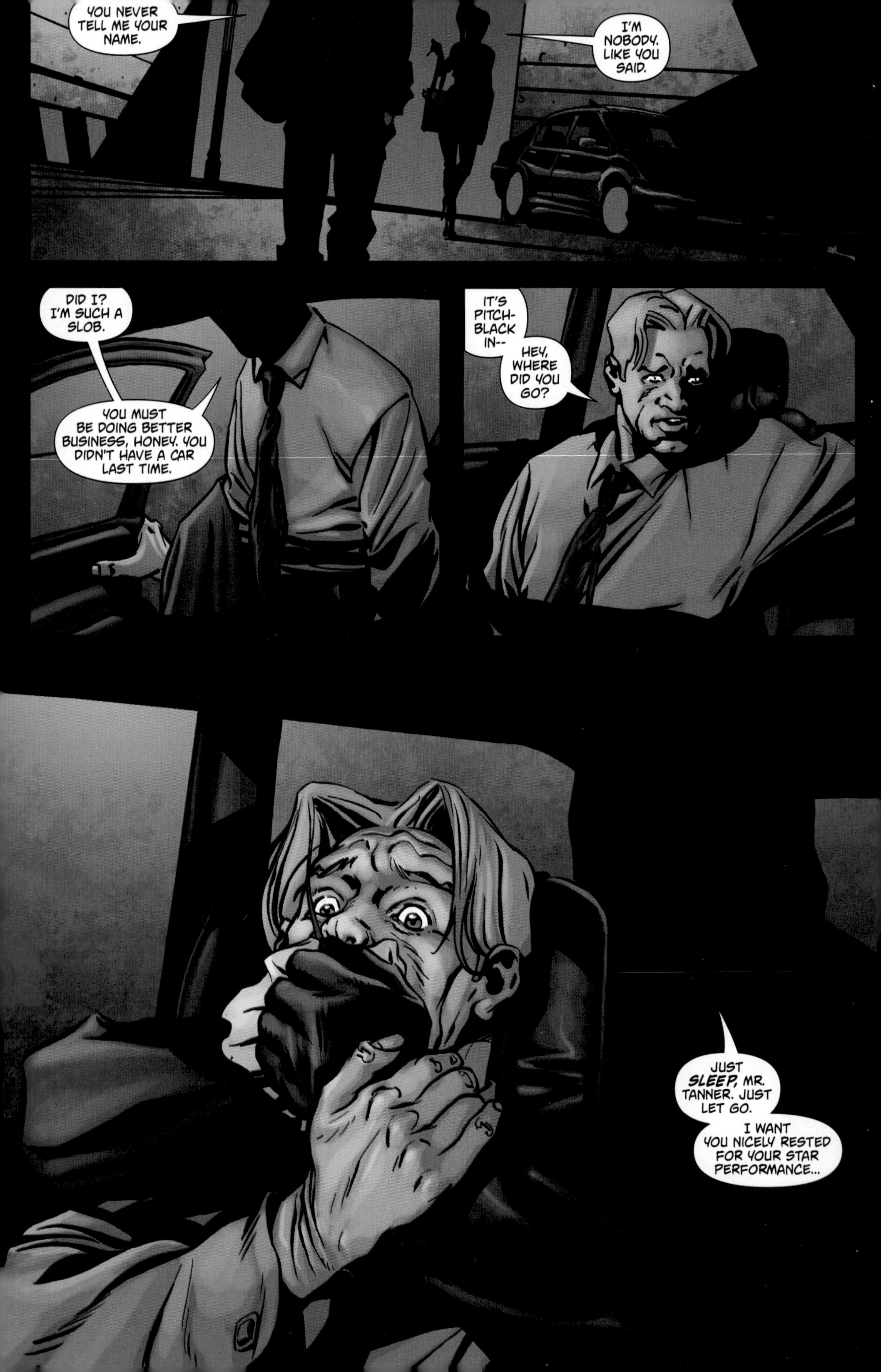
YOU NEVER TELL ME YOUR NAME.
I'M NOBODY. LIKE YOU SAID.
DID I? I'M SUCH A SLOB.
YOU MUST BE DOING BETTER BUSINESS, HONEY. YOU DIDN'T HAVE A CAR LAST TIME.
IT'S PITCH-BLACK IN--
HEY, WHERE DID YOU GO?
JUST SLEEP, MR. TANNER. JUST LET GO.
I WANT YOU NICELY RESTED FOR YOUR STAR PERFORMANCE...

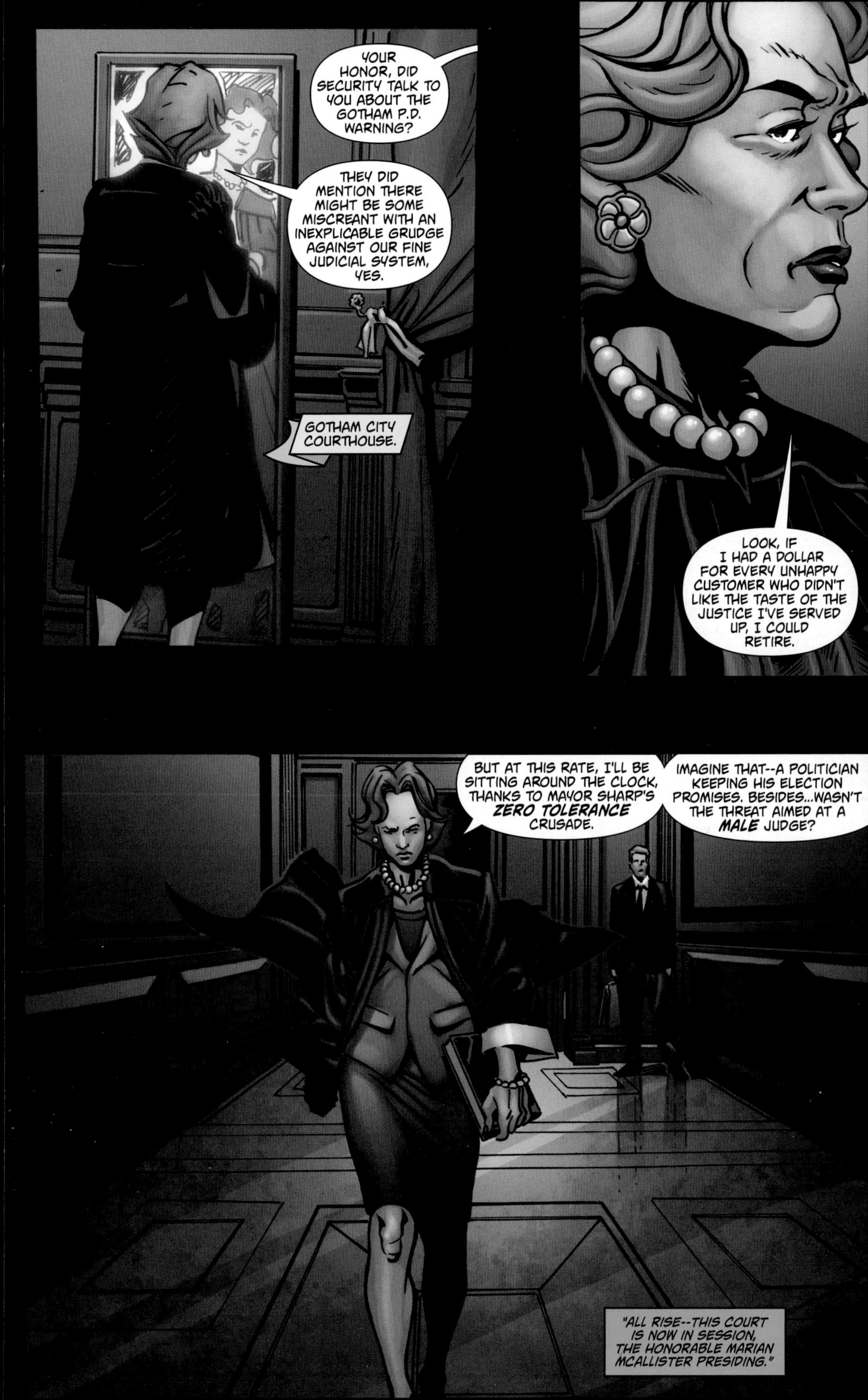
GOTHAM CITY COURTHOUSE.
YOUR HONOR, DID SECURITY TALK TO YOU ABOUT THE GOTHAM P.D. WARNING?
THEY DID MENTION THERE MIGHT BE SOME MISCREANT WITH AN INEXPLICABLE GRUDGE AGAINST OUR FINE JUDICIAL SYSTEM, YES.
LOOK, IF I HAD A DOLLAR FOR EVERY UNHAPPY CUSTOMER WHO DIDN'T LIKE THE TASTE OF THE JUSTICE I'VE SERVED UP, I COULD RETIRE.
BUT AT THIS RATE, I'LL BE SITTING AROUND THE CLOCK, THANKS TO MAYOR SHARP'S ZERO TOLERANCE CRUSADE.
IMAGINE THAT--A POLITICIAN KEEPING HIS ELECTION PROMISES. BESIDES...WASN'T THE THREAT AIMED AT A MALE JUDGE?
"ALL RISE--THIS COURT IS NOW IN SESSION, THE HONORABLE MARIAN MCALLISTER PRESIDING."

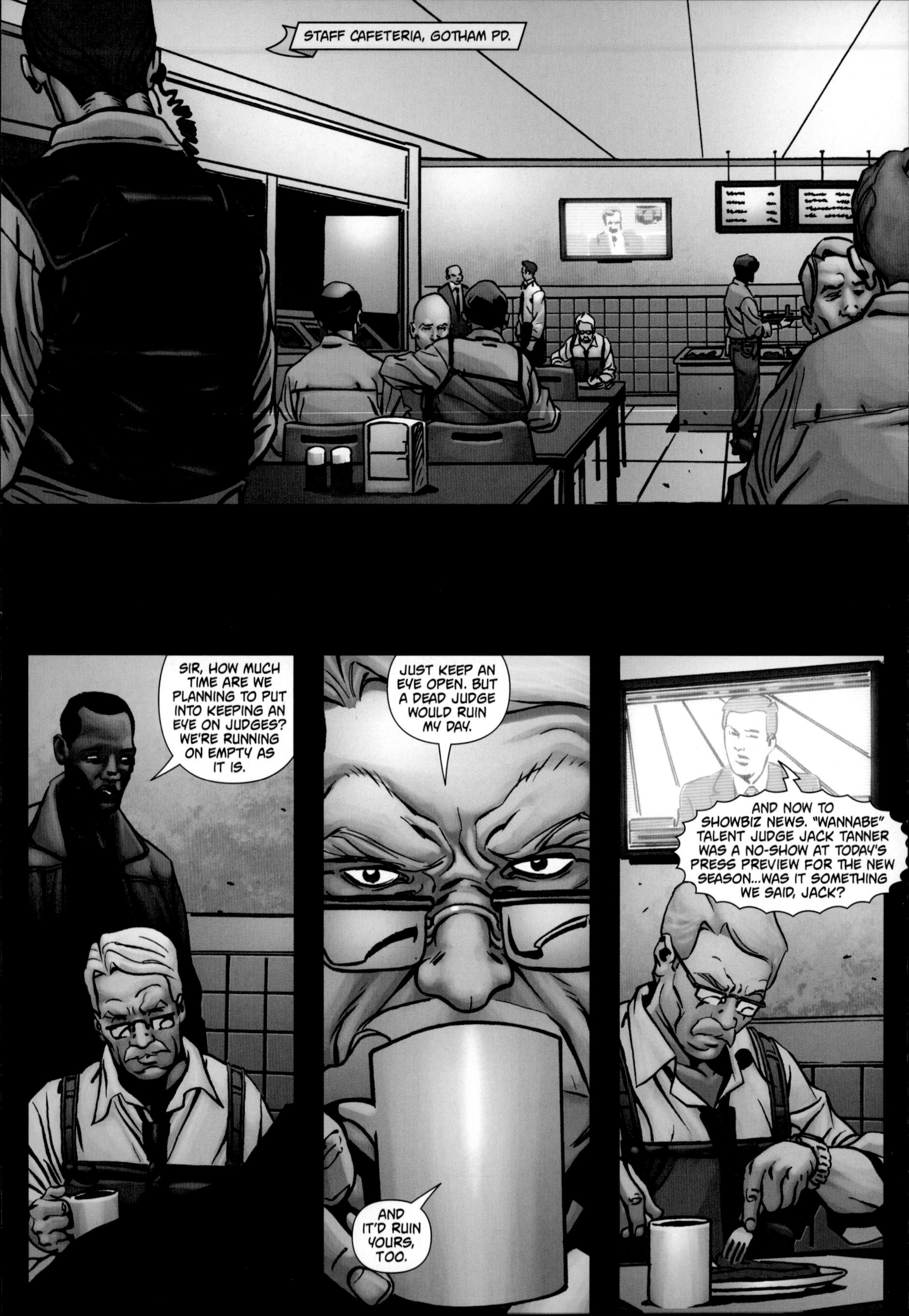
STAFF CAFETERIA, GOTHAM PD.
SIR, HOW MUCH TIME ARE WE PLANNING TO PUT INTO KEEPING AN EYE ON JUDGES? WE'RE RUNNING ON EMPTY AS IT IS.
JUST KEEP AN EYE OPEN. BUT A DEAD JUDGE WOULD RUIN MY DAY.
AND IT'D RUIN YOURS, TOO.
AND NOW TO SHOWBIZ NEWS. "WANNABE" TALENT JUDGE JACK TANNER WAS A NO-SHOW AT TODAY'S PRESS PREVIEW FOR THE NEW SEASON...WAS IT SOMETHING WE SAID, JACK?

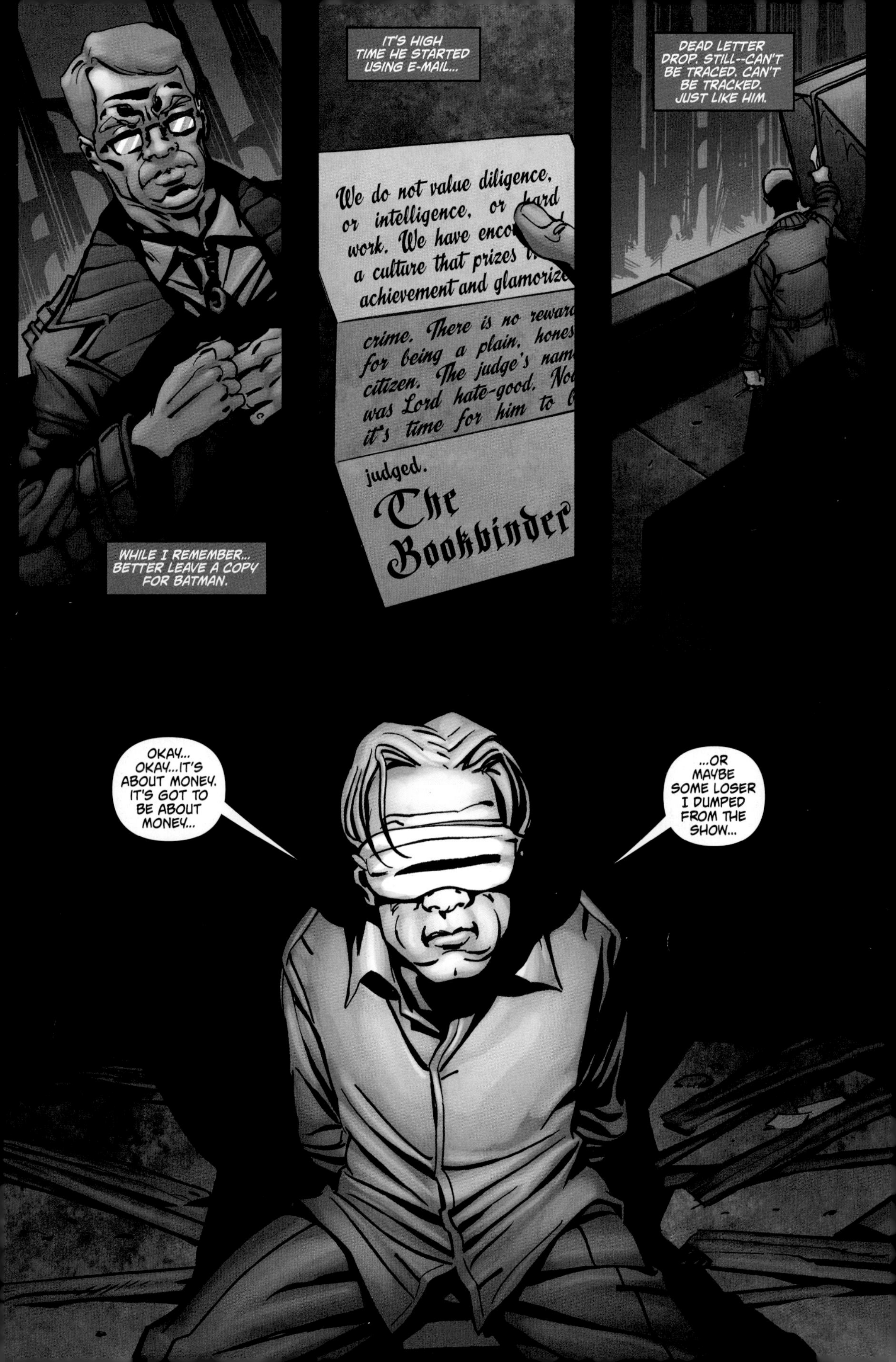
IT'S HIGH TIME HE STARTED USING E-MAIL...
We do not value diligence,
or intelligence, or ard
work. We have enco
a culture that prizes
achievement and glamorize
crime. There is no rewar
for being a plain, hones
citizen. The judge's nam
was Lord hate-good. No
it's time for him to
judged.
The Bookbinder
DEAD LETTER DROP. STILL--CAN'T BE TRACED. CAN'T BE TRACKED. JUST LIKE HIM.
WHILE I REMEMBER... BETTER LEAVE A COPY FOR BATMAN.
OKAY... OKAY...IT'S ABOUT MONEY. IT'S GOT TO BE ABOUT MONEY...
...OR MAYBE SOME LOSER I DUMPED FROM THE SHOW...

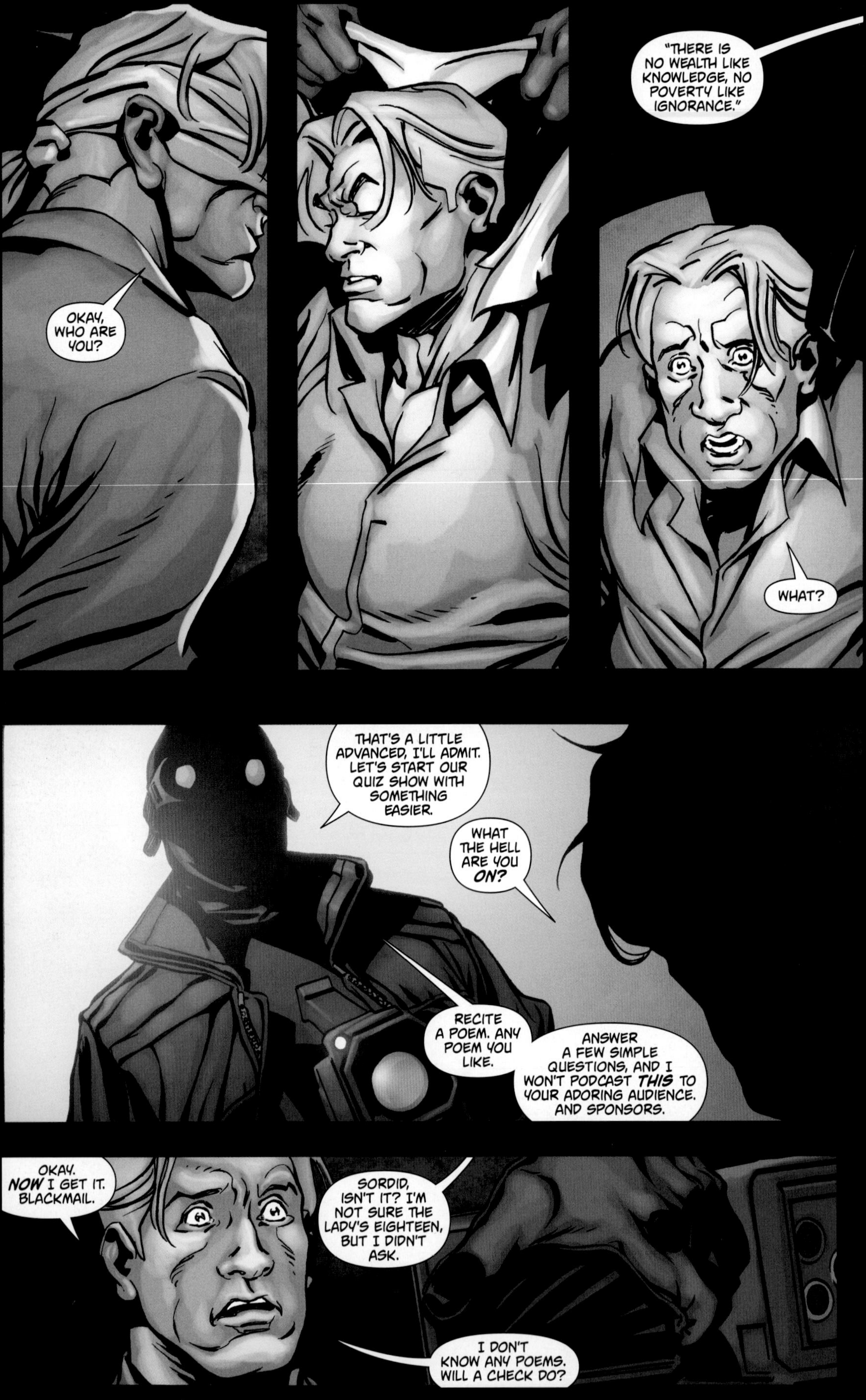
OKAY, WHO ARE YOU?
"THERE IS NO WEALTH LIKE KNOWLEDGE, NO POVERTY LIKE IGNORANCE."
WHAT?
THAT'S A LITTLE ADVANCED, I'LL ADMIT. LET'S START OUR QUIZ SHOW WITH SOMETHING EASIER.
WHAT THE HELL ARE YOU ON?
RECITE A POEM. ANY POEM YOU LIKE.
ANSWER A FEW SIMPLE QUESTIONS, AND I WON'T PODCAST THIS TO YOUR ADORING AUDIENCE. AND SPONSORS.
OKAY. NOW I GET IT. BLACKMAIL.
SORDID, ISN'T IT? I'M NOT SURE THE LADY'S EIGHTEEN, BUT I DIDN'T ASK.
I DON'T KNOW ANY POEMS. WILL A CHECK DO?

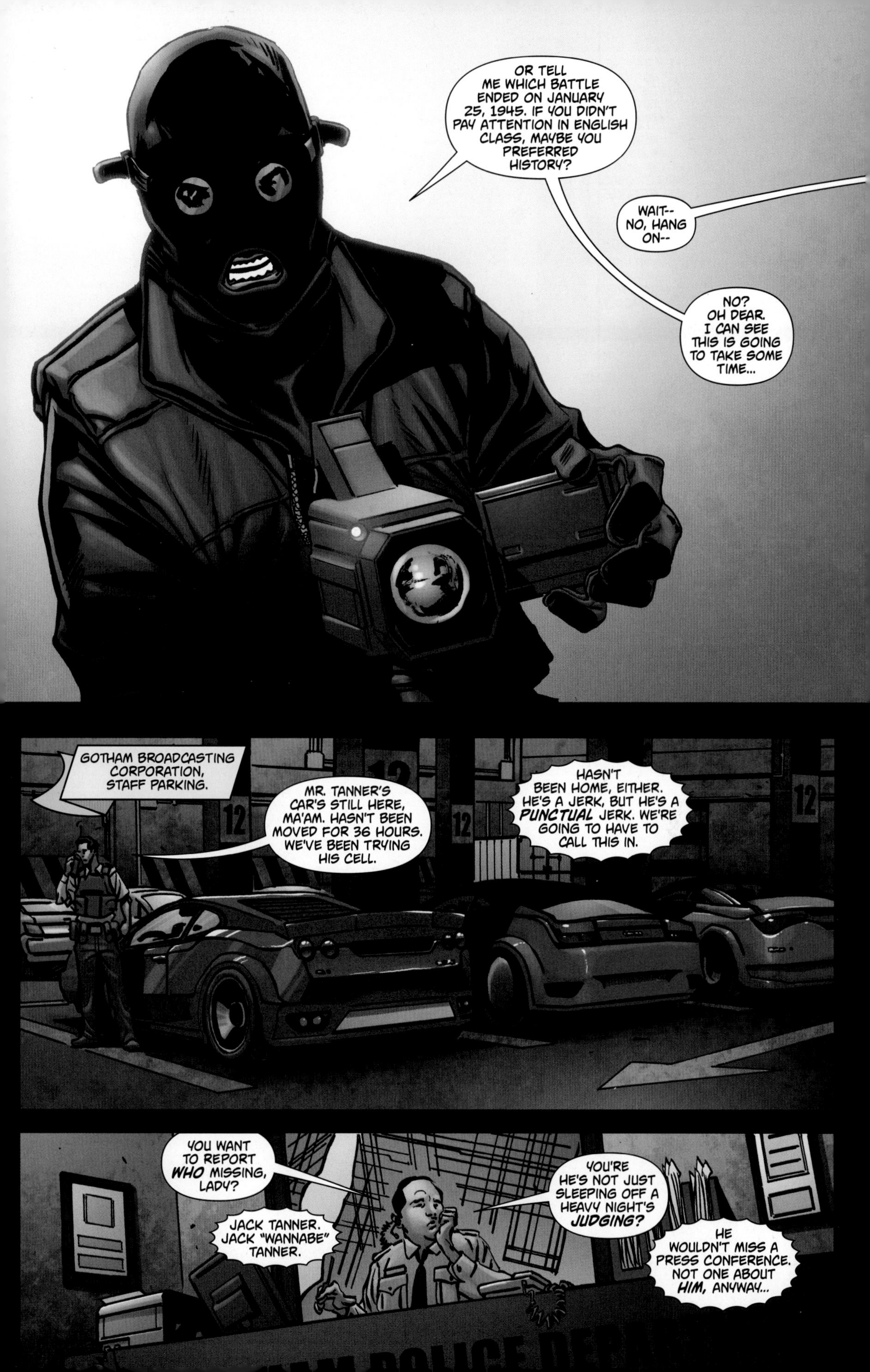
OR TELL ME WHICH BATTLE ENDED ON JANUARY 25, 1945. IF YOU DIDN'T PAY ATTENTION IN ENGLISH CLASS, MAYBE YOU PREFERRED HISTORY?
WAIT-- NO, HANG ON--
NO? OH DEAR. I CAN SEE THIS IS GOING TO TAKE SOME TIME...
GOTHAM BROADCASTING CORPORATION, STAFF PARKING.
MR. TANNER'S CAR'S STILL HERE, MA'AM. HASN'T BEEN MOVED FOR 36 HOURS. WE'VE BEEN TRYING HIS CELL.
HASN'T BEEN HOME, EITHER. HE'S A JERK, BUT HE'S A PUNCTUAL JERK. WE'RE GOING TO HAVE TO CALL THIS IN.
YOU WANT TO REPORT WHO MISSING, LADY?
JACK TANNER. JACK "WANNABE" TANNER.
YOU'RE HE'S NOT JUST SLEEPING OFF A HEAVY NIGHT'S JUDGING?
HE WOULDN'T MISS A PRESS CONFERENCE. NOT ONE ABOUT HIM, ANYWAY...

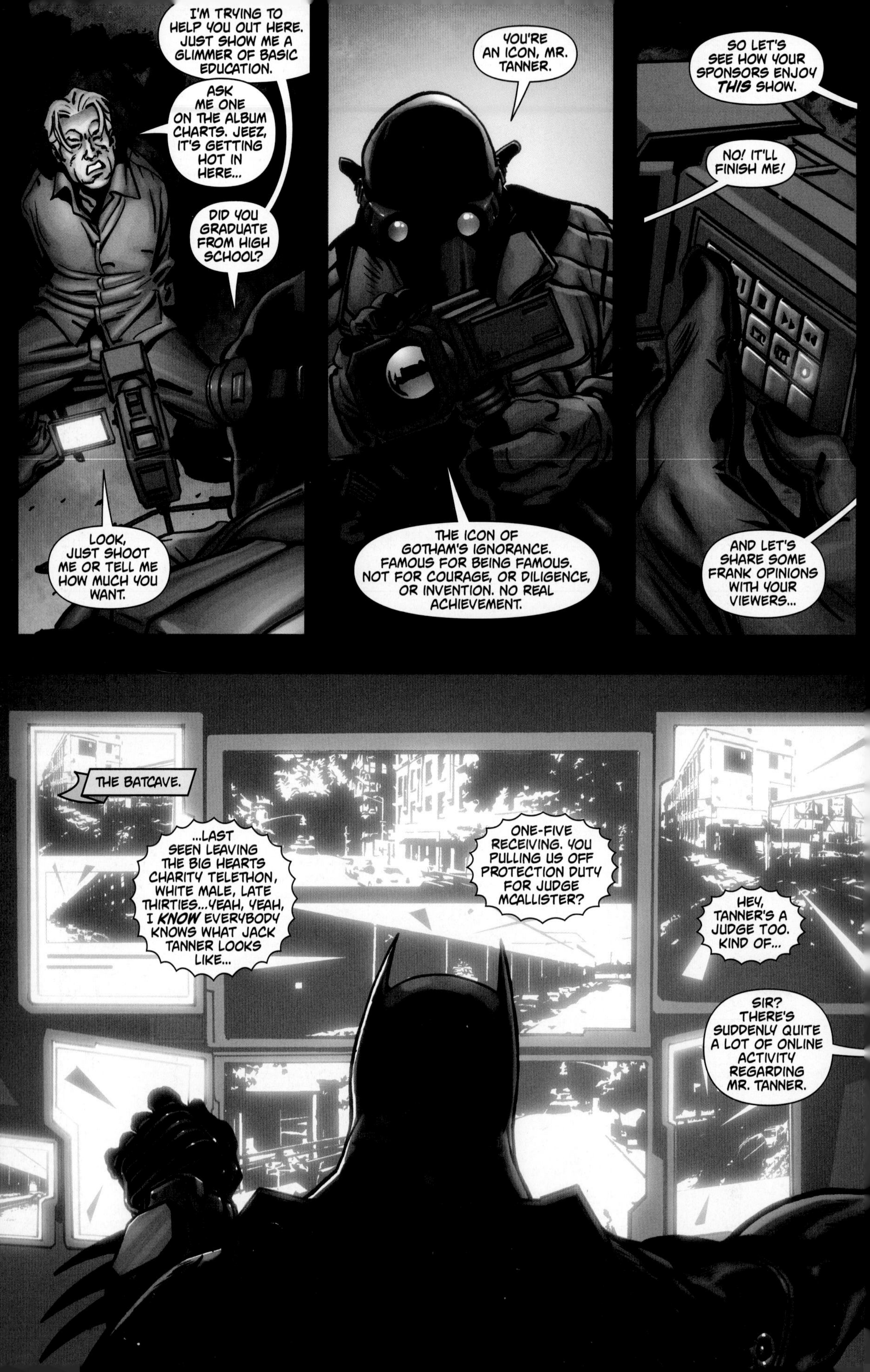

I'M TRYING TO HELP YOU OUT HERE. JUST SHOW ME A GLIMMER OF BASIC EDUCATION.
ASK ME ONE ON THE ALBUM CHARTS. JEEZ, IT'S GETTING HOT IN HERE...
DID YOU GRADUATE FROM HIGH SCHOOL?
LOOK, JUST SHOOT ME OR TELL ME HOW MUCH YOU WANT.
YOU'RE AN ICON, MR. TANNER.
THE ICON OF GOTHAM'S IGNORANCE. FAMOUS FOR BEING FAMOUS. NOT FOR COURAGE, OR DILIGENCE, OR INVENTION. NO REAL ACHIEVEMENT.
SO LET'S SEE HOW YOUR SPONSORS ENJOY *THIS* SHOW.
NO! IT'LL FINISH ME!
AND LET'S SHARE SOME FRANK OPINIONS WITH YOUR VIEWERS...
THE BATCAVE.
...LAST SEEN LEAVING THE BIG HEARTS CHARITY TELETHON, WHITE MALE, LATE THIRTIES...YEAH, YEAH, I *KNOW* EVERYBODY KNOWS WHAT JACK TANNER LOOKS LIKE...
ONE-FIVE RECEIVING. YOU PULLING US OFF PROTECTION DUTY FOR JUDGE MCALLISTER?
HEY, TANNER'S A JUDGE TOO. KIND OF...
SIR? THERE'S SUDDENLY QUITE A LOT OF ONLINE ACTIVITY REGARDING MR. TANNER.

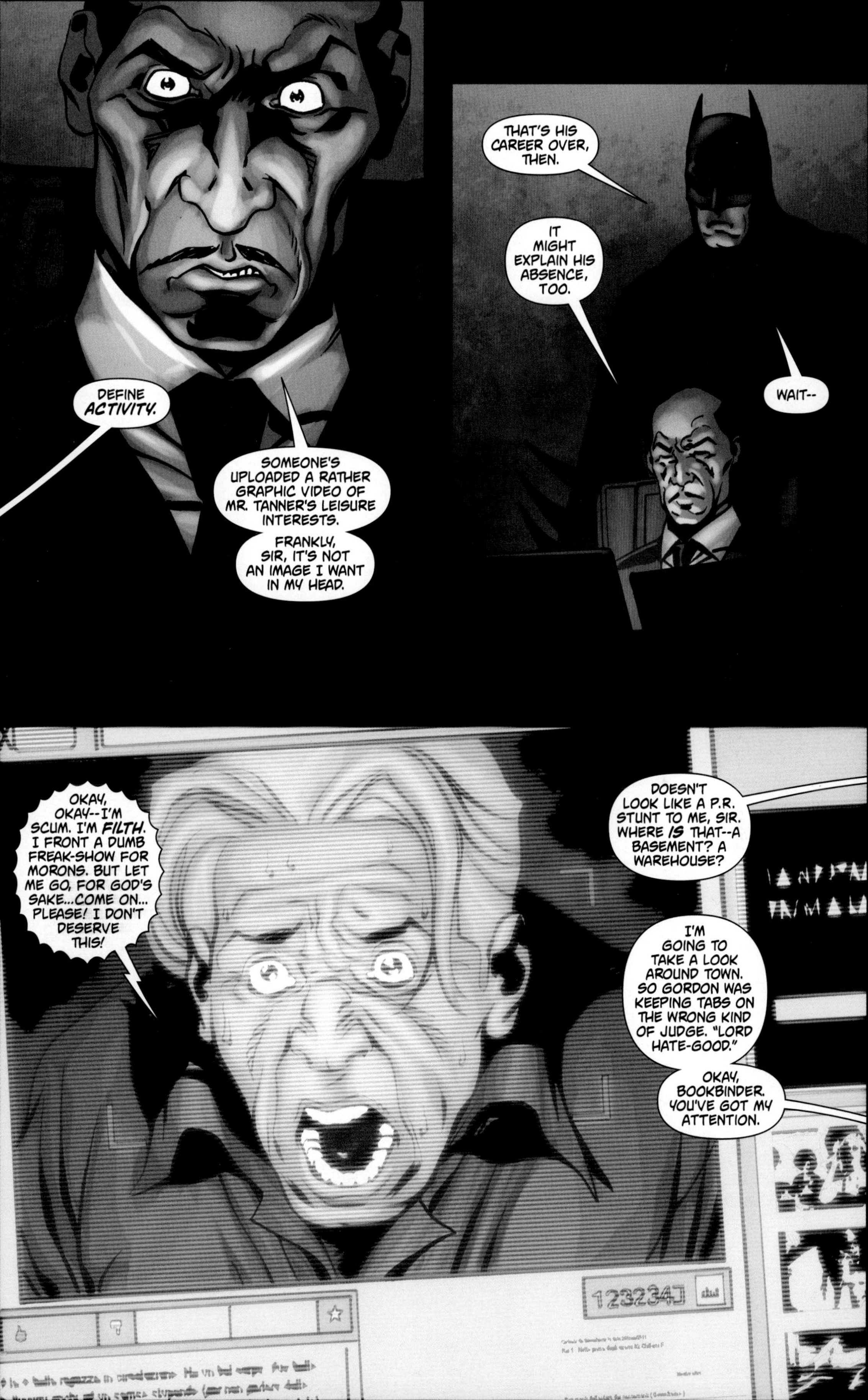
DEFINE *ACTIVITY.*
SOMEONE'S UPLOADED A RATHER GRAPHIC VIDEO OF MR. TANNER'S LEISURE INTERESTS.
FRANKLY, SIR, IT'S NOT AN IMAGE I WANT IN MY HEAD.
THAT'S HIS CAREER OVER, THEN.
IT MIGHT EXPLAIN HIS ABSENCE, TOO.
WAIT--
OKAY, OKAY--I'M SCUM. I'M *FILTH.* I FRONT A DUMB FREAK-SHOW FOR MORONS. BUT LET ME GO, FOR GOD'S SAKE...COME ON... PLEASE! I DON'T DESERVE THIS!
DOESN'T LOOK LIKE A P.R. STUNT TO ME, SIR. WHERE *IS* THAT--A BASEMENT? A WAREHOUSE?
I'M GOING TO TAKE A LOOK AROUND TOWN. SO GORDON WAS KEEPING TABS ON THE WRONG KIND OF JUDGE. "LORD HATE-GOOD."
OKAY, BOOKBINDER. YOU'VE GOT MY ATTENTION.

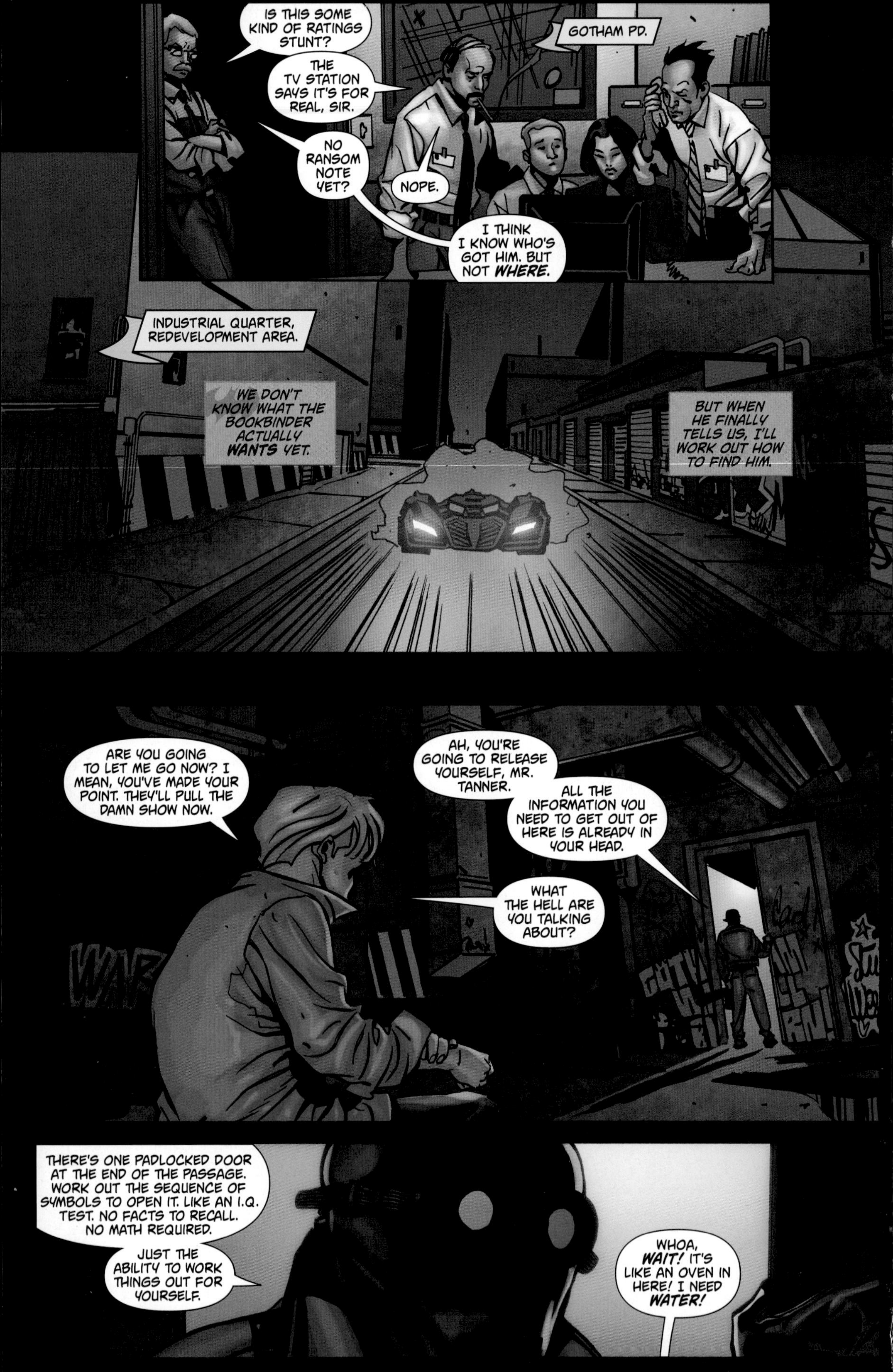

IS THIS SOME KIND OF RATINGS STUNT?
GOTHAM PD.
THE TV STATION SAYS IT'S FOR REAL, SIR.
NO RANSOM NOTE YET?
NOPE.
I THINK I KNOW WHO'S GOT HIM. BUT NOT WHERE.
INDUSTRIAL QUARTER, REDEVELOPMENT AREA.
WE DON'T KNOW WHAT THE BOOKBINDER ACTUALLY WANTS YET.
BUT WHEN HE FINALLY TELLS US, I'LL WORK OUT HOW TO FIND HIM.
ARE YOU GOING TO LET ME GO NOW? I MEAN, YOU'VE MADE YOUR POINT. THEY'LL PULL THE DAMN SHOW NOW.
AH, YOU'RE GOING TO RELEASE YOURSELF, MR. TANNER.
ALL THE INFORMATION YOU NEED TO GET OUT OF HERE IS ALREADY IN YOUR HEAD.
WHAT THE HELL ARE YOU TALKING ABOUT?
THERE'S ONE PADLOCKED DOOR AT THE END OF THE PASSAGE. WORK OUT THE SEQUENCE OF SYMBOLS TO OPEN IT. LIKE AN I.Q. TEST. NO FACTS TO RECALL. NO MATH REQUIRED.
JUST THE ABILITY TO WORK THINGS OUT FOR YOURSELF.
WHOA, WAIT! IT'S LIKE AN OVEN IN HERE! I NEED WATER!

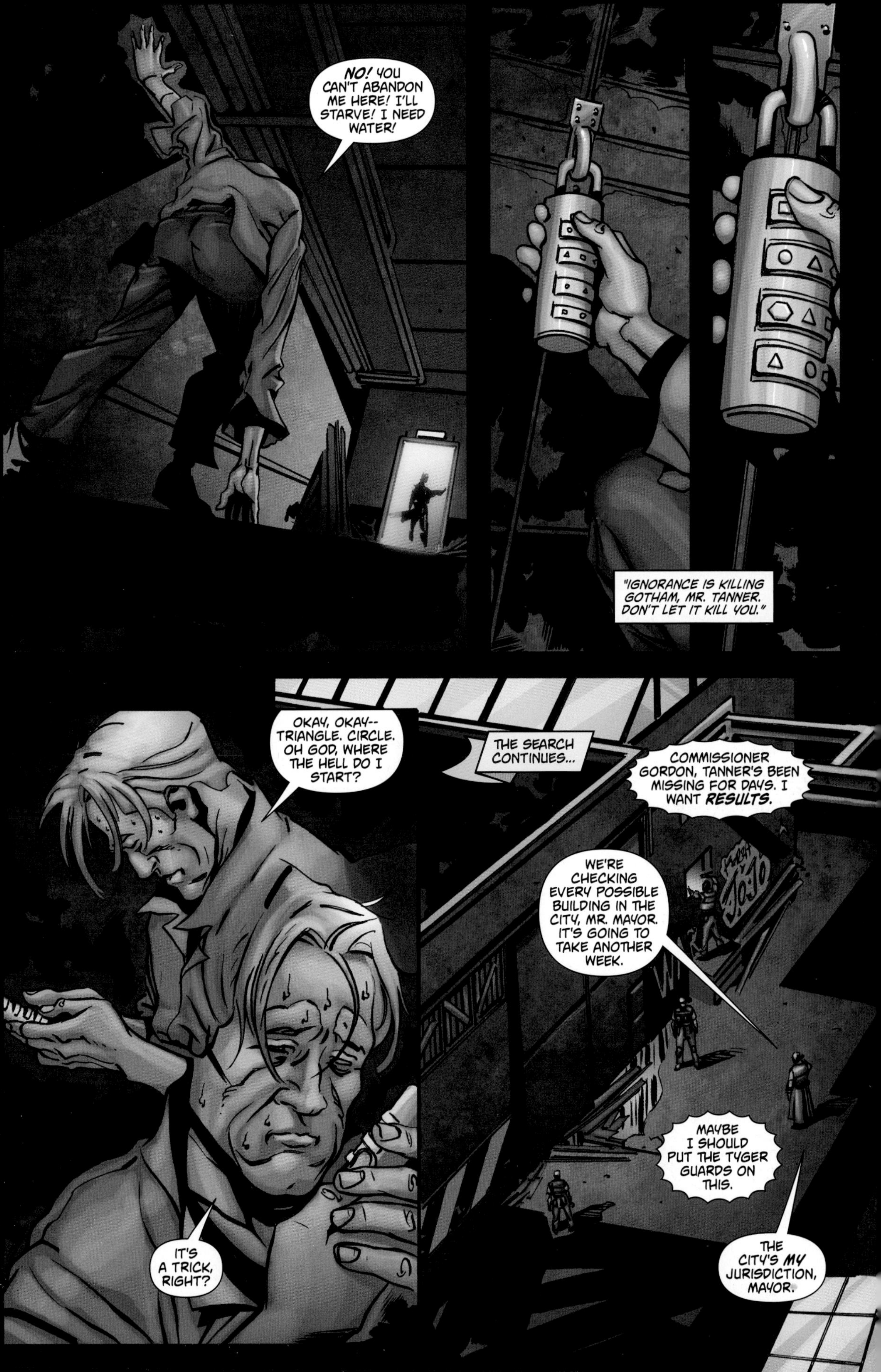
NO! YOU CAN'T ABANDON ME HERE! I'LL STARVE! I NEED WATER!
"IGNORANCE IS KILLING GOTHAM, MR. TANNER. DON'T LET IT KILL YOU."
OKAY, OKAY-- TRIANGLE. CIRCLE. OH GOD, WHERE THE HELL DO I START?
IT'S A TRICK, RIGHT?
THE SEARCH CONTINUES...
COMMISSIONER GORDON, TANNER'S BEEN MISSING FOR DAYS. I WANT RESULTS.
WE'RE CHECKING EVERY POSSIBLE BUILDING IN THE CITY, MR. MAYOR. IT'S GOING TO TAKE ANOTHER WEEK.
MAYBE I SHOULD PUT THE TYGER GUARDS ON THIS.
THE CITY'S MY JURISDICTION, MAYOR.

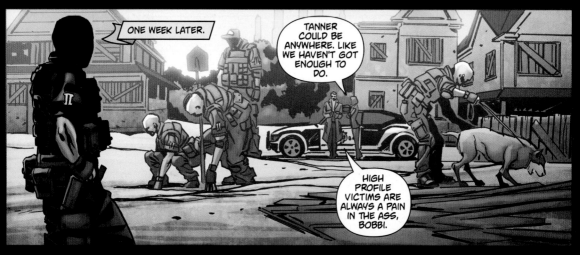

ONE WEEK LATER.

TANNER COULD BE ANYWHERE. LIKE WE HAVEN'T GOT ENOUGH TO DO.

HIGH PROFILE VICTIMS ARE ALWAYS A PAIN IN THE ASS, BOBBI.

HEADS UP. JAKE'S A CORPSE DOG, RIGHT?

AFRAID SO, SIR. HE ONLY REACTS LIKE THAT WHEN HE SCENTS A STIFF.

HERE WE GO...

COMMISSIONER? DETECTIVE RHEE? WE'VE GOT SOMETHING!

CALL OFF THE SEARCH. GET FORENSIC DOWN HERE *NOW.*

LOOKS LIKE WE'VE GOT A NEW LUNATIC IN TOWN.

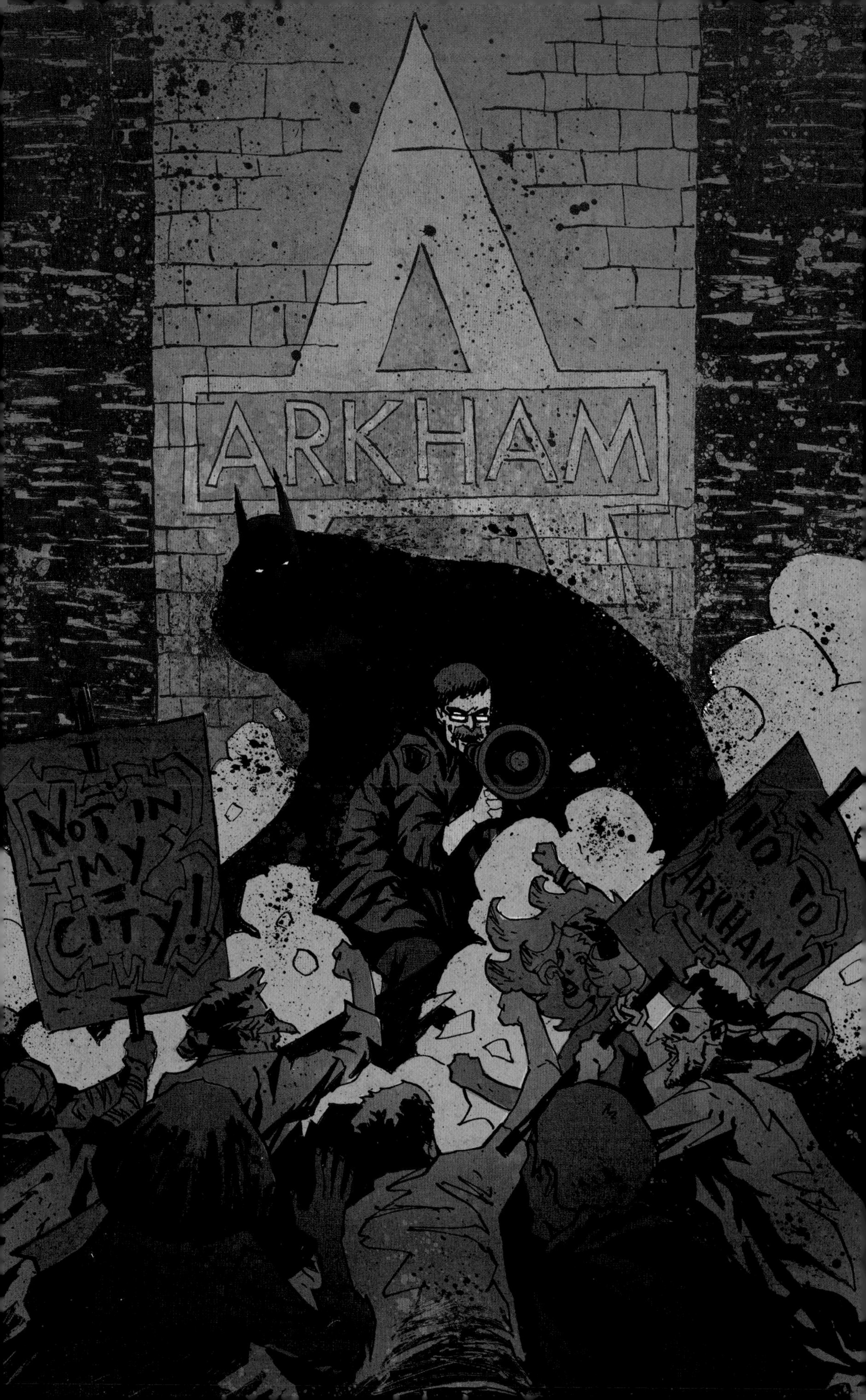
ARKHAM
NOT IN MY CITY!
NO TO ARKHAM!

WELCOME
TO THE SLOUGH OF DESPOND
PART TWO

WRITTEN BY: KAREN TRAVISS
ART BY: CHRISTIAN DUCE
COLORS BY: ALEJANDRO SANCHEZ
LETTERS BY: TRAVIS LANHAM
COVER BY: CHRIS MITTEN

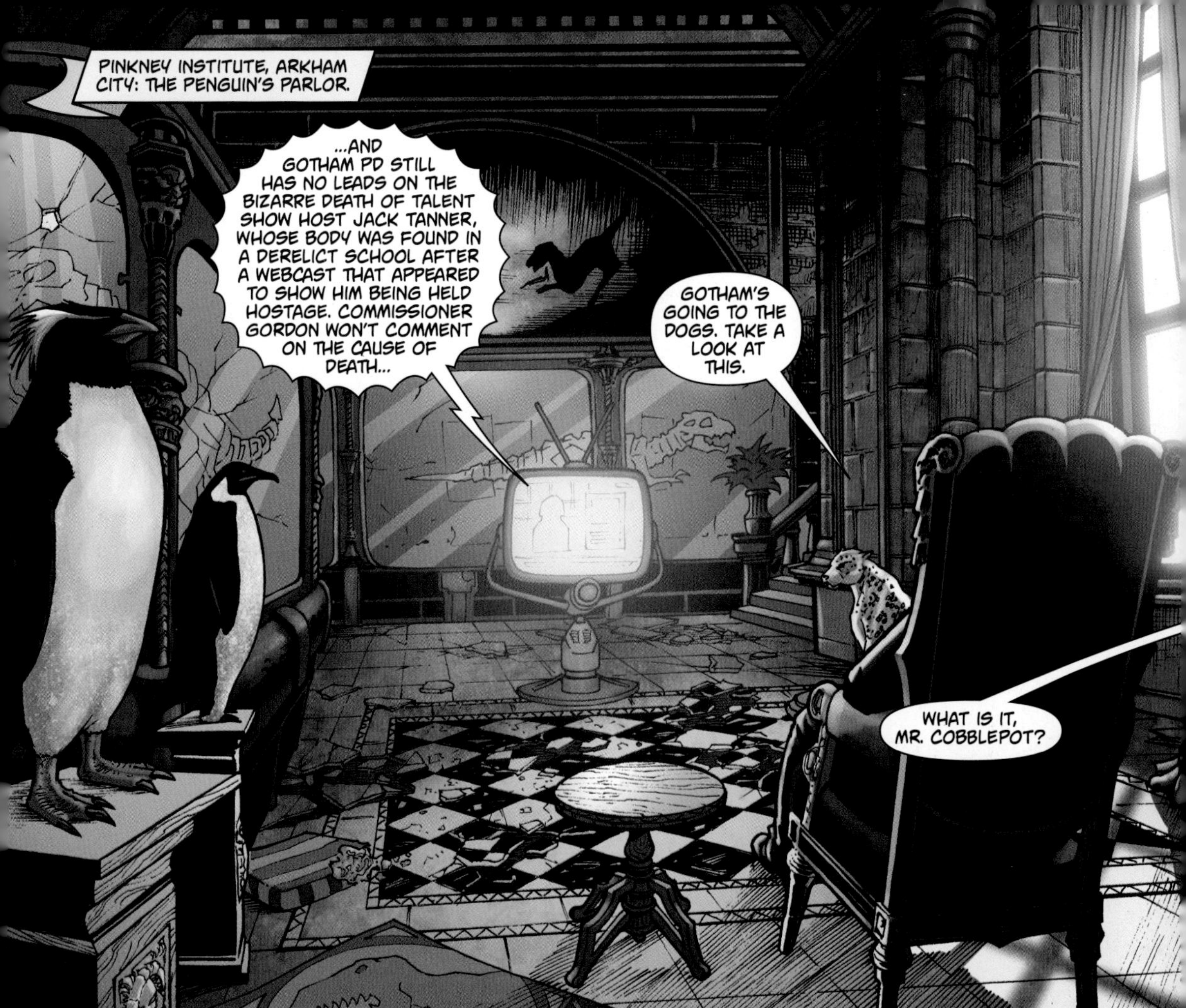
PINKNEY INSTITUTE, ARKHAM CITY: THE PENGUIN'S PARLOR.
...AND GOTHAM PD STILL HAS NO LEADS ON THE BIZARRE DEATH OF TALENT SHOW HOST JACK TANNER, WHOSE BODY WAS FOUND IN A DERELICT SCHOOL AFTER A WEBCAST THAT APPEARED TO SHOW HIM BEING HELD HOSTAGE. COMMISSIONER GORDON WON'T COMMENT ON THE CAUSE OF DEATH...
GOTHAM'S GOING TO THE DOGS. TAKE A LOOK AT THIS.
WHAT IS IT, MR. COBBLEPOT?
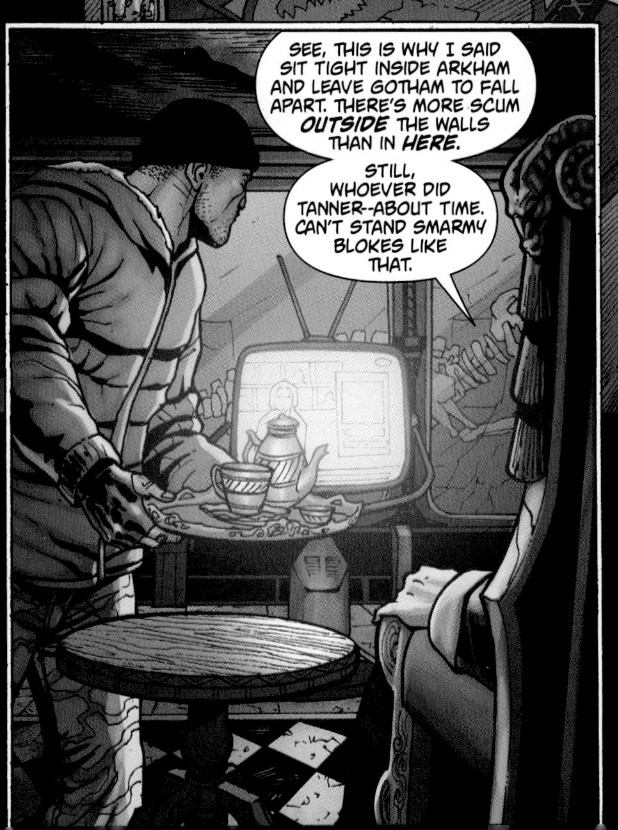
SEE, THIS IS WHY I SAID SIT TIGHT INSIDE ARKHAM AND LEAVE GOTHAM TO FALL APART. THERE'S MORE SCUM **OUTSIDE** THE WALLS THAN IN **HERE.**
STILL, WHOEVER DID TANNER--ABOUT TIME. CAN'T STAND SMARMY BLOKES LIKE THAT.
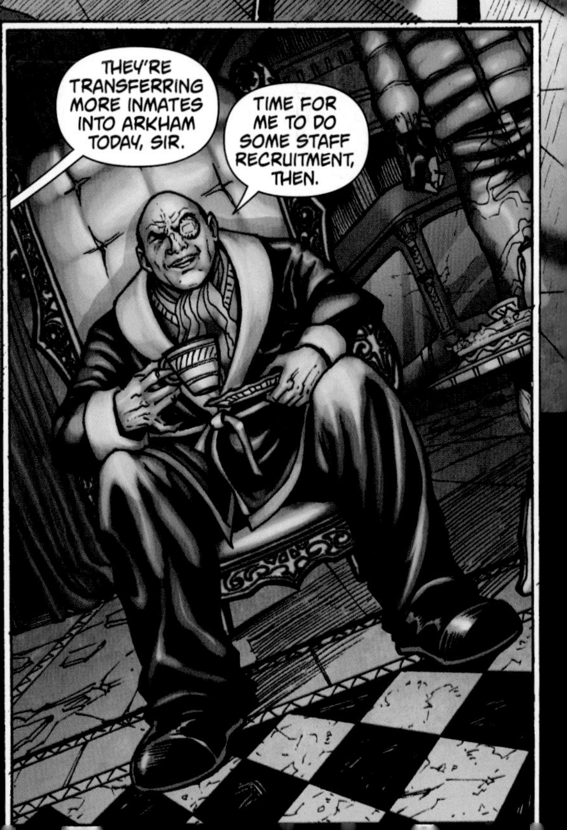
THEY'RE TRANSFERRING MORE INMATES INTO ARKHAM TODAY, SIR.
TIME FOR ME TO DO SOME STAFF RECRUITMENT, THEN.

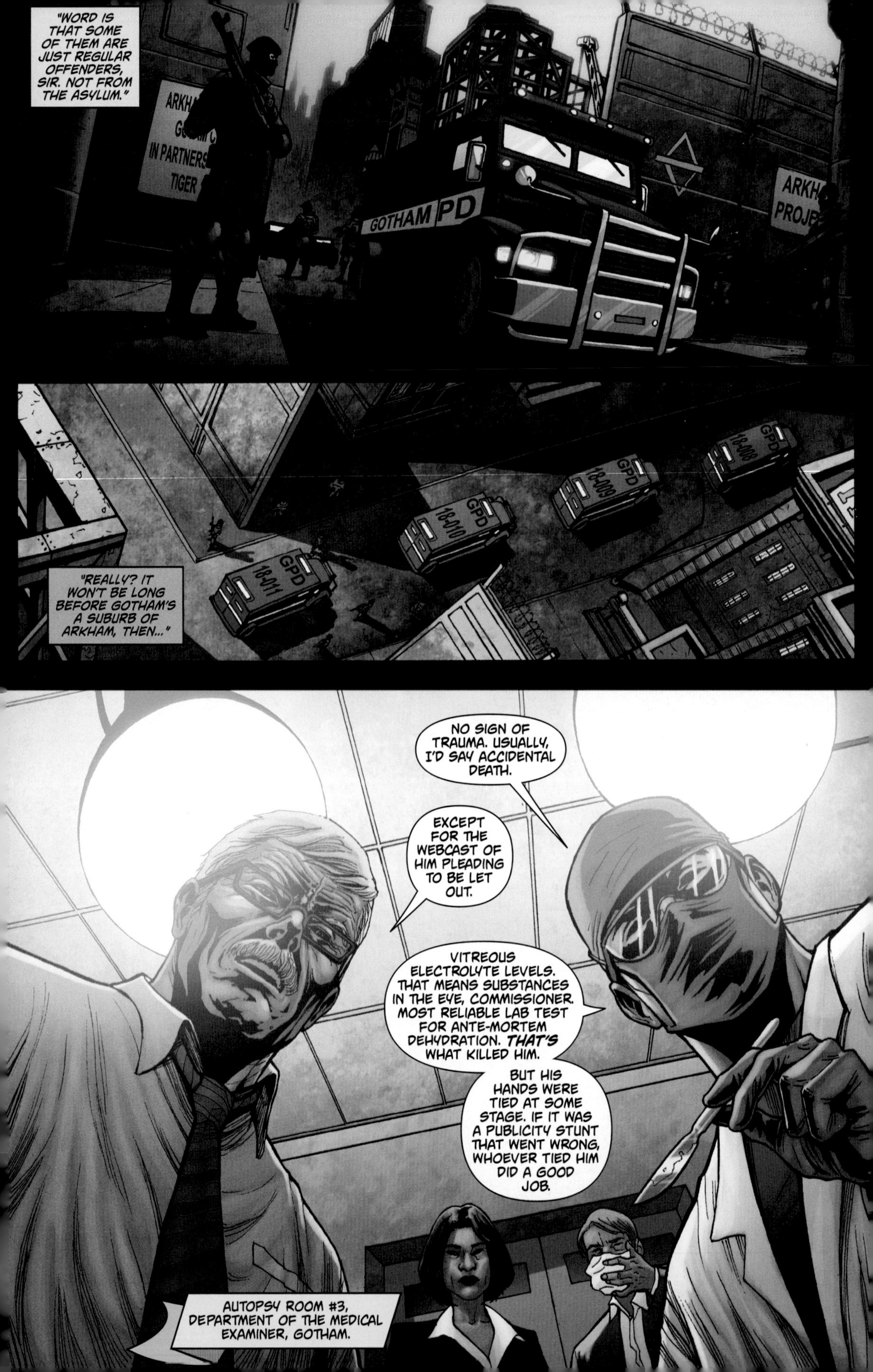
"WORD IS THAT SOME OF THEM ARE JUST REGULAR OFFENDERS, SIR. NOT FROM THE ASYLUM."
GOTHAM PD
GPD 18-008
GPD 18-009
GPD 18-010
GPD 18-011
"REALLY? IT WON'T BE LONG BEFORE GOTHAM'S A SUBURB OF ARKHAM, THEN..."
NO SIGN OF TRAUMA. USUALLY, I'D SAY ACCIDENTAL DEATH.
EXCEPT FOR THE WEBCAST OF HIM PLEADING TO BE LET OUT.
VITREOUS ELECTROLYTE LEVELS. THAT MEANS SUBSTANCES IN THE EYE, COMMISSIONER. MOST RELIABLE LAB TEST FOR ANTE-MORTEM DEHYDRATION. THAT'S WHAT KILLED HIM.
BUT HIS HANDS WERE TIED AT SOME STAGE. IF IT WAS A PUBLICITY STUNT THAT WENT WRONG, WHOEVER TIED HIM DID A GOOD JOB.
AUTOPSY ROOM #3, DEPARTMENT OF THE MEDICAL EXAMINER, GOTHAM.

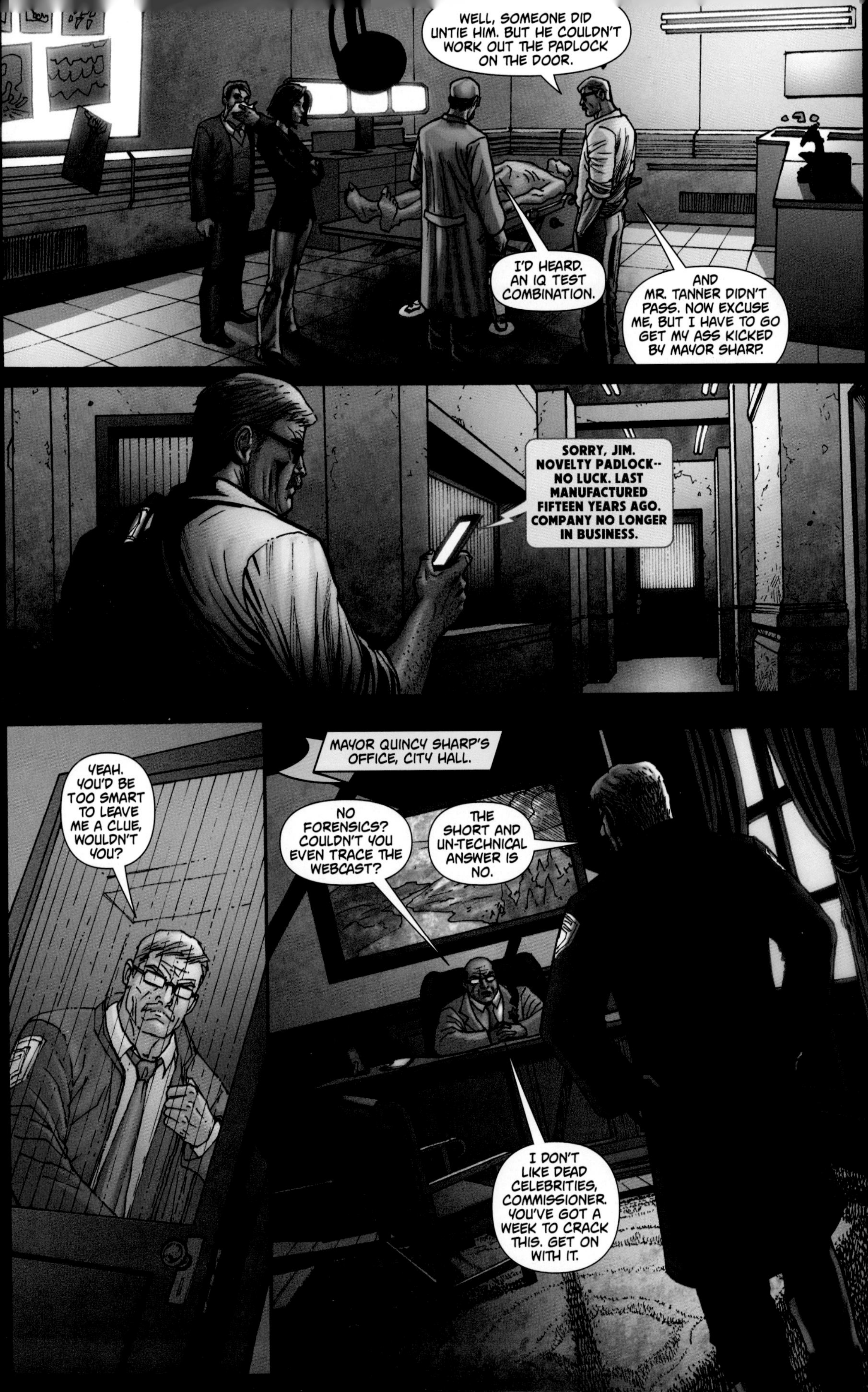
WELL, SOMEONE DID UNTIE HIM. BUT HE COULDN'T WORK OUT THE PADLOCK ON THE DOOR.
I'D HEARD. AN IQ TEST COMBINATION.
AND MR. TANNER DIDN'T PASS. NOW EXCUSE ME, BUT I HAVE TO GO GET MY ASS KICKED BY MAYOR SHARP.
SORRY, JIM. NOVELTY PADLOCK-- NO LUCK. LAST MANUFACTURED FIFTEEN YEARS AGO. COMPANY NO LONGER IN BUSINESS.
YEAH. YOU'D BE TOO SMART TO LEAVE ME A CLUE, WOULDN'T YOU?
MAYOR QUINCY SHARP'S OFFICE, CITY HALL.
NO FORENSICS? COULDN'T YOU EVEN TRACE THE WEBCAST?
THE SHORT AND UN-TECHNICAL ANSWER IS NO.
I DON'T LIKE DEAD CELEBRITIES, COMMISSIONER. YOU'VE GOT A WEEK TO CRACK THIS. GET ON WITH IT.

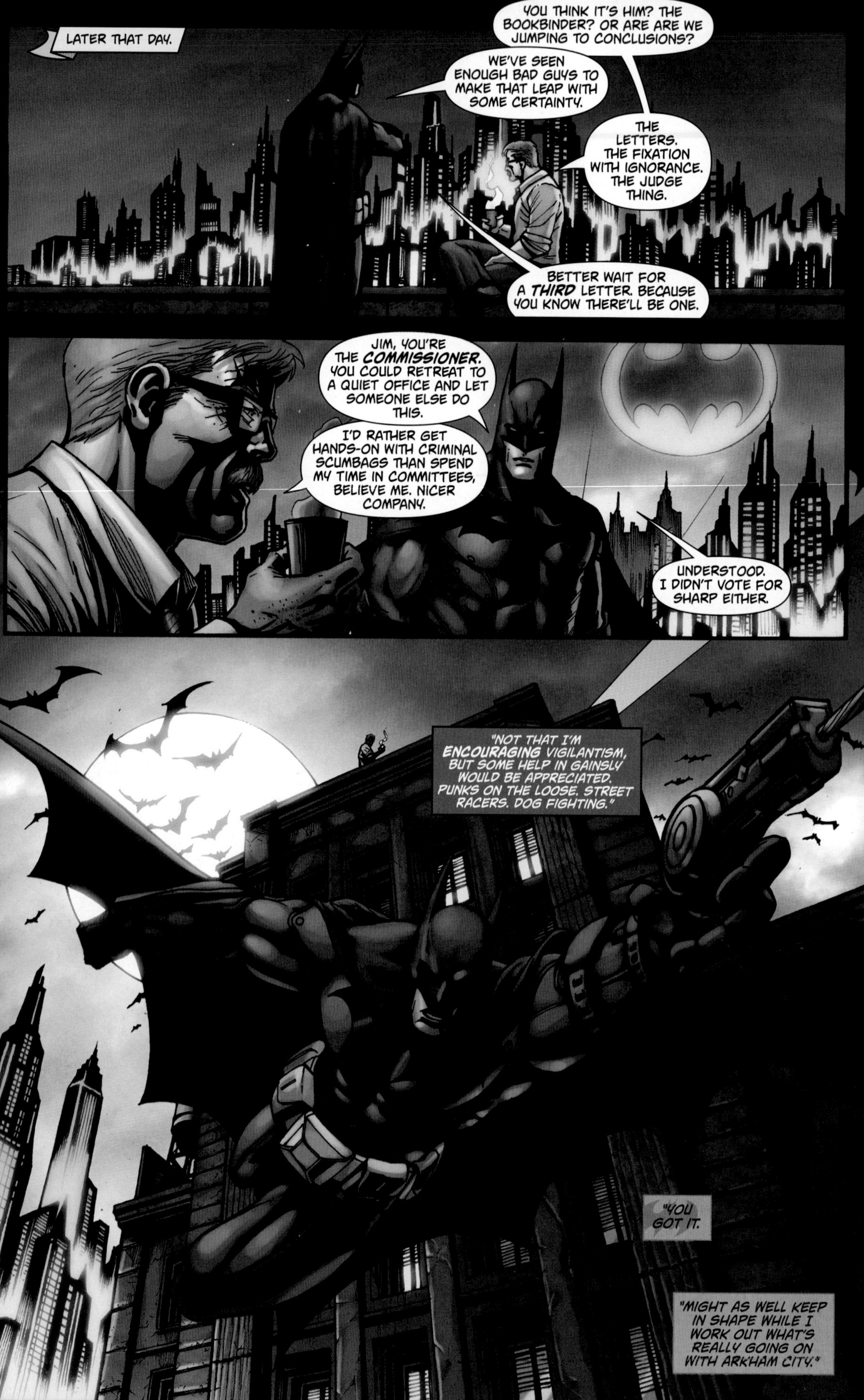
LATER THAT DAY.
YOU THINK IT'S HIM? THE BOOKBINDER? OR ARE ARE WE JUMPING TO CONCLUSIONS?
WE'VE SEEN ENOUGH BAD GUYS TO MAKE THAT LEAP WITH SOME CERTAINTY.
THE LETTERS. THE FIXATION WITH IGNORANCE. THE JUDGE THING.
BETTER WAIT FOR A THIRD LETTER. BECAUSE YOU KNOW THERE'LL BE ONE.
JIM, YOU'RE THE COMMISSIONER. YOU COULD RETREAT TO A QUIET OFFICE AND LET SOMEONE ELSE DO THIS.
I'D RATHER GET HANDS-ON WITH CRIMINAL SCUMBAGS THAN SPEND MY TIME IN COMMITTEES, BELIEVE ME. NICER COMPANY.
UNDERSTOOD. I DIDN'T VOTE FOR SHARP EITHER.
"NOT THAT I'M ENCOURAGING VIGILANTISM, BUT SOME HELP IN GAINSLY WOULD BE APPRECIATED. PUNKS ON THE LOOSE. STREET RACERS. DOG FIGHTING."
"YOU GOT IT.
"MIGHT AS WELL KEEP IN SHAPE WHILE I WORK OUT WHAT'S REALLY GOING ON WITH ARKHAM CITY."

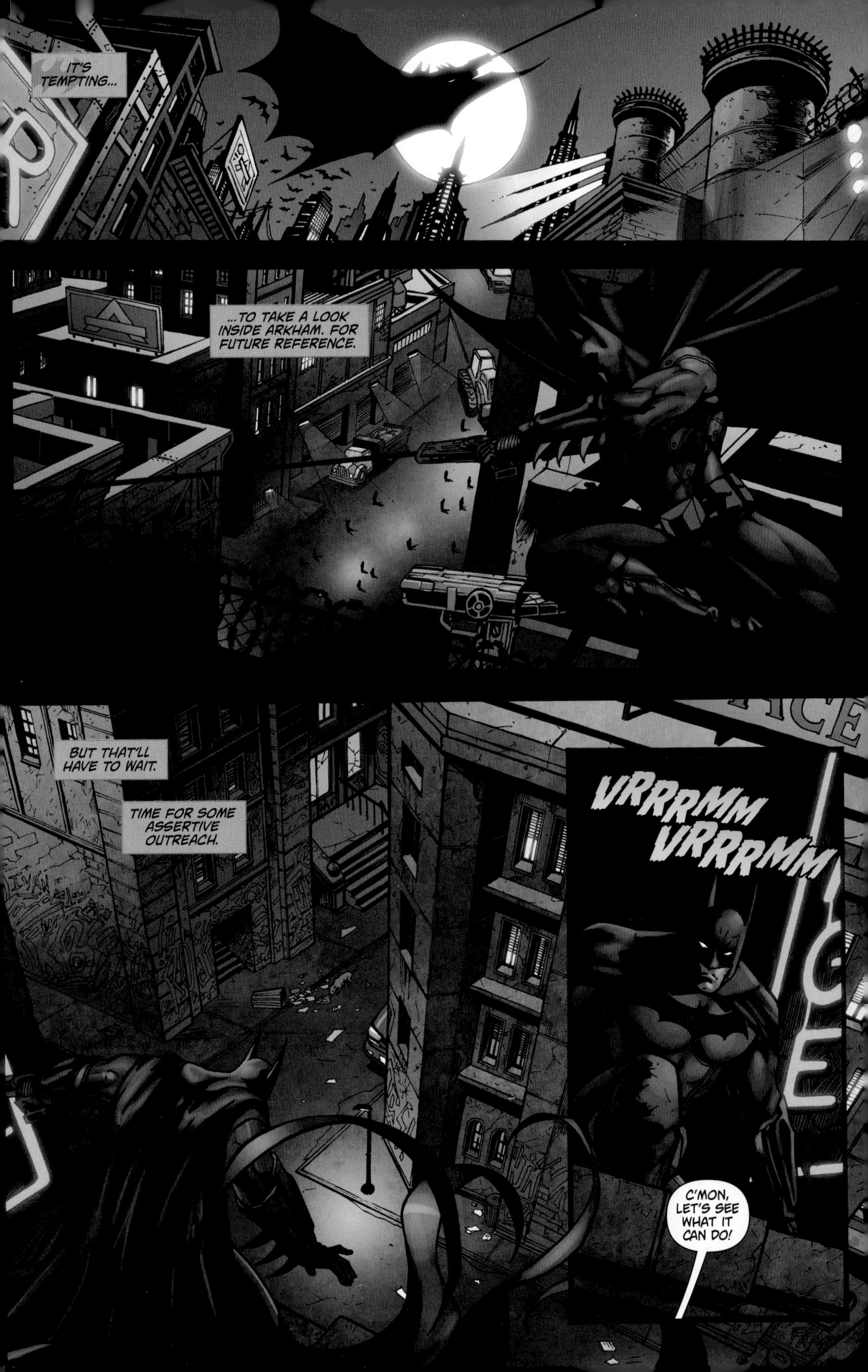
IT'S TEMPTING...
...TO TAKE A LOOK INSIDE ARKHAM. FOR FUTURE REFERENCE.
BUT THAT'LL HAVE TO WAIT.
TIME FOR SOME ASSERTIVE OUTREACH.
VRRRMM VRRRMM
C'MON, LET'S SEE WHAT IT CAN DO!

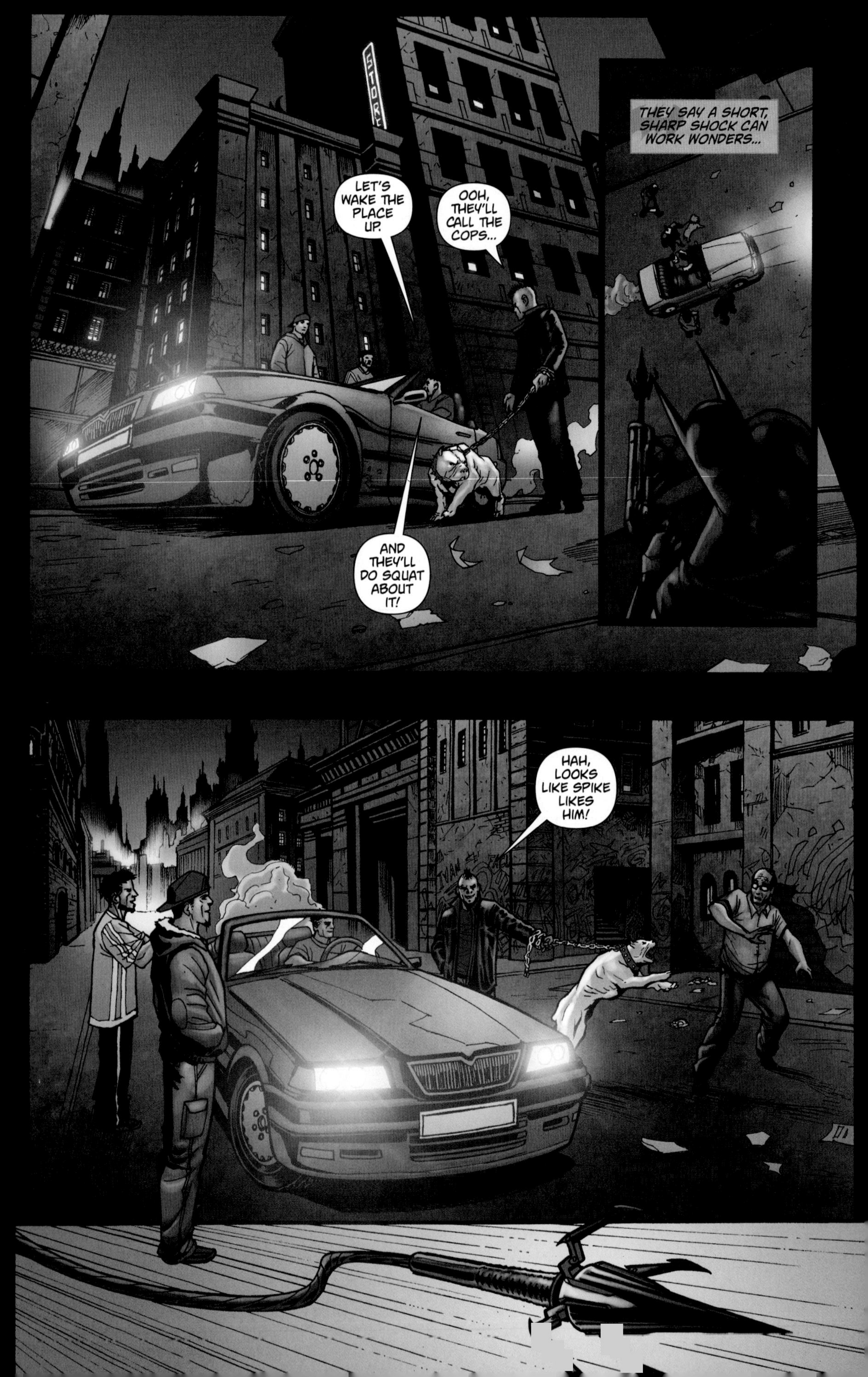
STORE
LET'S WAKE THE PLACE UP.
OOH, THEY'LL CALL THE COPS...
AND THEY'LL DO SQUAT ABOUT IT!
THEY SAY A SHORT, SHARP SHOCK CAN WORK WONDERS...
HAH, LOOKS LIKE SPIKE LIKES HIM!

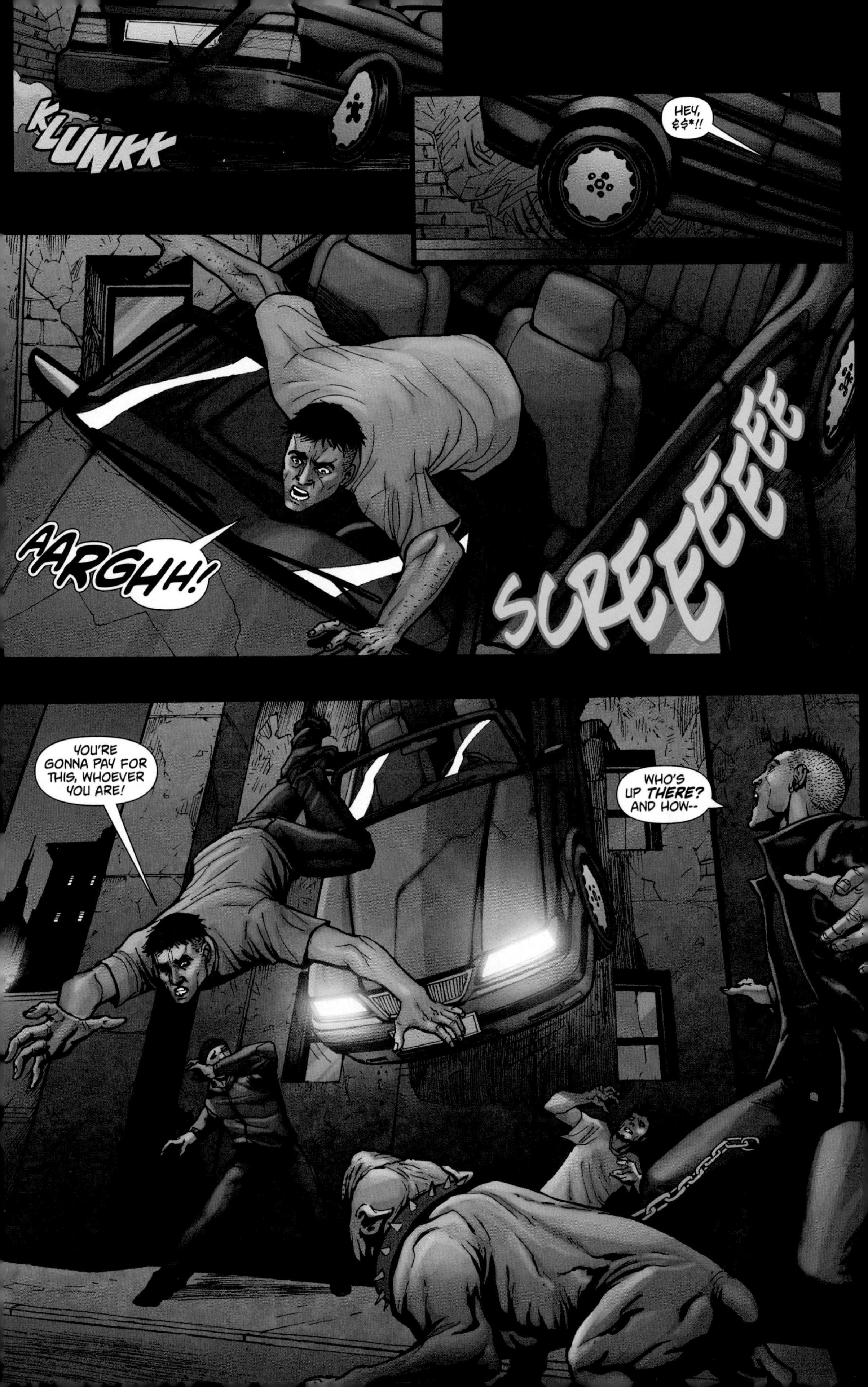
KLUNKK
HEY, $$*!!
AARGHH!
SCREEEEEE
YOU'RE GONNA PAY FOR THIS, WHOEVER YOU ARE!
WHO'S UP THERE? AND HOW--

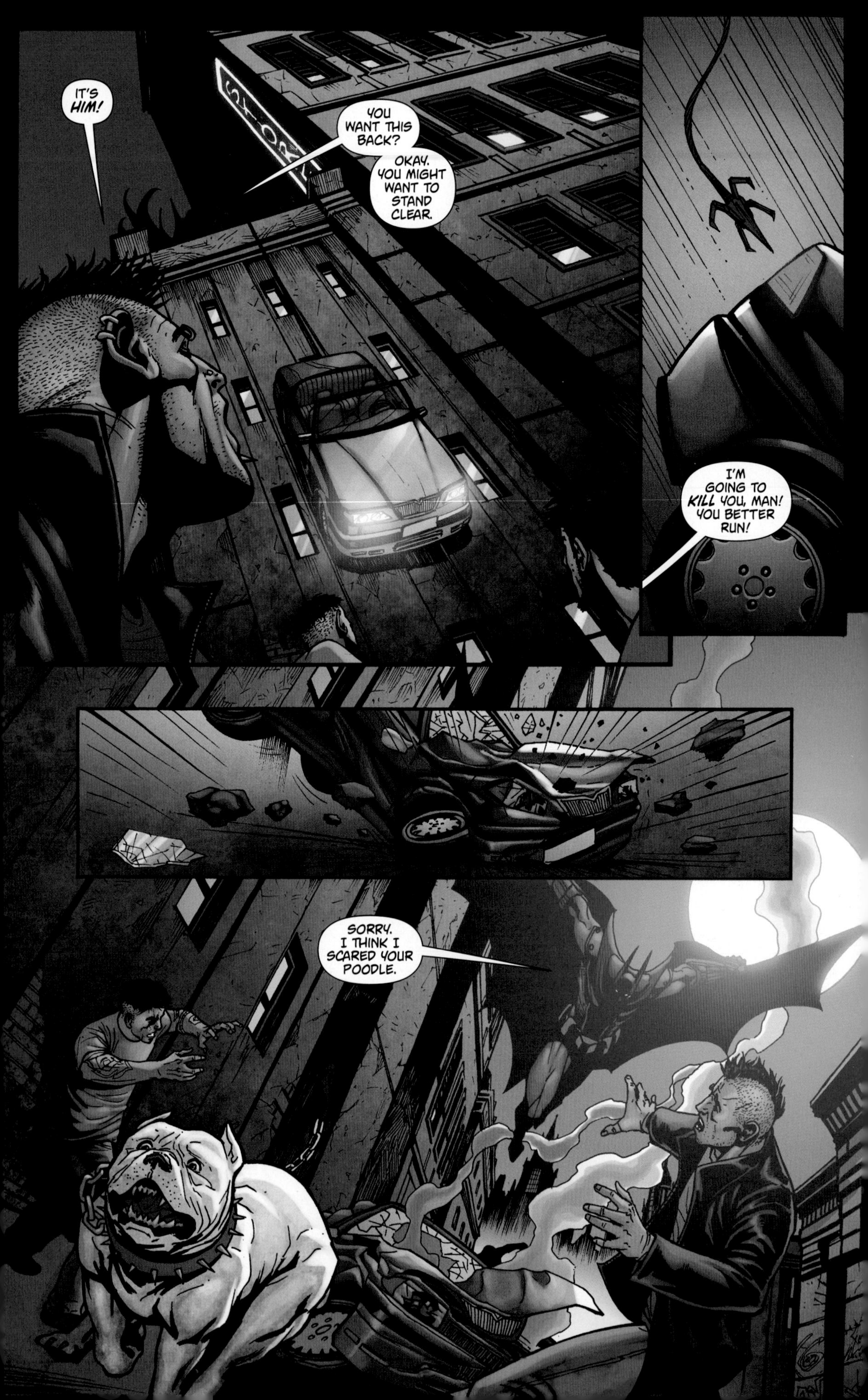
IT'S HIM!
YOU WANT THIS BACK?
OKAY. YOU MIGHT WANT TO STAND CLEAR.
I'M GOING TO KILL YOU, MAN! YOU BETTER RUN!
SORRY. I THINK I SCARED YOUR POODLE.

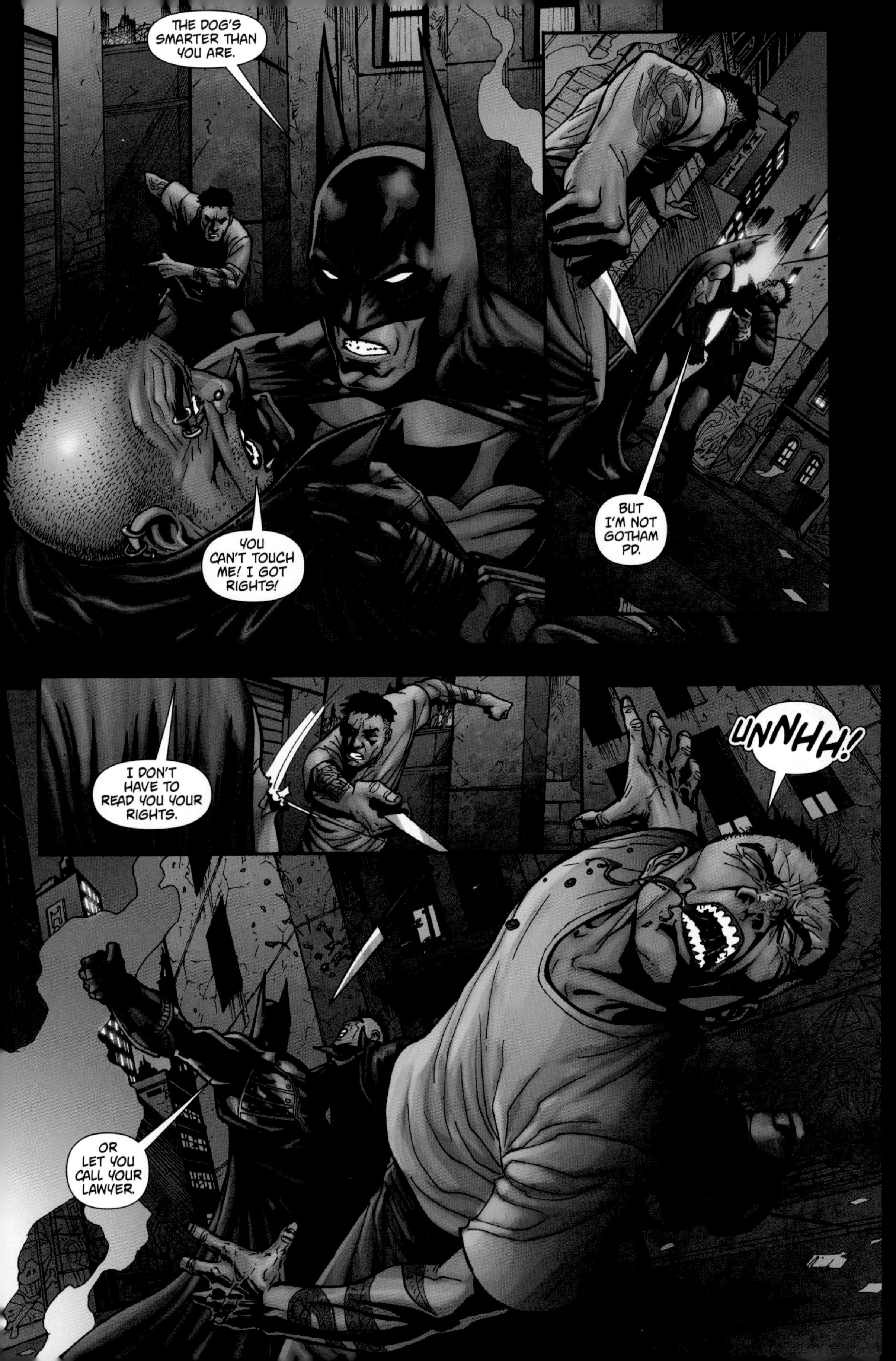
THE DOG'S SMARTER THAN YOU ARE.
YOU CAN'T TOUCH ME! I GOT RIGHTS!
BUT I'M NOT GOTHAM PD.
I DON'T HAVE TO READ YOU YOUR RIGHTS.
UNNHH!
OR LET YOU CALL YOUR LAWYER.

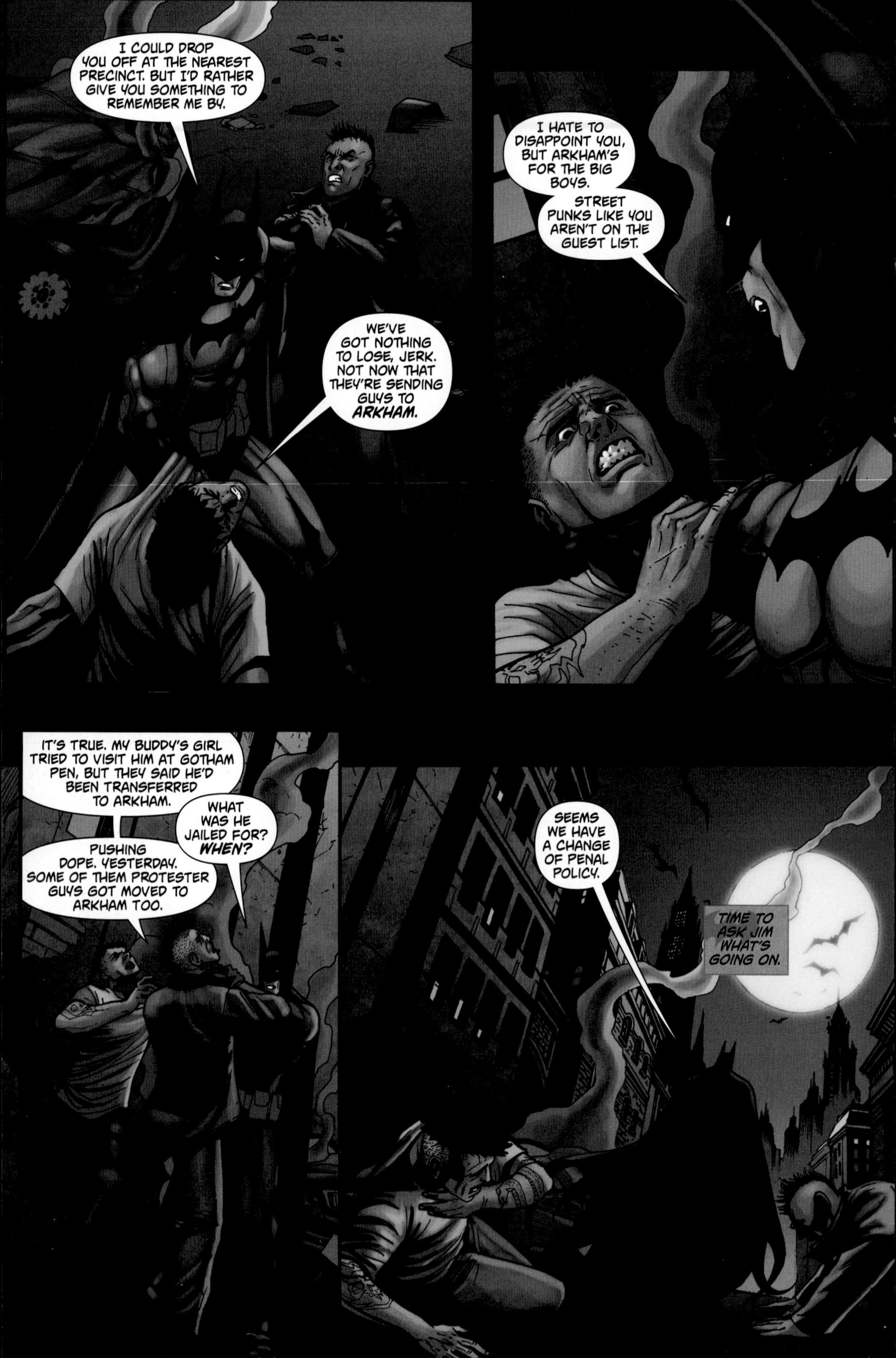
I COULD DROP YOU OFF AT THE NEAREST PRECINCT. BUT I'D RATHER GIVE YOU SOMETHING TO REMEMBER ME BY.
WE'VE GOT NOTHING TO LOSE, JERK. NOT NOW THAT THEY'RE SENDING GUYS TO ARKHAM.
I HATE TO DISAPPOINT YOU, BUT ARKHAM'S FOR THE BIG BOYS.
STREET PUNKS LIKE YOU AREN'T ON THE GUEST LIST.
IT'S TRUE. MY BUDDY'S GIRL TRIED TO VISIT HIM AT GOTHAM PEN, BUT THEY SAID HE'D BEEN TRANSFERRED TO ARKHAM.
WHAT WAS HE JAILED FOR? WHEN?
PUSHING DOPE. YESTERDAY. SOME OF THEM PROTESTER GUYS GOT MOVED TO ARKHAM TOO.
SEEMS WE HAVE A CHANGE OF PENAL POLICY.
TIME TO ASK JIM WHAT'S GOING ON.

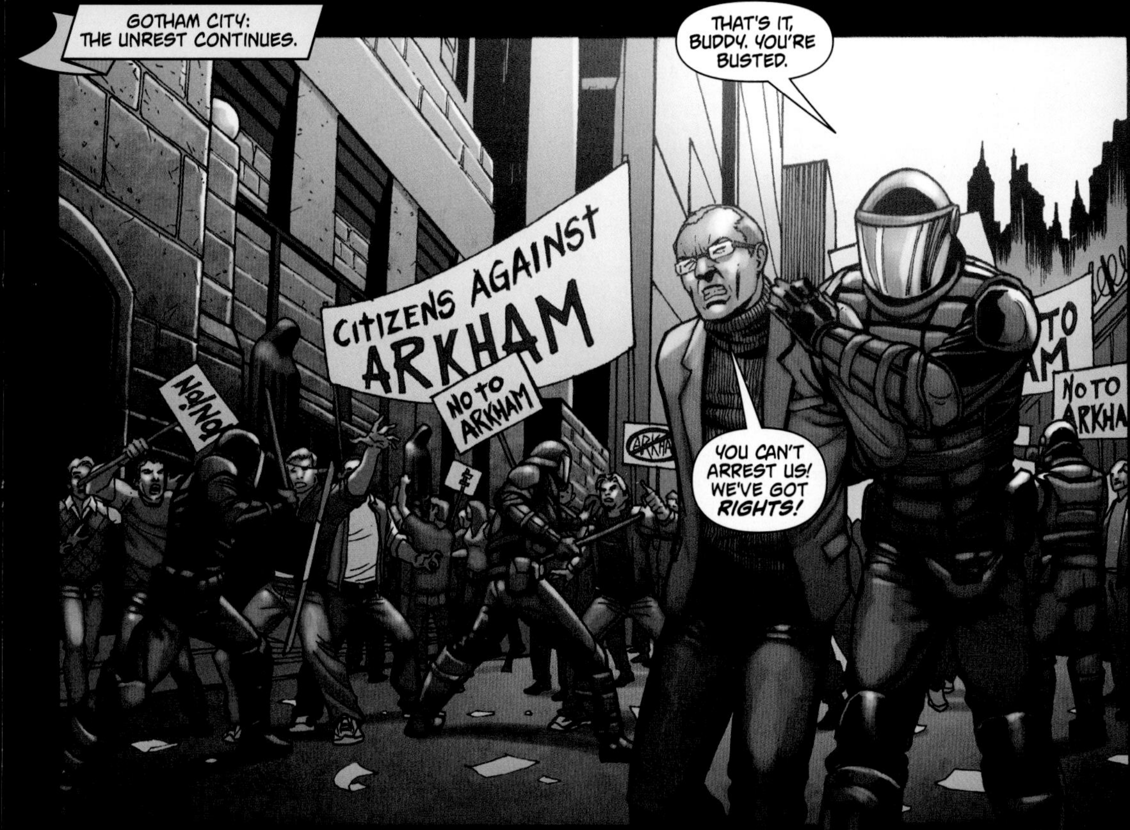
GOTHAM CITY: THE UNREST CONTINUES.
THAT'S IT, BUDDY. YOU'RE BUSTED.
CITIZENS AGAINST ARKHAM
NO TO ARKHAM
YOU CAN'T ARREST US! WE'VE GOT RIGHTS!

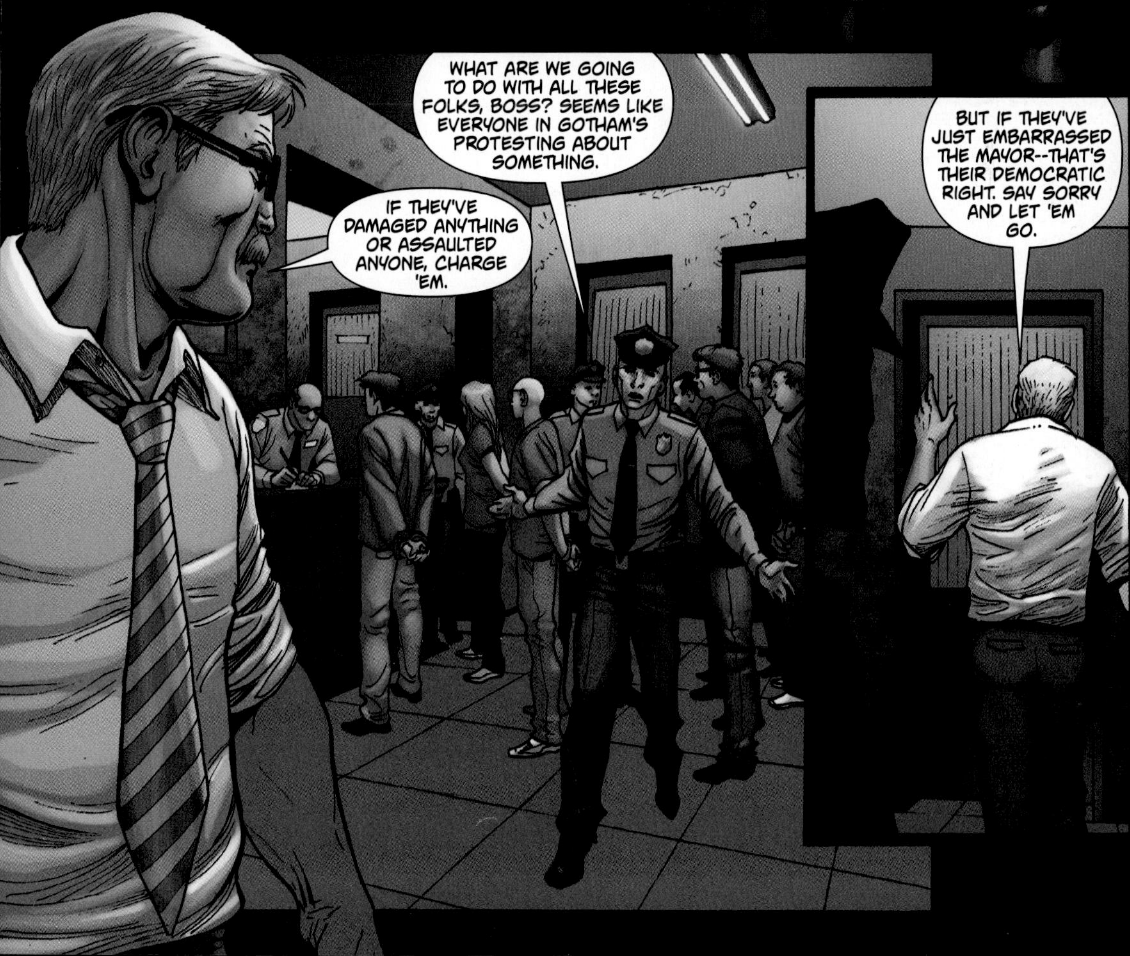
WHAT ARE WE GOING TO DO WITH ALL THESE FOLKS, BOSS? SEEMS LIKE EVERYONE IN GOTHAM'S PROTESTING ABOUT SOMETHING.
IF THEY'VE DAMAGED ANYTHING OR ASSAULTED ANYONE, CHARGE 'EM.
BUT IF THEY'VE JUST EMBARRASSED THE MAYOR--THAT'S THEIR DEMOCRATIC RIGHT. SAY SORRY AND LET 'EM GO.

THE BATCAVE.

DON'T WORRY. THIS IS UNTRACEABLE. YOU CAN'T DISAPPEAR TO THE ROOF SO OFTEN NOW THAT YOU'VE QUIT SMOKING.

SO, JIM... TELL ME WHY PROTESTERS ARE GETTING CONVICTED AND SENTENCED TO ARKHAM.

AND SINCE WHEN DID HAVING A POLITICAL OPINION LAND YOU IN JAIL?

I DIDN'T DAMN WELL KNOW ABOUT ARKHAM. AND WE'RE NOT BOOKING PEOPLE JUST FOR PROTESTING.

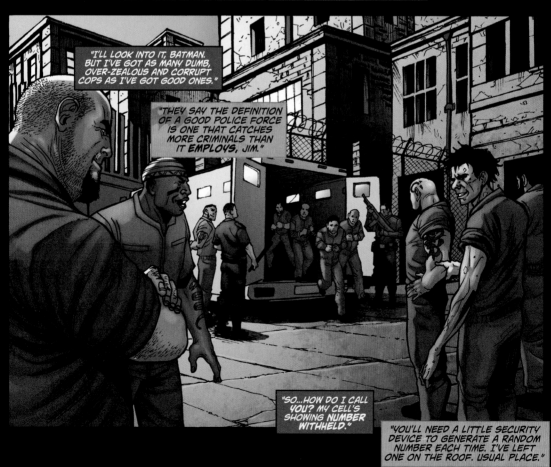

"I'LL LOOK INTO IT, BATMAN. BUT I'VE GOT AS MANY DUMB, OVER-ZEALOUS AND CORRUPT COPS AS I'VE GOT GOOD ONES."

"THEY SAY THE DEFINITION OF A GOOD POLICE FORCE IS ONE THAT CATCHES MORE CRIMINALS THAN IT EMPLOYS, JIM."

"SO...HOW DO I CALL YOU? MY CELL'S SHOWING NUMBER WITHHELD."

"YOU'LL NEED A LITTLE SECURITY DEVICE TO GENERATE A RANDOM NUMBER EACH TIME. I'VE LEFT ONE ON THE ROOF. USUAL PLACE."

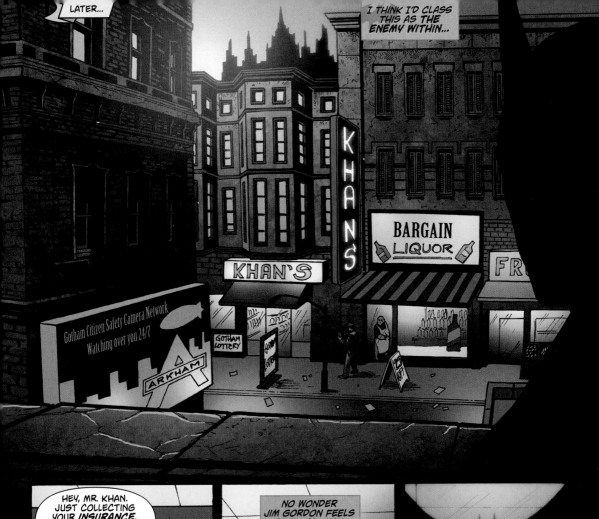

LATER...

I THINK I'D CLASS THIS AS THE ENEMY WITHIN...

KHAN'S

KHAN'S

BARGAIN LIQUOR

Gotham Citizen Safety Camera Network
Watching over you 24/7

ARKHAM

GOTHAM LOTTERY

HEY, MR. KHAN. JUST COLLECTING YOUR *INSURANCE*. FOR EXTRA PROTECTION IN THESE UNCERTAIN TIMES, RIGHT?

NO WONDER JIM GORDON FEELS LIKE IT'S JUST HIM AND ME.

BECAUSE SOME DAYS, IT IS

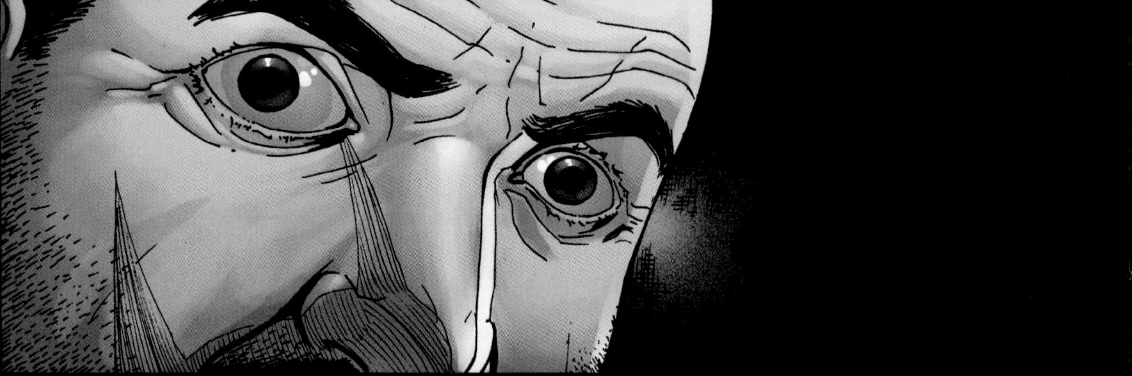

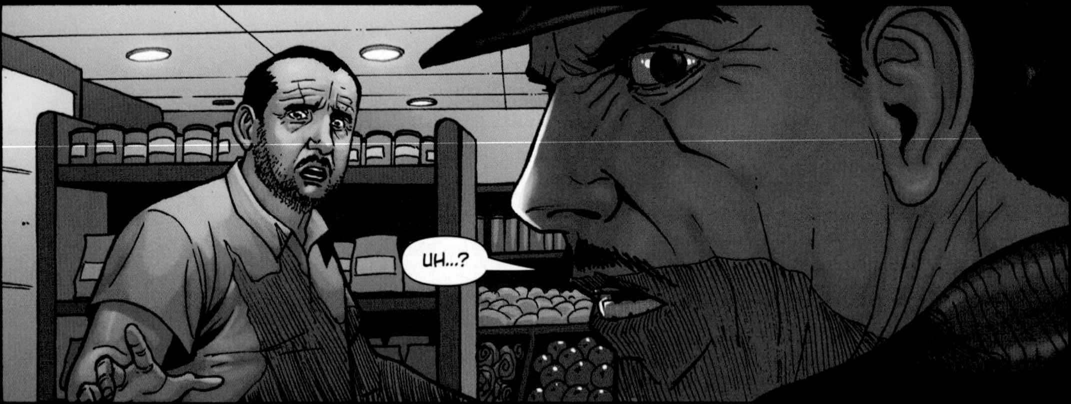
UH...?

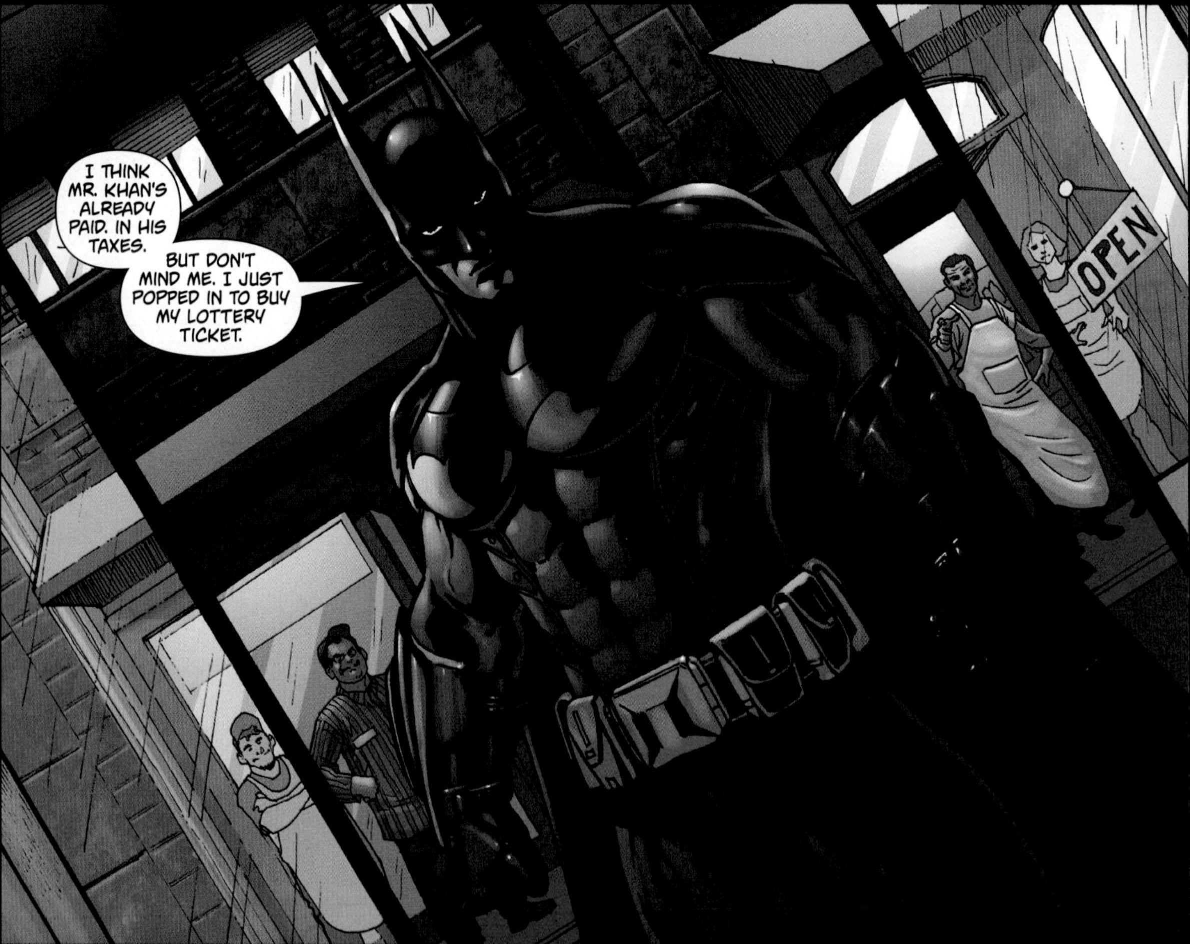
I THINK MR. KHAN'S ALREADY PAID. IN HIS TAXES.
BUT DON'T MIND ME. I JUST POPPED IN TO BUY MY LOTTERY TICKET.
OPEN

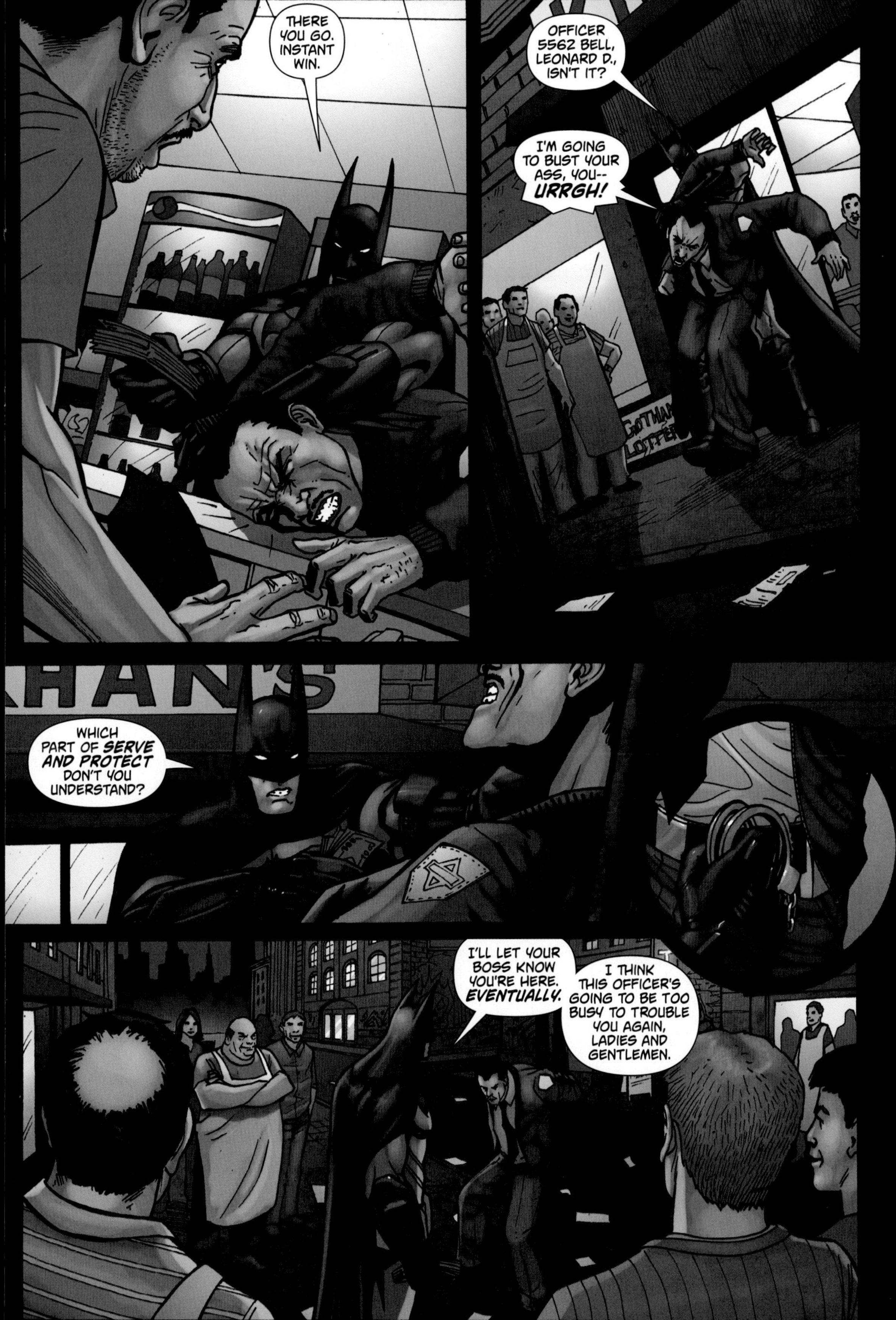
THERE YOU GO. INSTANT WIN.
OFFICER 5562 BELL, LEONARD D., ISN'T IT?
I'M GOING TO BUST YOUR ASS, YOU-- **URRGH!**
GOTHAM LOTTER
KHAN'S
WHICH PART OF ***SERVE AND PROTECT*** DON'T YOU UNDERSTAND?
I'LL LET YOUR BOSS KNOW YOU'RE HERE. ***EVENTUALLY.***
I THINK THIS OFFICER'S GOING TO BE TOO BUSY TO TROUBLE YOU AGAIN, LADIES AND GENTLEMEN.

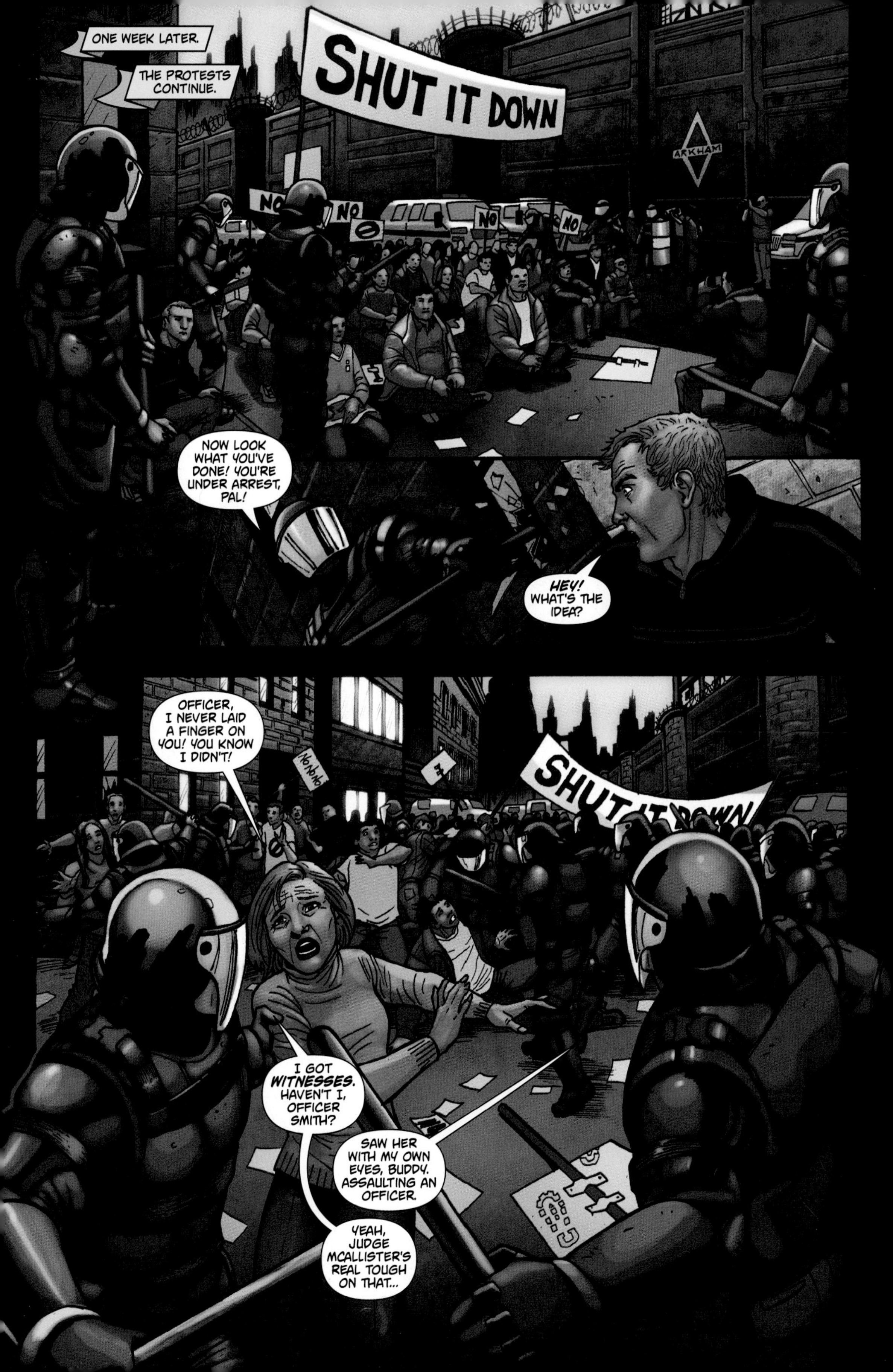
ONE WEEK LATER.
THE PROTESTS CONTINUE.
SHUT IT DOWN
ARKHAM
NO
NO
NO
NO
NOW LOOK WHAT YOU'VE DONE! YOU'RE UNDER ARREST, PAL!
HEY! WHAT'S THE IDEA?
OFFICER, I NEVER LAID A FINGER ON YOU! YOU KNOW I DIDN'T!
SHUT IT DOWN
I GOT WITNESSES. HAVEN'T I, OFFICER SMITH?
SAW HER WITH MY OWN EYES, BUDDY. ASSAULTING AN OFFICER.
YEAH, JUDGE MCALLISTER'S REAL TOUGH ON THAT...

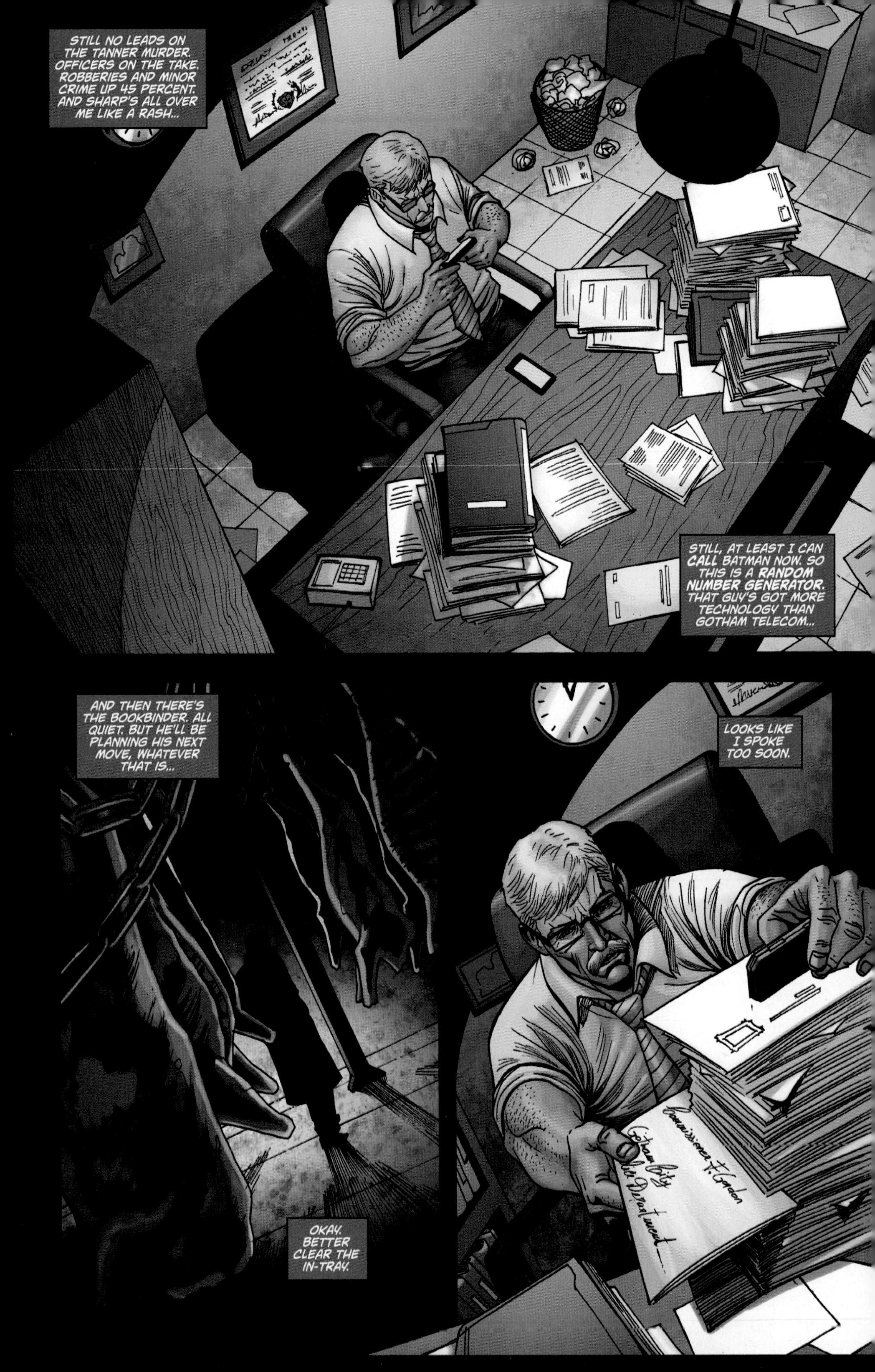
STILL NO LEADS ON THE TANNER MURDER. OFFICERS ON THE TAKE. ROBBERIES AND MINOR CRIME UP 45 PERCENT. AND SHARP'S ALL OVER ME LIKE A RASH...
STILL, AT LEAST I CAN **CALL** BATMAN NOW. SO THIS IS A **RANDOM NUMBER GENERATOR.** THAT GUY'S GOT MORE TECHNOLOGY THAN GOTHAM TELECOM...
AND THEN THERE'S THE BOOKBINDER. ALL QUIET. BUT HE'LL BE PLANNING HIS NEXT MOVE, WHATEVER THAT IS...
OKAY. BETTER CLEAR THE IN-TRAY.
LOOKS LIKE I SPOKE TOO SOON.

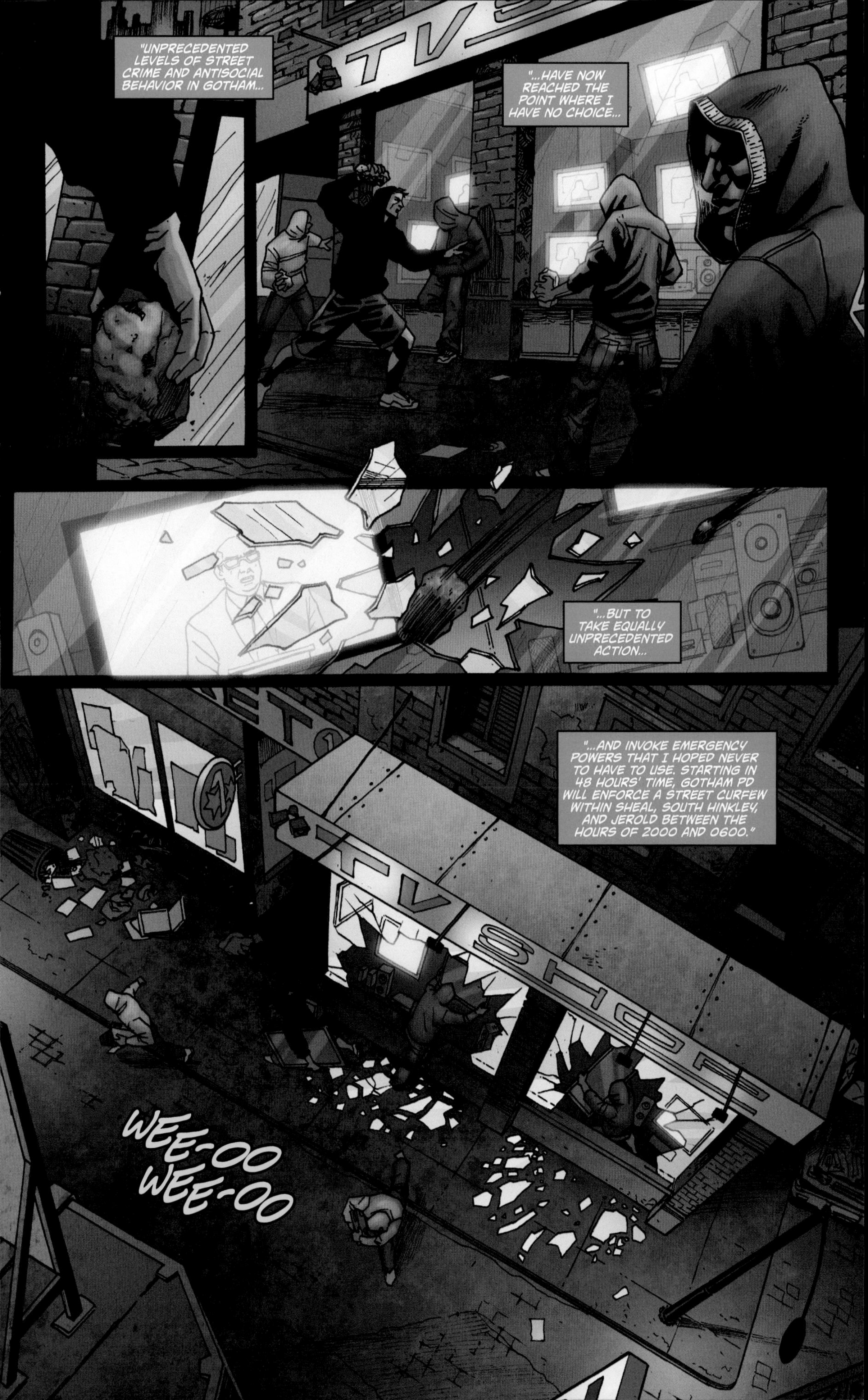
"UNPRECEDENTED LEVELS OF STREET CRIME AND ANTISOCIAL BEHAVIOR IN GOTHAM...
"...HAVE NOW REACHED THE POINT WHERE I HAVE NO CHOICE...
"...BUT TO TAKE EQUALLY UNPRECEDENTED ACTION...
"...AND INVOKE EMERGENCY POWERS THAT I HOPED NEVER TO HAVE TO USE. STARTING IN 48 HOURS' TIME, GOTHAM PD WILL ENFORCE A STREET CURFEW WITHIN SHEAL, SOUTH HINKLEY, AND JEROLD BETWEEN THE HOURS OF 2000 AND 0600."
WEE-OO WEE-OO

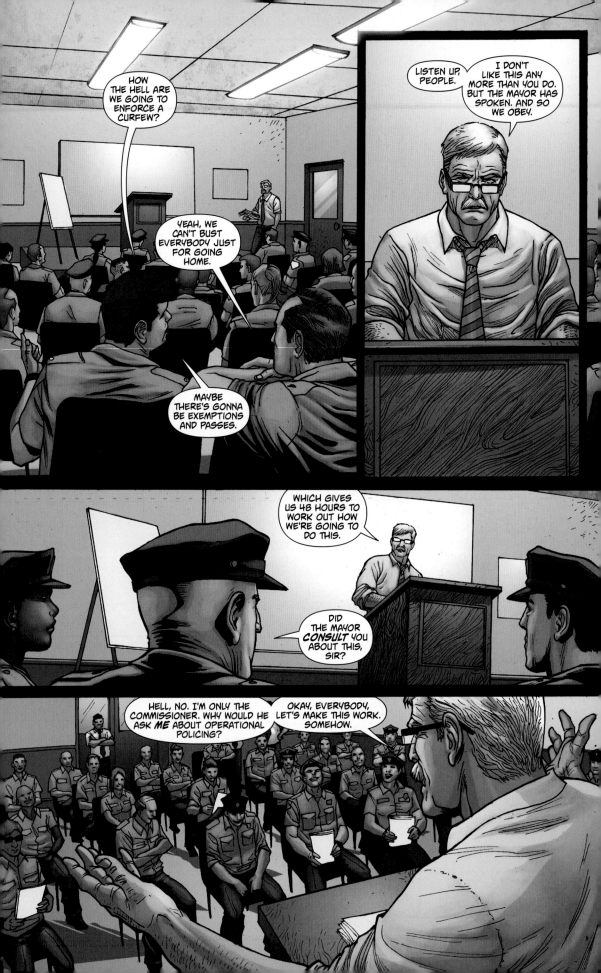

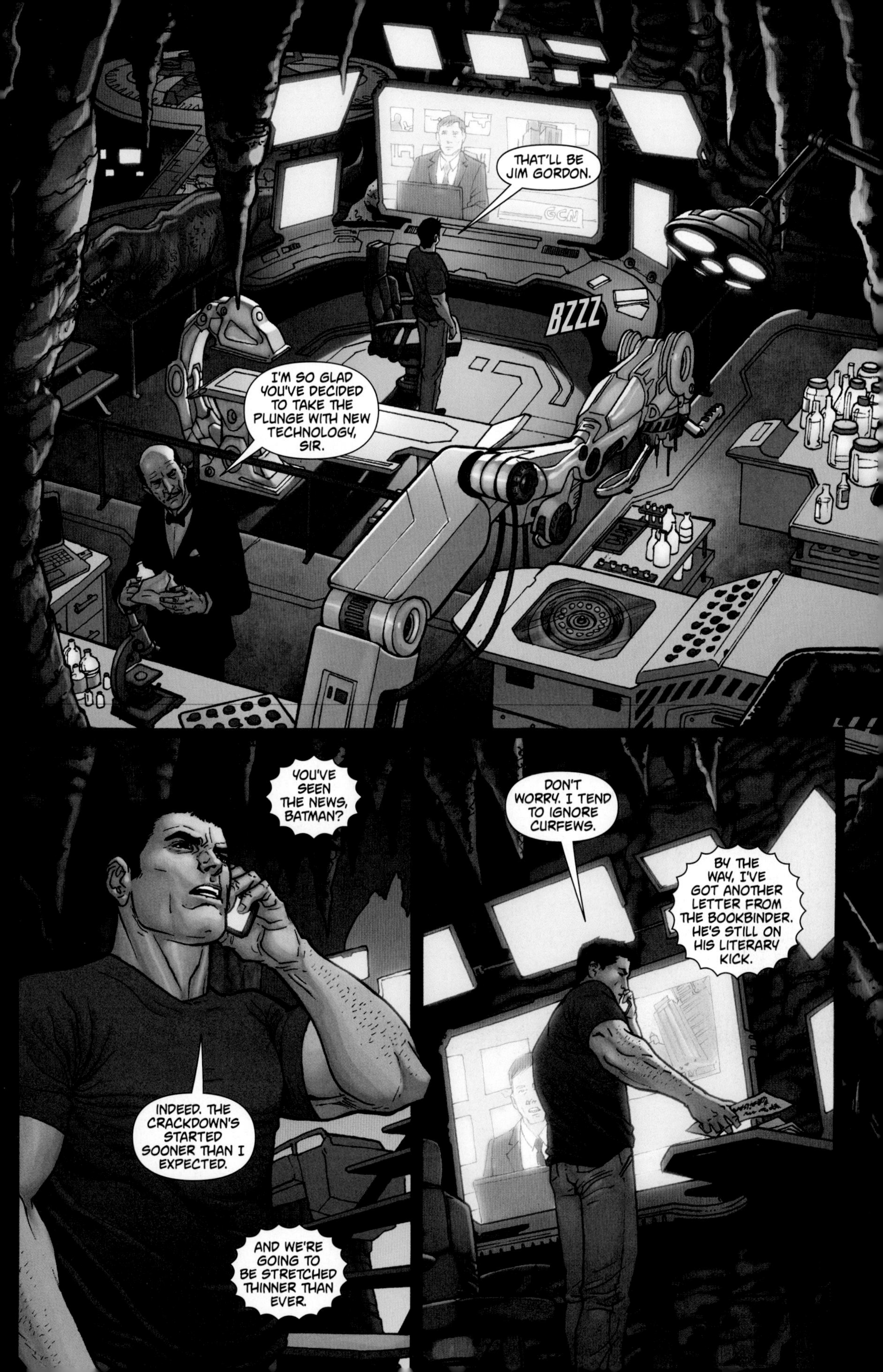
THAT'LL BE JIM GORDON.
BZZZ
I'M SO GLAD YOU'VE DECIDED TO TAKE THE PLUNGE WITH NEW TECHNOLOGY, SIR.
YOU'VE SEEN THE NEWS, BATMAN?
INDEED. THE CRACKDOWN'S STARTED SOONER THAN I EXPECTED.
AND WE'RE GOING TO BE STRETCHED THINNER THAN EVER.
DON'T WORRY. I TEND TO IGNORE CURFEWS.
BY THE WAY, I'VE GOT ANOTHER LETTER FROM THE BOOKBINDER. HE'S STILL ON HIS LITERARY KICK.

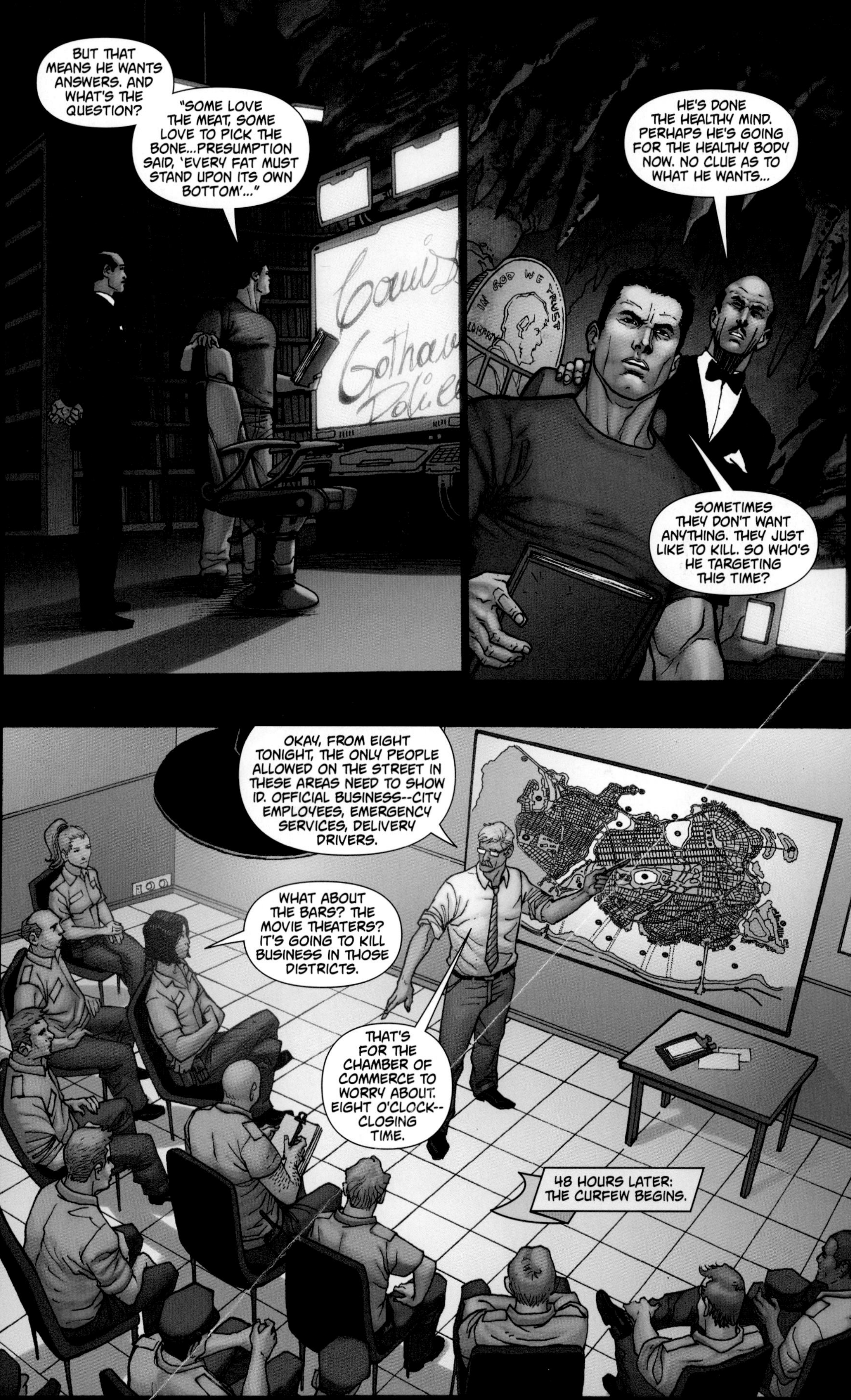
BUT THAT MEANS HE WANTS ANSWERS. AND WHAT'S THE QUESTION?
"SOME LOVE THE MEAT, SOME LOVE TO PICK THE BONE...PRESUMPTION SAID, 'EVERY FAT MUST STAND UPON ITS OWN BOTTOM'..."
HE'S DONE THE HEALTHY MIND. PERHAPS HE'S GOING FOR THE HEALTHY BODY NOW. NO CLUE AS TO WHAT HE WANTS...
IN GOD WE TRUST
SOMETIMES THEY DON'T WANT ANYTHING. THEY JUST LIKE TO KILL. SO WHO'S HE TARGETING THIS TIME?
OKAY, FROM EIGHT TONIGHT, THE ONLY PEOPLE ALLOWED ON THE STREET IN THESE AREAS NEED TO SHOW ID. OFFICIAL BUSINESS--CITY EMPLOYEES, EMERGENCY SERVICES, DELIVERY DRIVERS.
WHAT ABOUT THE BARS? THE MOVIE THEATERS? IT'S GOING TO KILL BUSINESS IN THOSE DISTRICTS.
THAT'S FOR THE CHAMBER OF COMMERCE TO WORRY ABOUT. EIGHT O'CLOCK--CLOSING TIME.
48 HOURS LATER: THE CURFEW BEGINS.

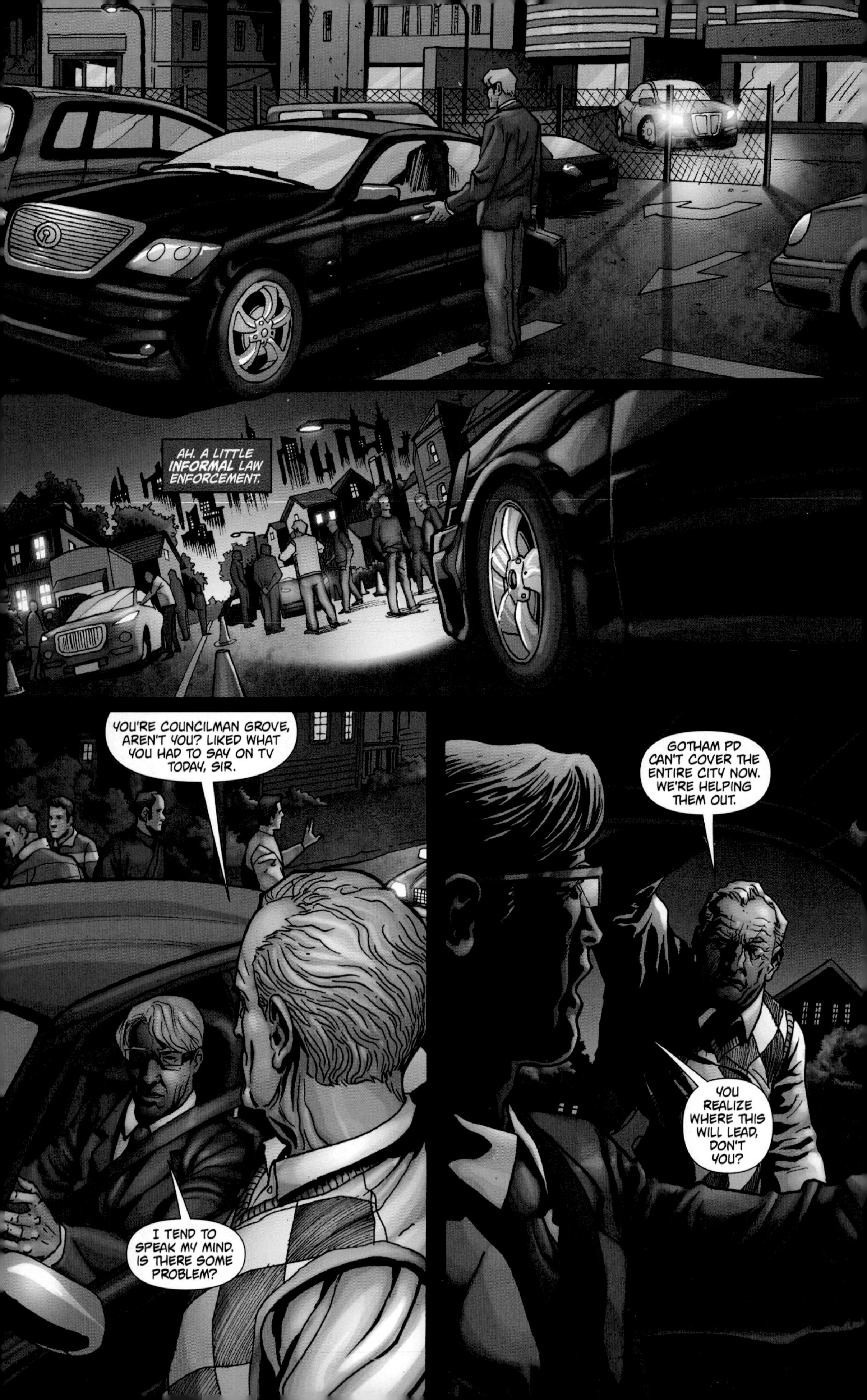
AH. A LITTLE INFORMAL LAW ENFORCEMENT.
YOU'RE COUNCILMAN GROVE, AREN'T YOU? LIKED WHAT YOU HAD TO SAY ON TV TODAY, SIR.
I TEND TO SPEAK MY MIND. IS THERE SOME PROBLEM?
GOTHAM PD CAN'T COVER THE ENTIRE CITY NOW. WE'RE HELPING THEM OUT.
YOU REALIZE WHERE THIS WILL LEAD, DON'T YOU?

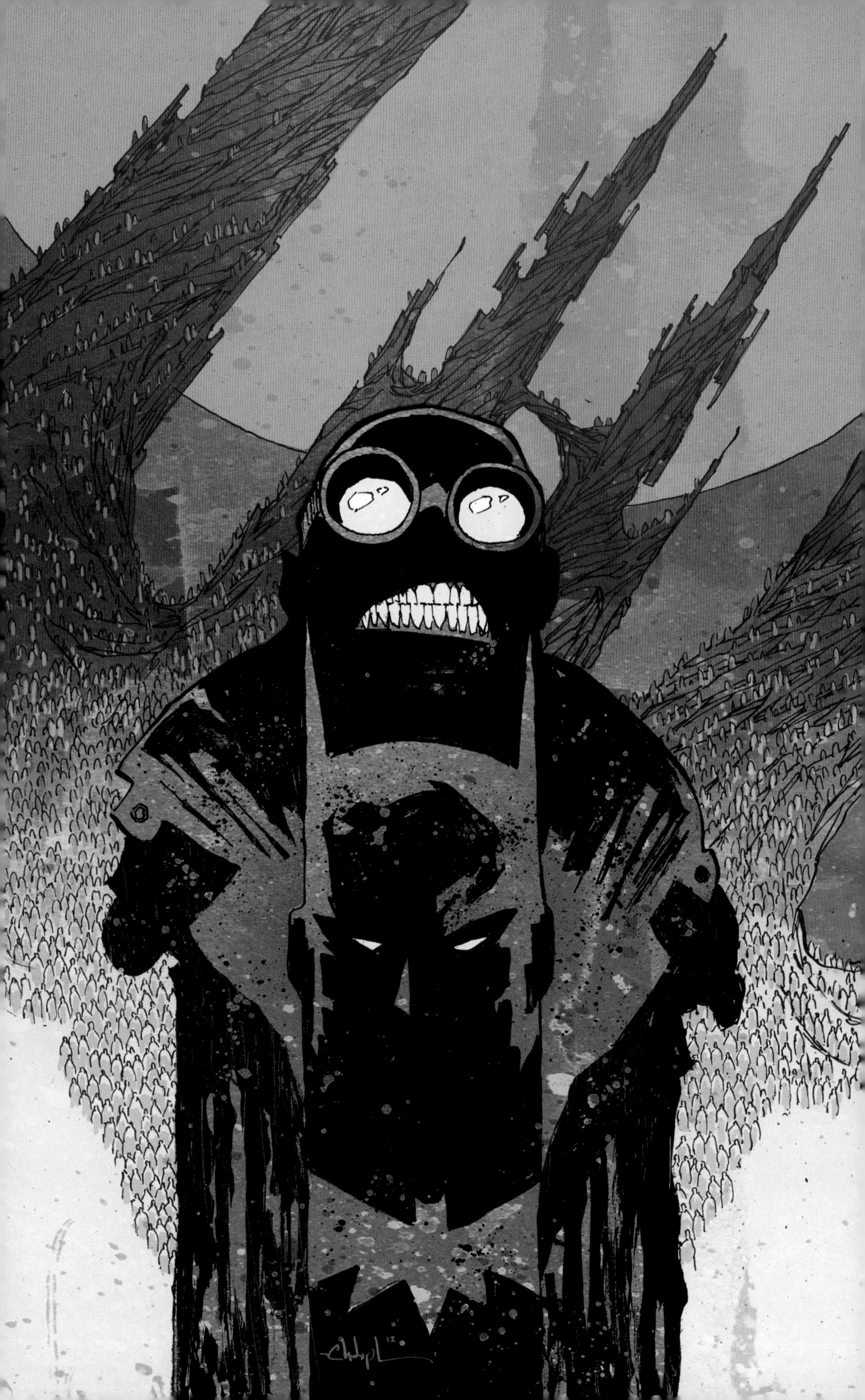

WELCOME
TO THE SLOUGH OF DESPOND
PART THREE

WRITTEN BY: KAREN TRAVISS
ART BY: FEDERICO DALLOCCHIO
COLORS BY: ALEJANDRO SANCHEZ
LETTERS BY: TRAVIS LANHAM
COVER BY: CHRIS MITTEN

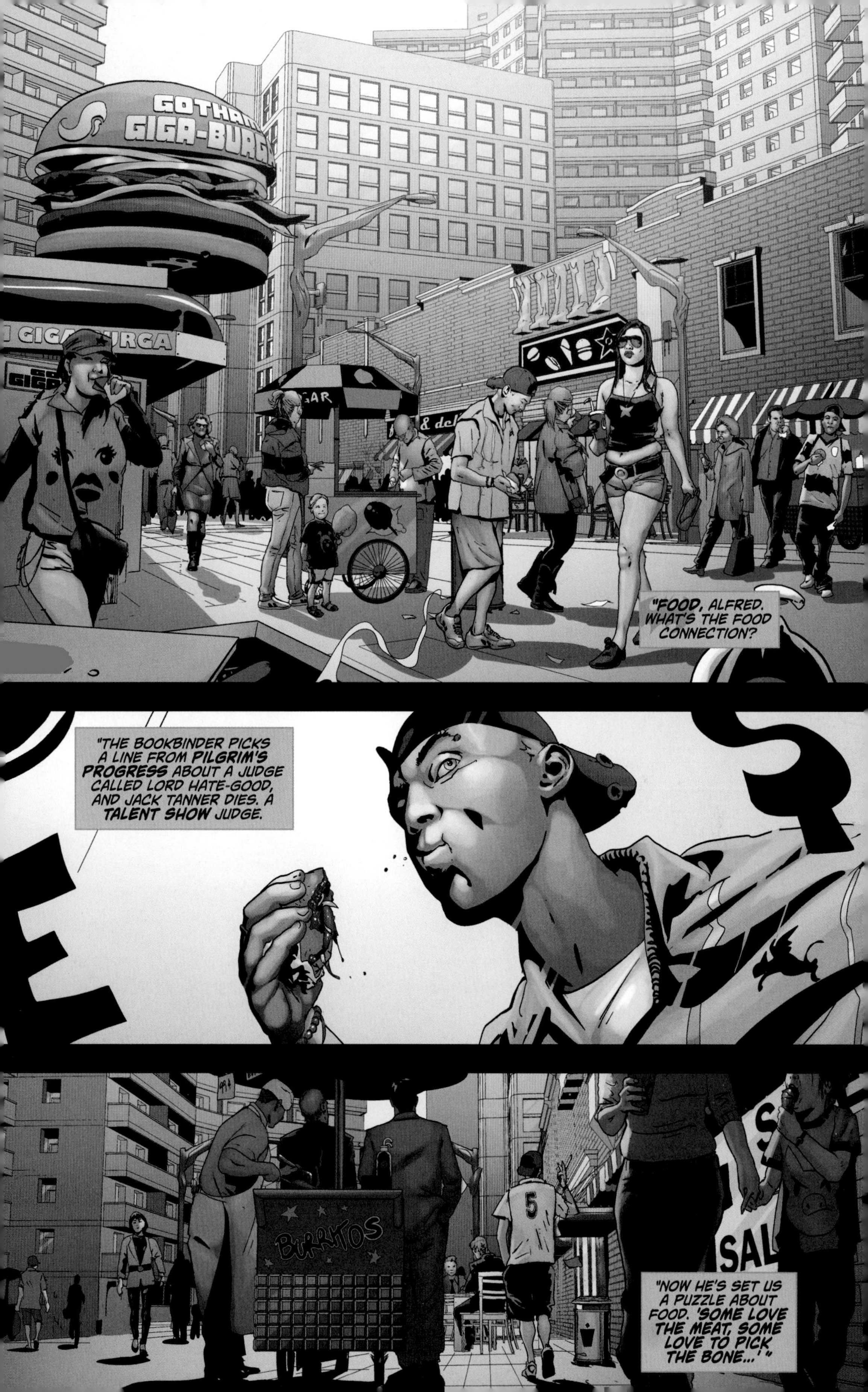
"FOOD, ALFRED. WHAT'S THE FOOD CONNECTION?
"THE BOOKBINDER PICKS A LINE FROM PILGRIM'S PROGRESS ABOUT A JUDGE CALLED LORD HATE-GOOD, AND JACK TANNER DIES. A TALENT SHOW JUDGE.
BURRITOS
"NOW HE'S SET US A PUZZLE ABOUT FOOD. 'SOME LOVE THE MEAT, SOME LOVE TO PICK THE BONE...'"

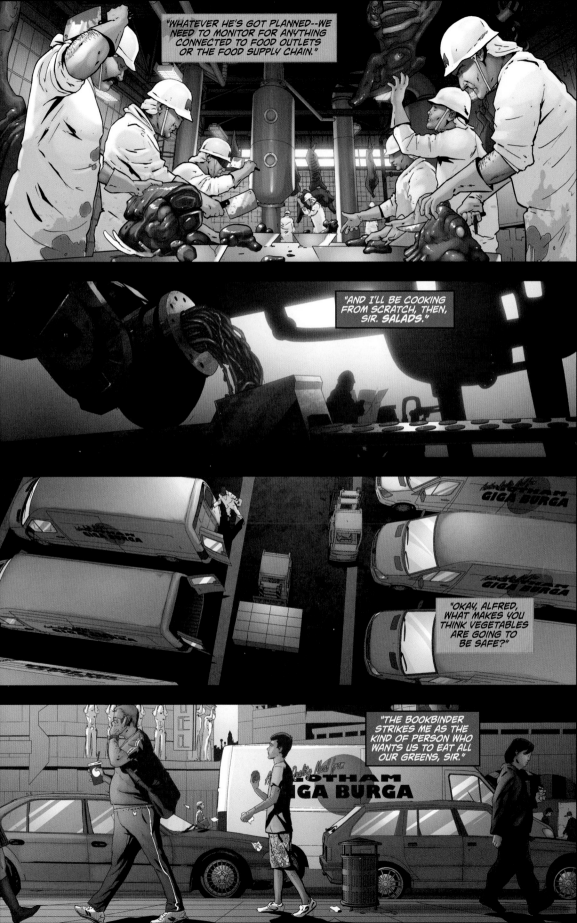

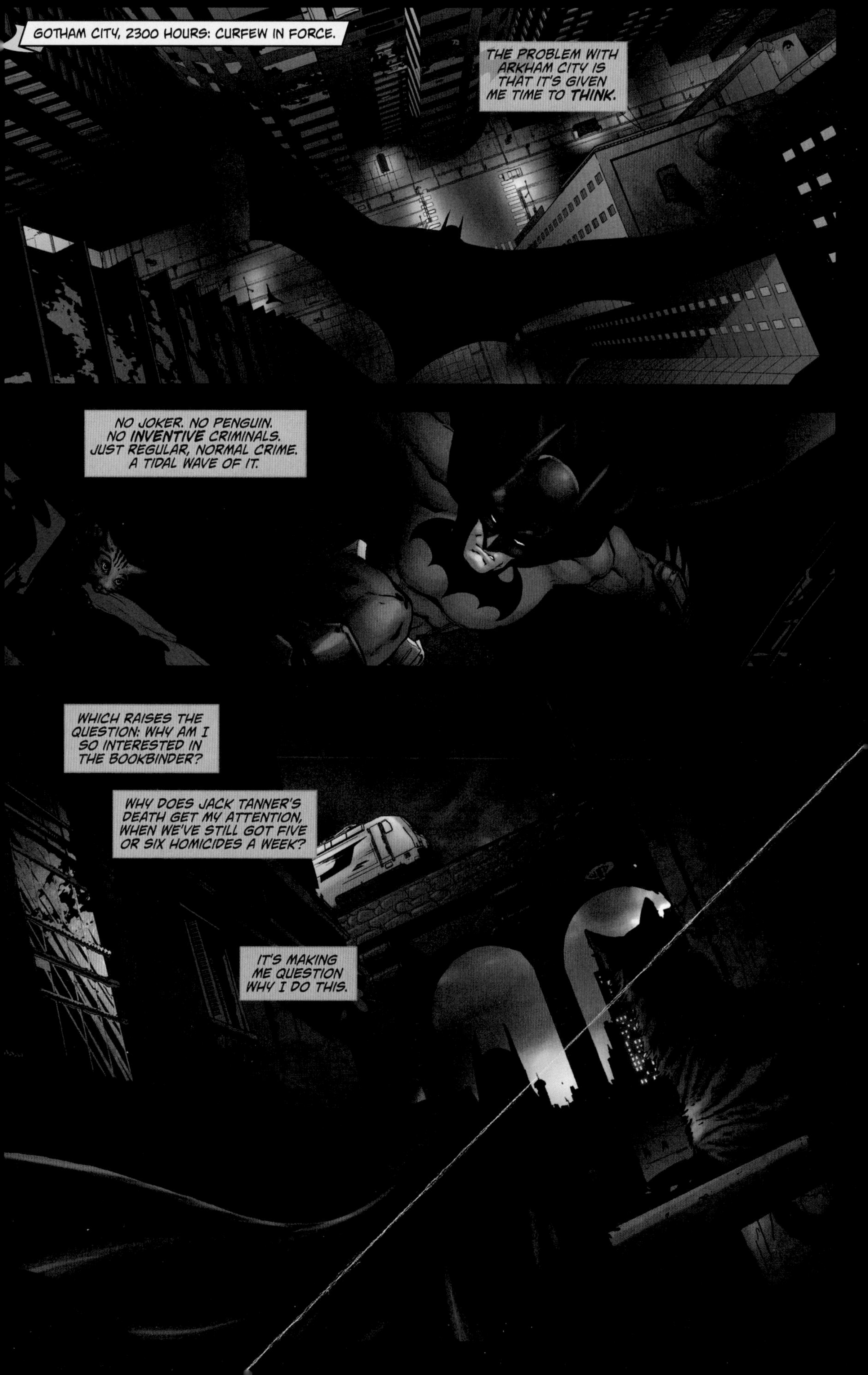
GOTHAM CITY, 2300 HOURS: CURFEW IN FORCE.
THE PROBLEM WITH ARKHAM CITY IS THAT IT'S GIVEN ME TIME TO THINK.
NO JOKER. NO PENGUIN. NO INVENTIVE CRIMINALS. JUST REGULAR, NORMAL CRIME. A TIDAL WAVE OF IT.
WHICH RAISES THE QUESTION: WHY AM I SO INTERESTED IN THE BOOKBINDER?
WHY DOES JACK TANNER'S DEATH GET MY ATTENTION, WHEN WE'VE STILL GOT FIVE OR SIX HOMICIDES A WEEK?
IT'S MAKING ME QUESTION WHY I DO THIS.

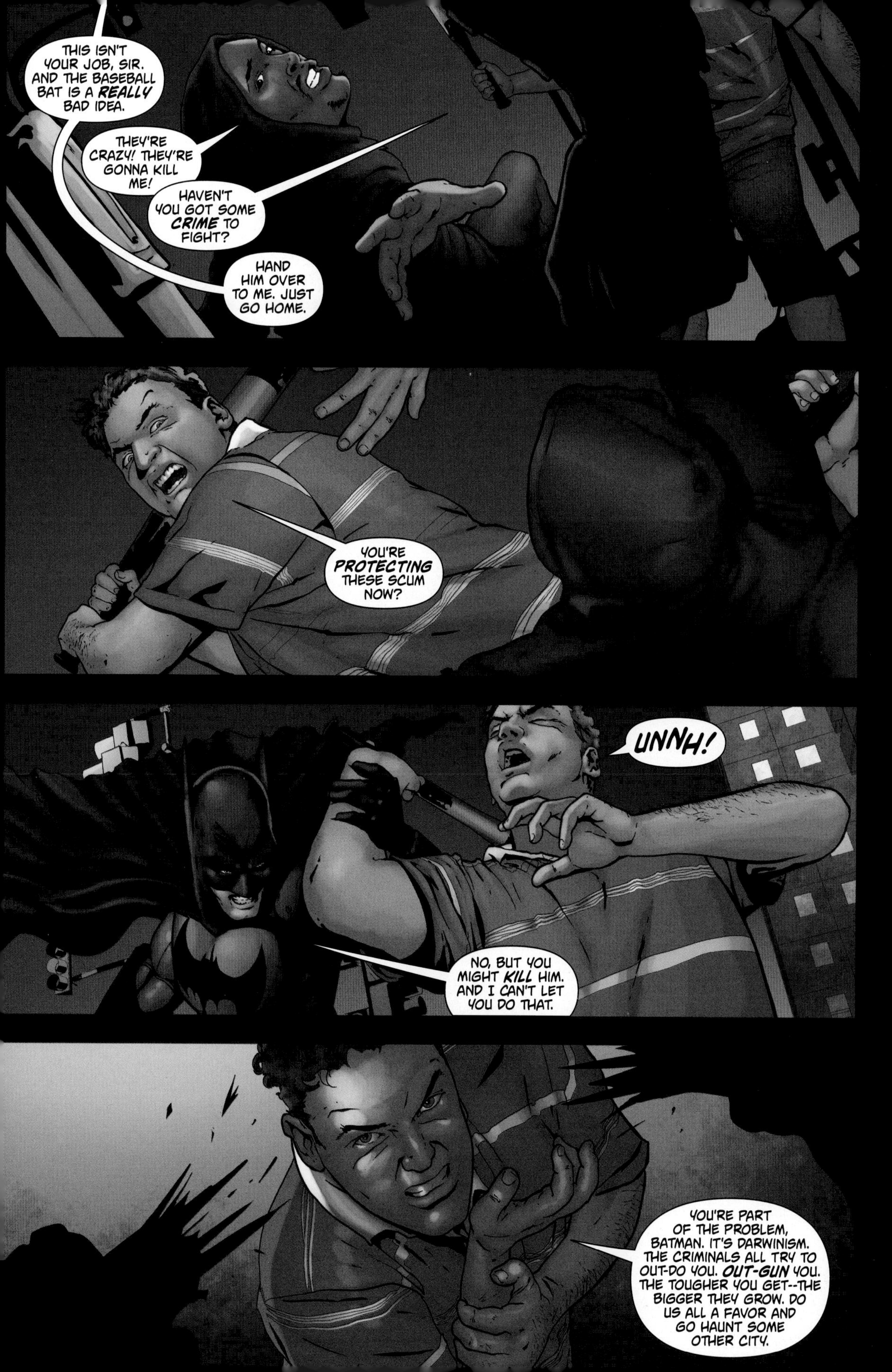
THIS ISN'T YOUR JOB, SIR. AND THE BASEBALL BAT IS A *REALLY* BAD IDEA.
THEY'RE CRAZY! THEY'RE GONNA KILL ME!
HAVEN'T YOU GOT SOME *CRIME* TO FIGHT?
HAND HIM OVER TO ME. JUST GO HOME.
YOU'RE *PROTECTING* THESE SCUM NOW?
UNNH!
NO, BUT YOU MIGHT *KILL* HIM. AND I CAN'T LET YOU DO THAT.
YOU'RE PART OF THE PROBLEM, BATMAN. IT'S DARWINISM. THE CRIMINALS ALL TRY TO OUT-DO YOU. *OUT-GUN* YOU. THE TOUGHER YOU GET--THE BIGGER THEY GROW. DO US ALL A FAVOR AND GO HAUNT SOME OTHER CITY.

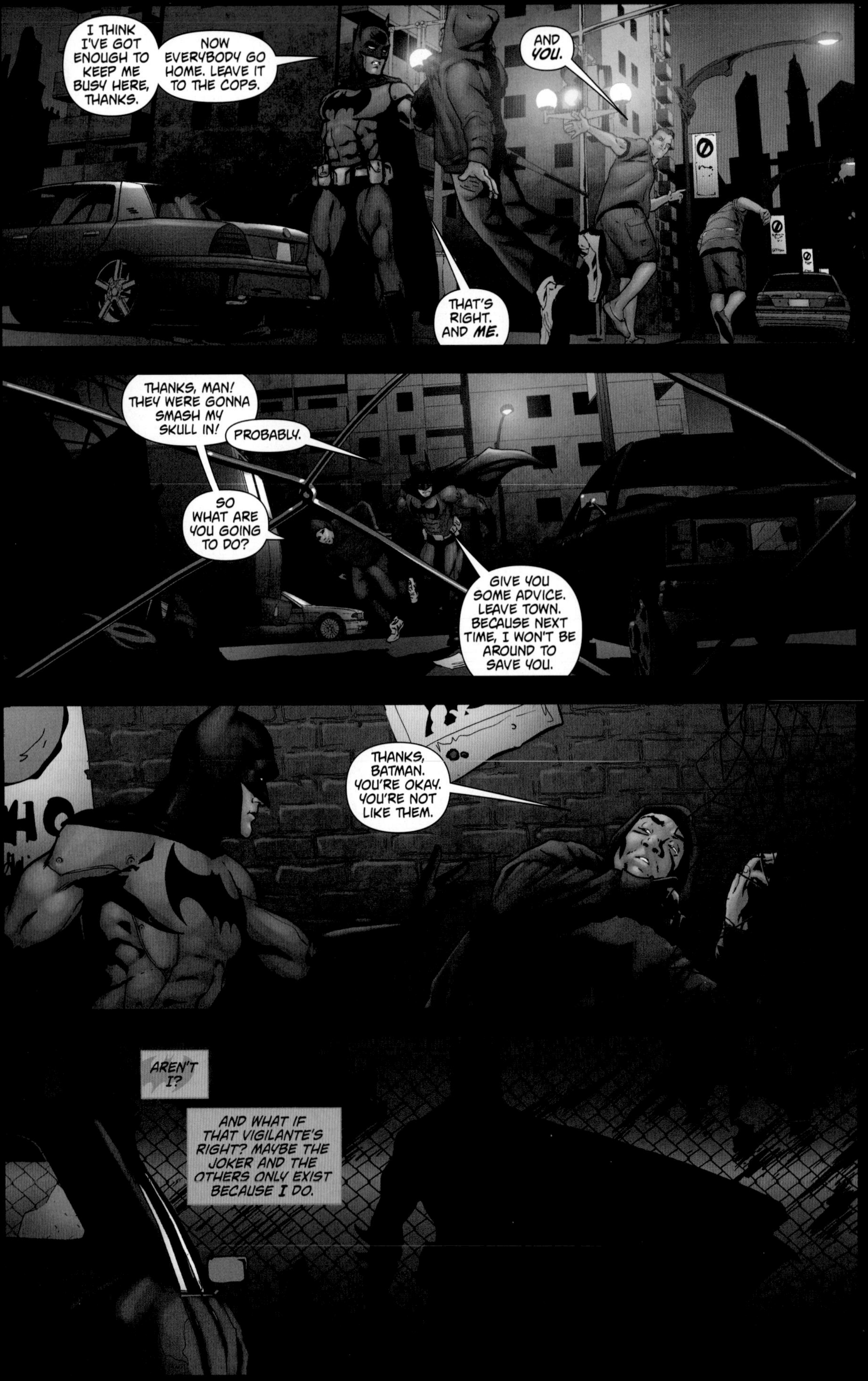
I THINK I'VE GOT ENOUGH TO KEEP ME BUSY HERE, THANKS.
NOW EVERYBODY GO HOME. LEAVE IT TO THE COPS.
AND *YOU*.
THAT'S RIGHT. AND *ME*.
THANKS, MAN! THEY WERE GONNA SMASH MY SKULL IN!
PROBABLY.
SO WHAT ARE YOU GOING TO DO?
GIVE YOU SOME ADVICE. LEAVE TOWN. BECAUSE NEXT TIME, I WON'T BE AROUND TO SAVE YOU.
THANKS, BATMAN. YOU'RE OKAY. YOU'RE NOT LIKE THEM.
AREN'T I?
AND WHAT IF THAT VIGILANTE'S RIGHT? MAYBE THE JOKER AND THE OTHERS ONLY EXIST BECAUSE *I* DO.

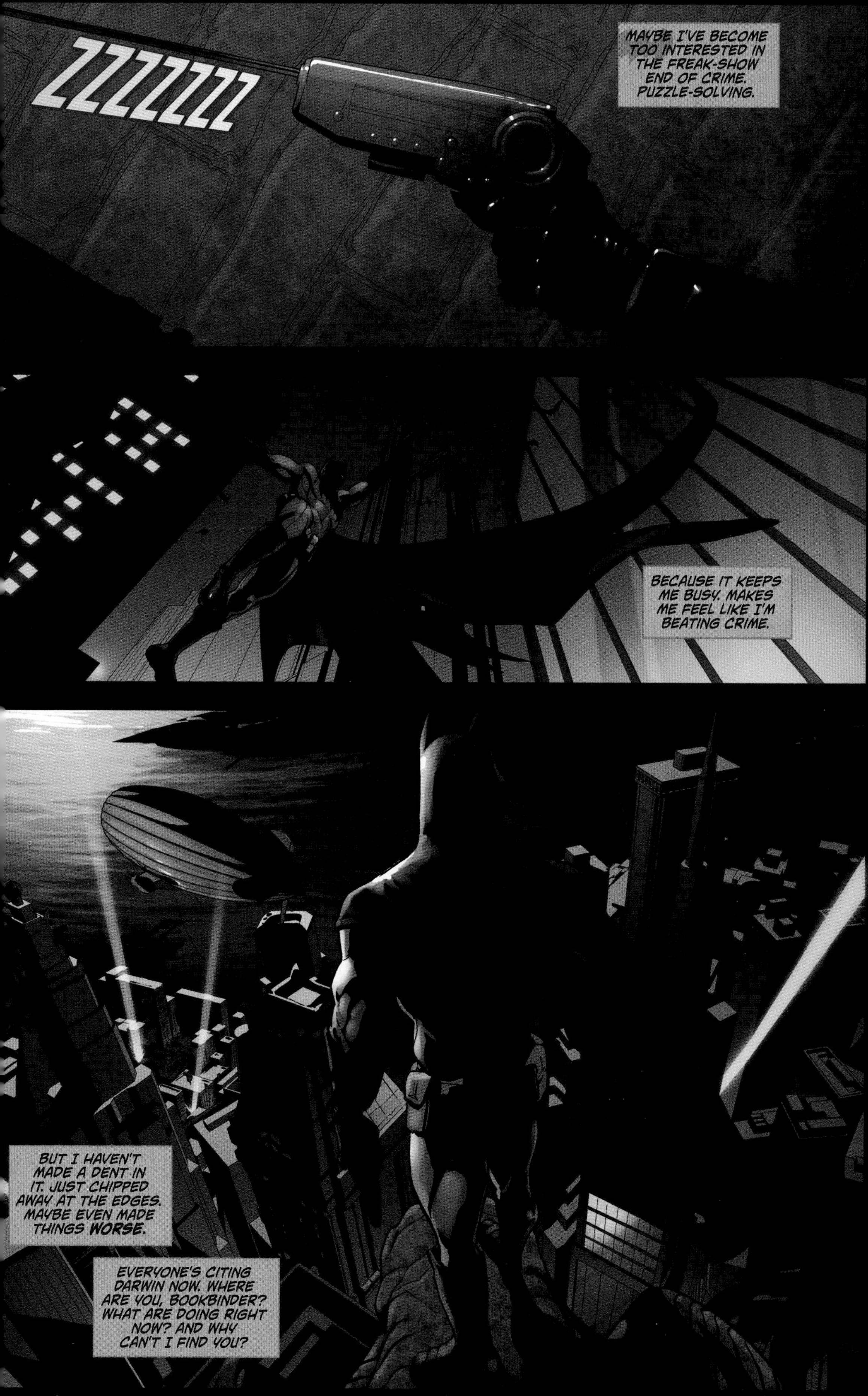
ZZZZZZZZ
MAYBE I'VE BECOME TOO INTERESTED IN THE FREAK-SHOW END OF CRIME. PUZZLE-SOLVING.
BECAUSE IT KEEPS ME BUSY. MAKES ME FEEL LIKE I'M BEATING CRIME.
BUT I HAVEN'T MADE A DENT IN IT. JUST CHIPPED AWAY AT THE EDGES. MAYBE EVEN MADE THINGS WORSE.
EVERYONE'S CITING DARWIN NOW. WHERE ARE YOU, BOOKBINDER? WHAT ARE DOING RIGHT NOW? AND WHY CAN'T I FIND YOU?

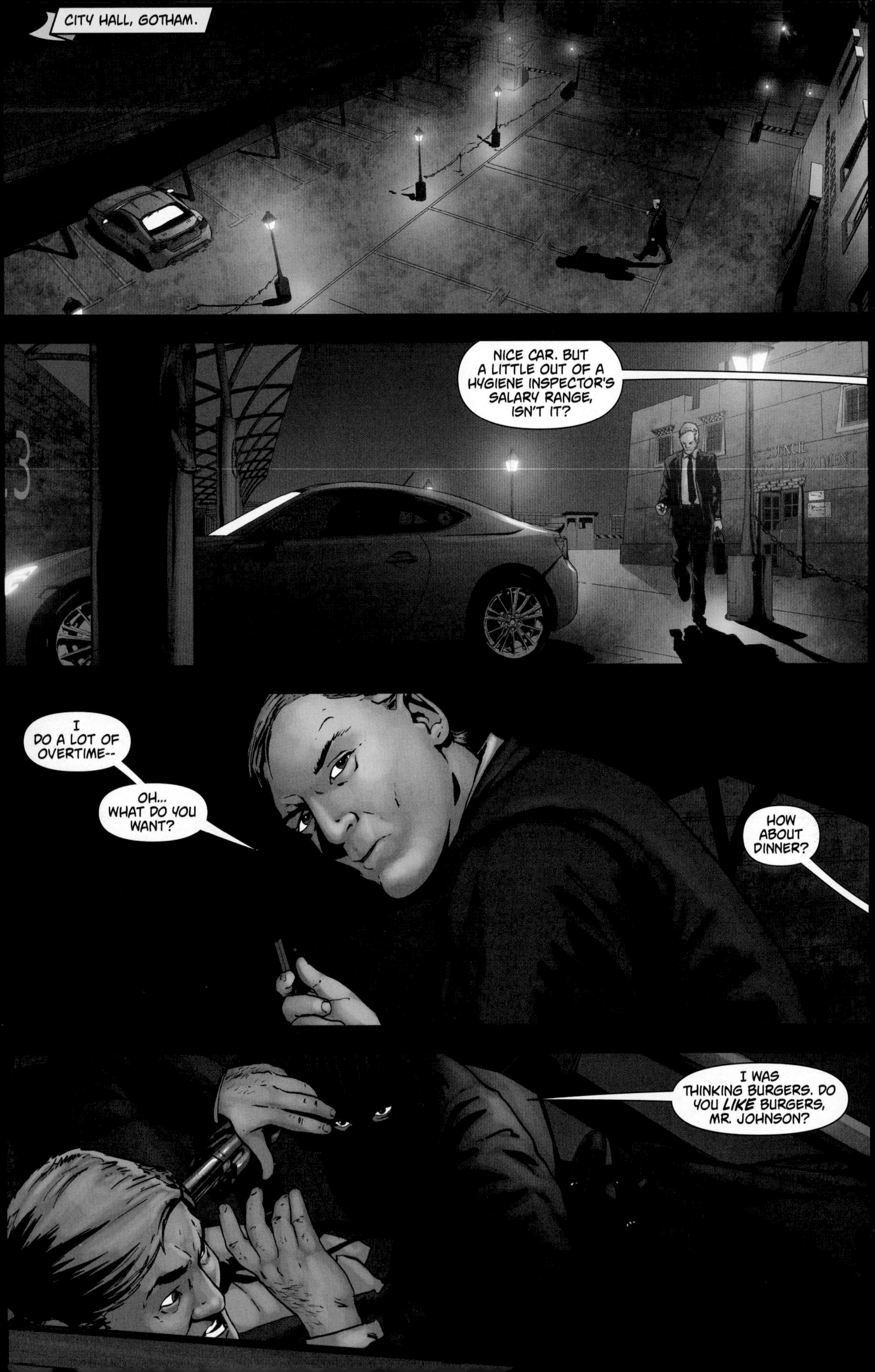
CITY HALL, GOTHAM.
NICE CAR. BUT A LITTLE OUT OF A HYGIENE INSPECTOR'S SALARY RANGE, ISN'T IT?
I DO A LOT OF OVERTIME--
OH... WHAT DO YOU WANT?
HOW ABOUT DINNER?
I WAS THINKING BURGERS. DO YOU *LIKE* BURGERS, MR. JOHNSON?

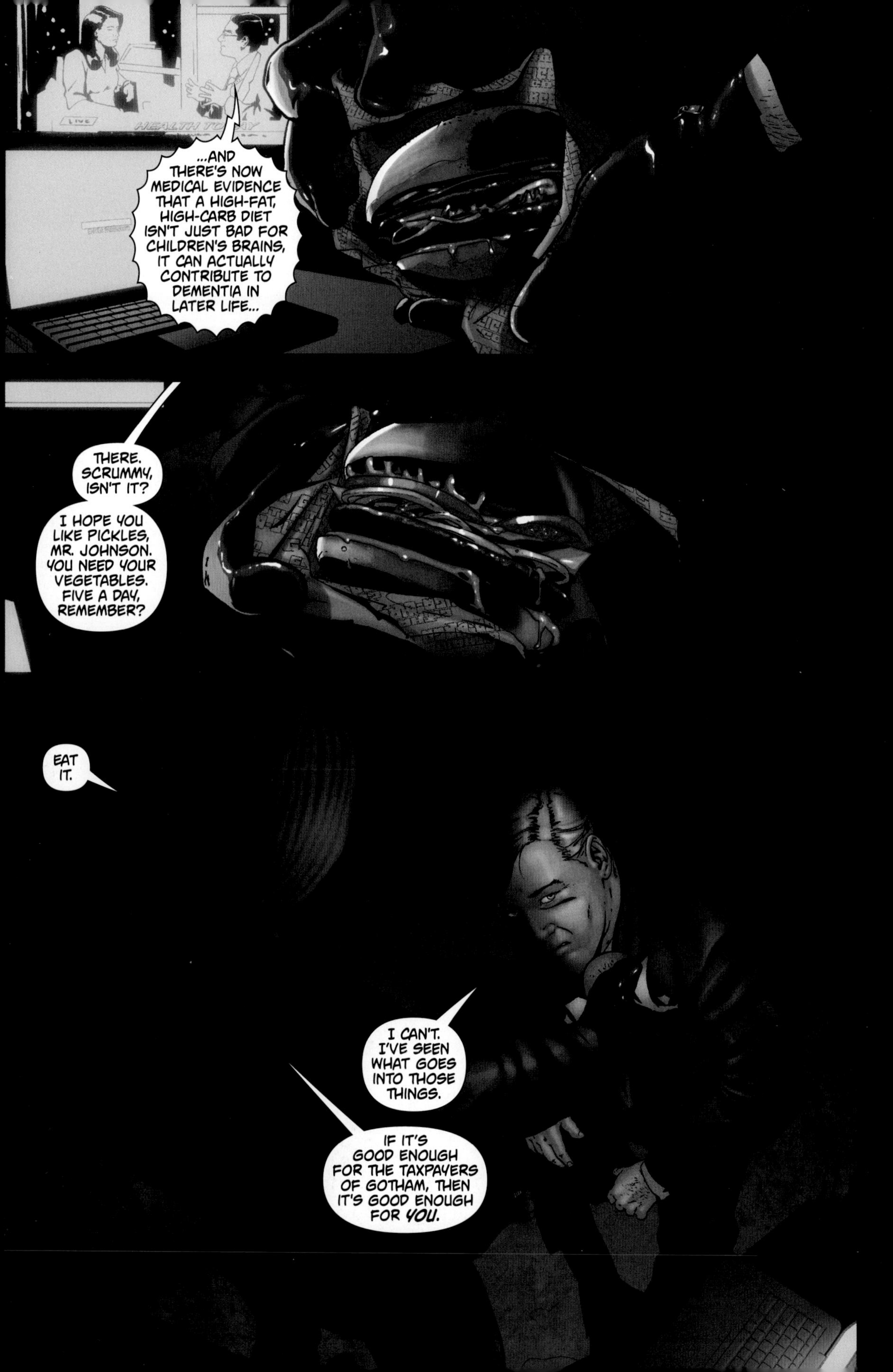
LIVE
HEALTH TODAY
...AND THERE'S NOW MEDICAL EVIDENCE THAT A HIGH-FAT, HIGH-CARB DIET ISN'T JUST BAD FOR CHILDREN'S BRAINS, IT CAN ACTUALLY CONTRIBUTE TO DEMENTIA IN LATER LIFE...
THERE. SCRUMMY, ISN'T IT?
I HOPE YOU LIKE PICKLES, MR. JOHNSON. YOU NEED YOUR VEGETABLES. FIVE A DAY, REMEMBER?
EAT IT.
I CAN'T. I'VE SEEN WHAT GOES INTO THOSE THINGS.
IF IT'S GOOD ENOUGH FOR THE TAXPAYERS OF GOTHAM, THEN IT'S GOOD ENOUGH FOR *YOU*.

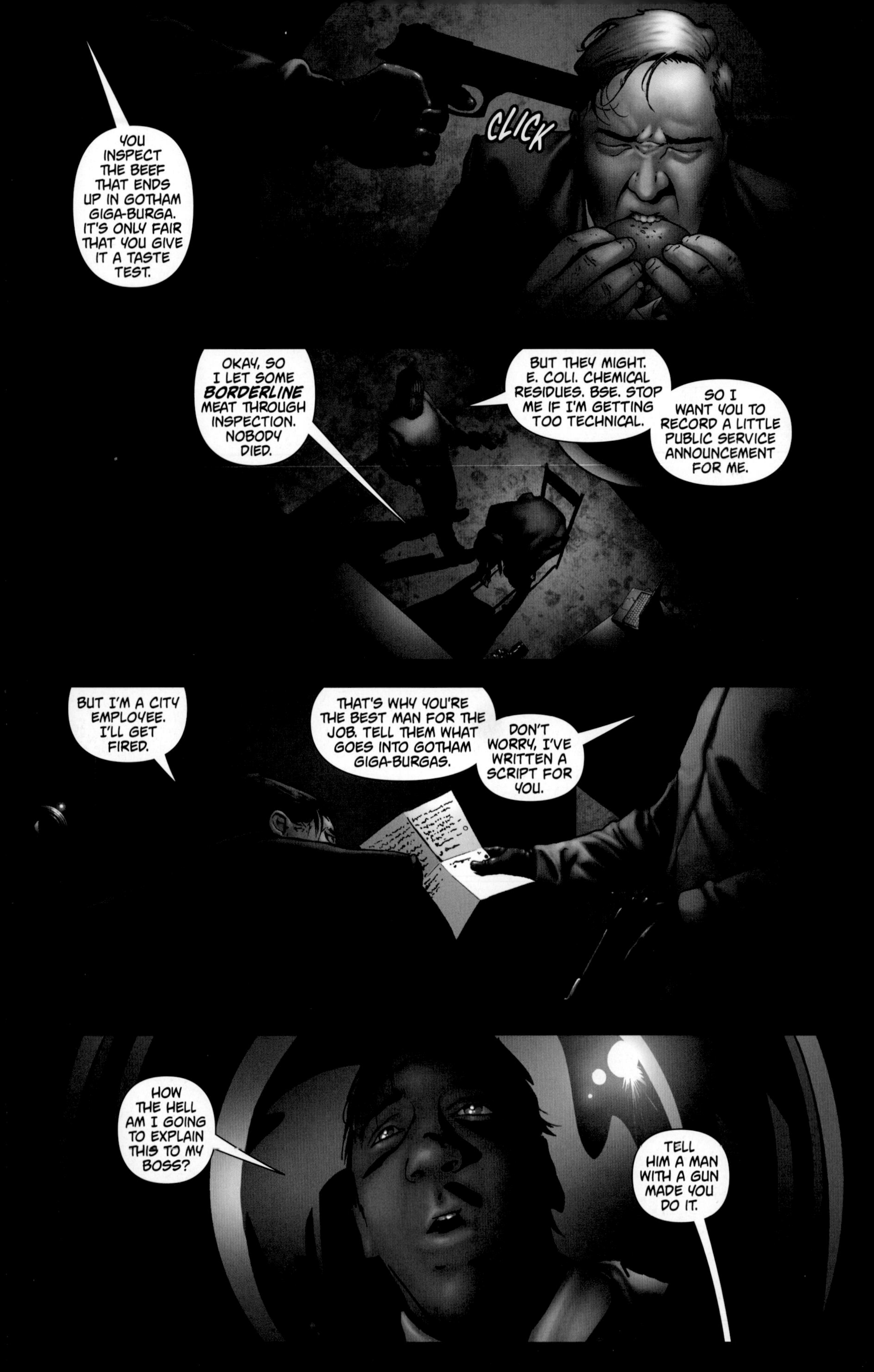
CLICK
YOU INSPECT THE BEEF THAT ENDS UP IN GOTHAM GIGA-BURGA. IT'S ONLY FAIR THAT YOU GIVE IT A TASTE TEST.
OKAY, SO I LET SOME BORDERLINE MEAT THROUGH INSPECTION. NOBODY DIED.
BUT THEY MIGHT. E. COLI. CHEMICAL RESIDUES. BSE. STOP ME IF I'M GETTING TOO TECHNICAL.
SO I WANT YOU TO RECORD A LITTLE PUBLIC SERVICE ANNOUNCEMENT FOR ME.
BUT I'M A CITY EMPLOYEE. I'LL GET FIRED.
THAT'S WHY YOU'RE THE BEST MAN FOR THE JOB. TELL THEM WHAT GOES INTO GOTHAM GIGA-BURGAS.
DON'T WORRY, I'VE WRITTEN A SCRIPT FOR YOU.
HOW THE HELL AM I GOING TO EXPLAIN THIS TO MY BOSS?
TELL HIM A MAN WITH A GUN MADE YOU DO IT.

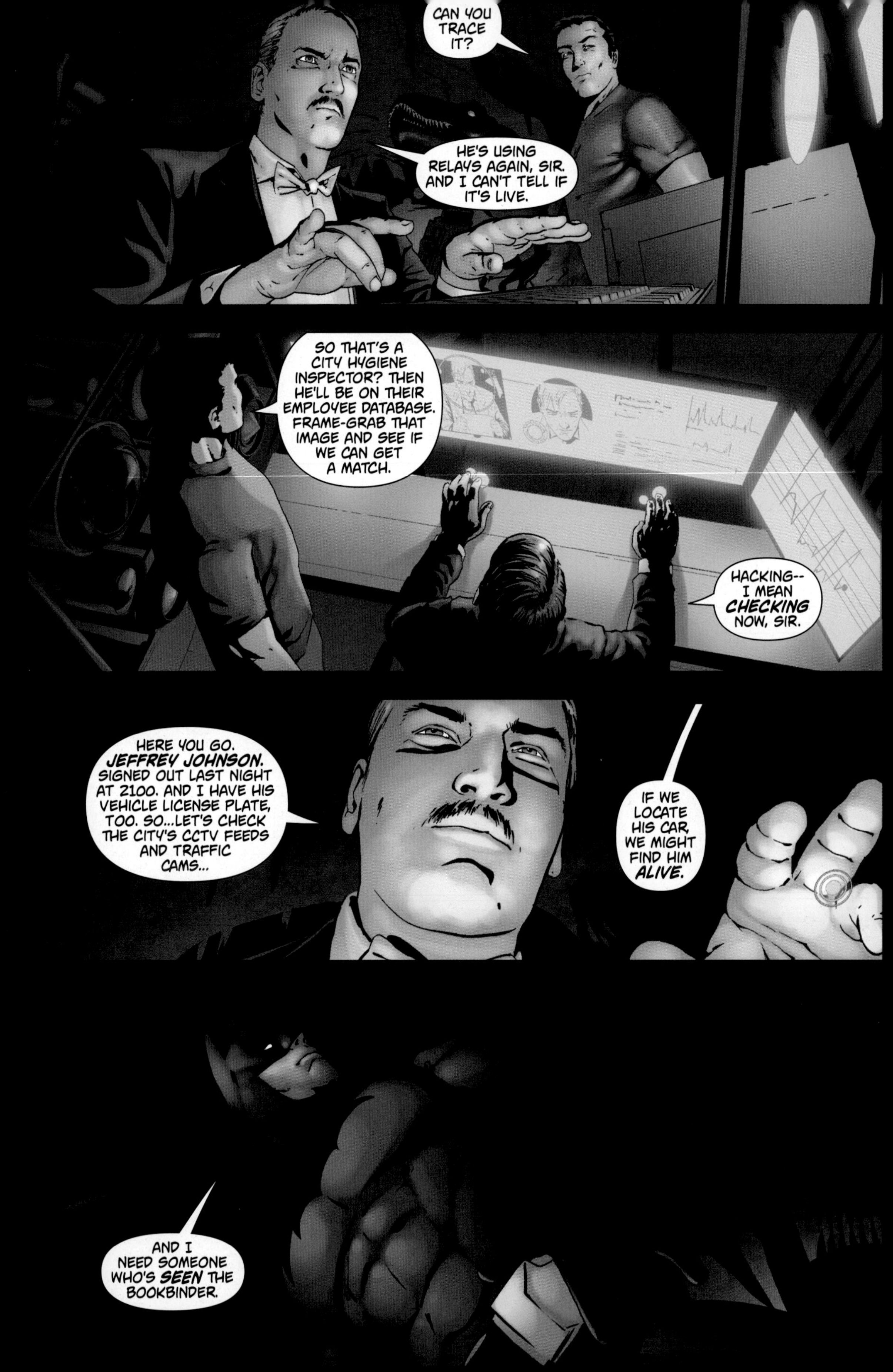
CAN YOU TRACE IT?
HE'S USING RELAYS AGAIN, SIR. AND I CAN'T TELL IF IT'S LIVE.
SO THAT'S A CITY HYGIENE INSPECTOR? THEN HE'LL BE ON THEIR EMPLOYEE DATABASE. FRAME-GRAB THAT IMAGE AND SEE IF WE CAN GET A MATCH.
HACKING-- I MEAN CHECKING NOW, SIR.
HERE YOU GO. JEFFREY JOHNSON. SIGNED OUT LAST NIGHT AT 2100. AND I HAVE HIS VEHICLE LICENSE PLATE, TOO. SO...LET'S CHECK THE CITY'S CCTV FEEDS AND TRAFFIC CAMS...
IF WE LOCATE HIS CAR, WE MIGHT FIND HIM ALIVE.
AND I NEED SOMEONE WHO'S SEEN THE BOOKBINDER.

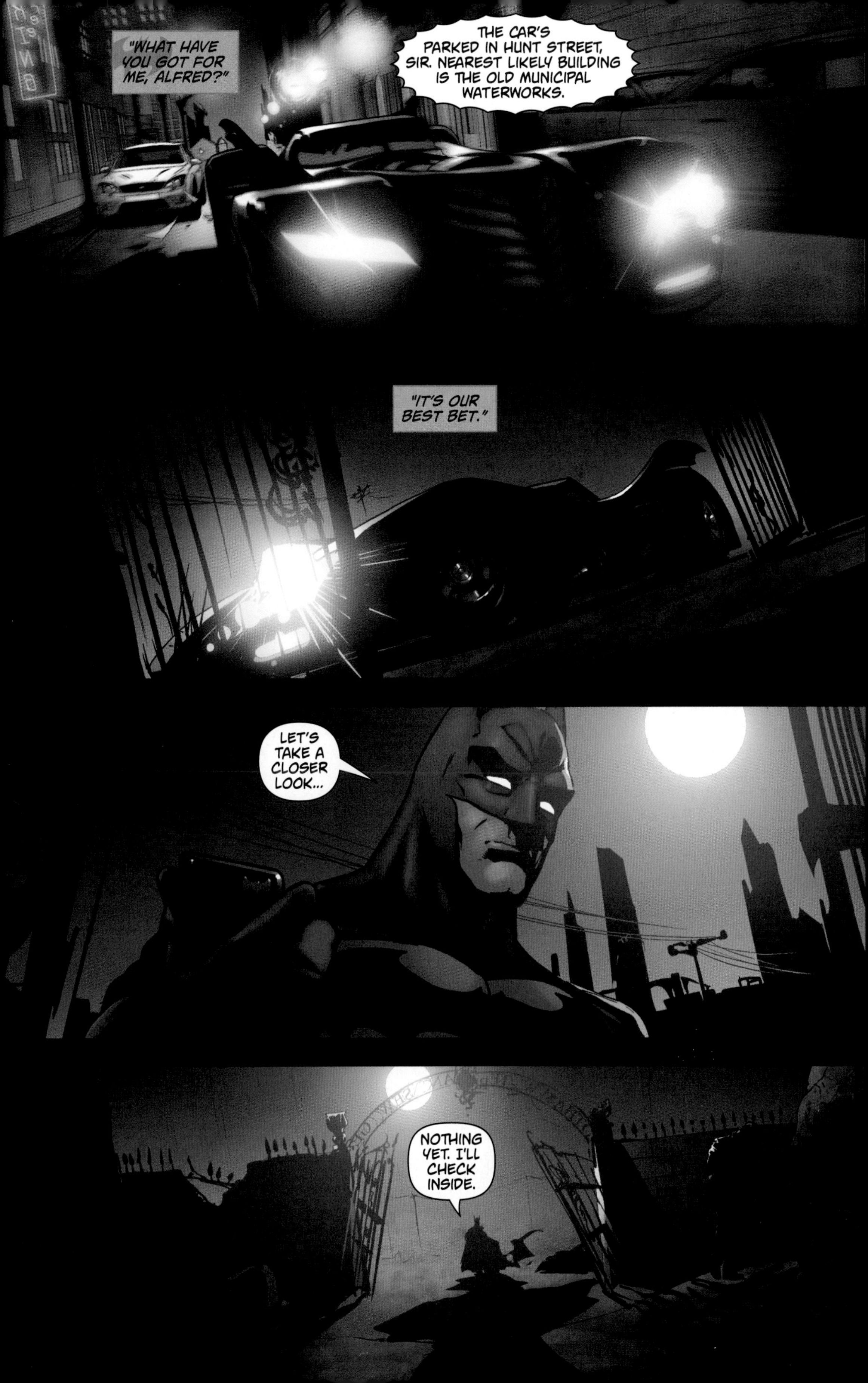
"WHAT HAVE YOU GOT FOR ME, ALFRED?"
THE CAR'S PARKED IN HUNT STREET, SIR. NEAREST LIKELY BUILDING IS THE OLD MUNICIPAL WATERWORKS.
"IT'S OUR BEST BET."
LET'S TAKE A CLOSER LOOK...
NOTHING YET. I'LL CHECK INSIDE.

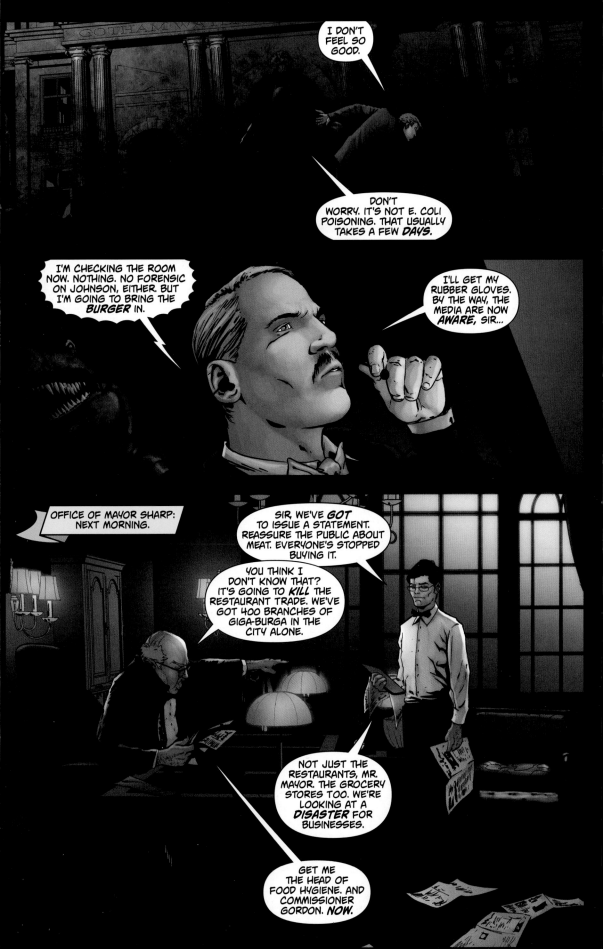

LUNCH TIME, CENTRAL GOTHAM.

THE BOOKBINDER'S TAKEN ONE TRASHY SHOW OFF THE AIR. NOW HE'S TAKEN BEEF OFF THE MENU--AND FOLKS ARE TOO SCARED TO BUY OTHER MEATS, TOO. WHAT ARE WE DEALING WITH HERE, BATMAN?

I'M STILL WORKING THAT OUT. FIRST, THERE'S THE ECONOMICS ANGLE. THIS IS COSTING BUSINESSES *MONEY.*

AND APART FROM TANNER, NOBODY'S BEEN *HURT* YET. HE'S STILL GIVING EVERYONE A CHOICE. TO BE *SMART* AND SURVIVE-- WHAT HE REGARDS AS SMART, ANYWAY.

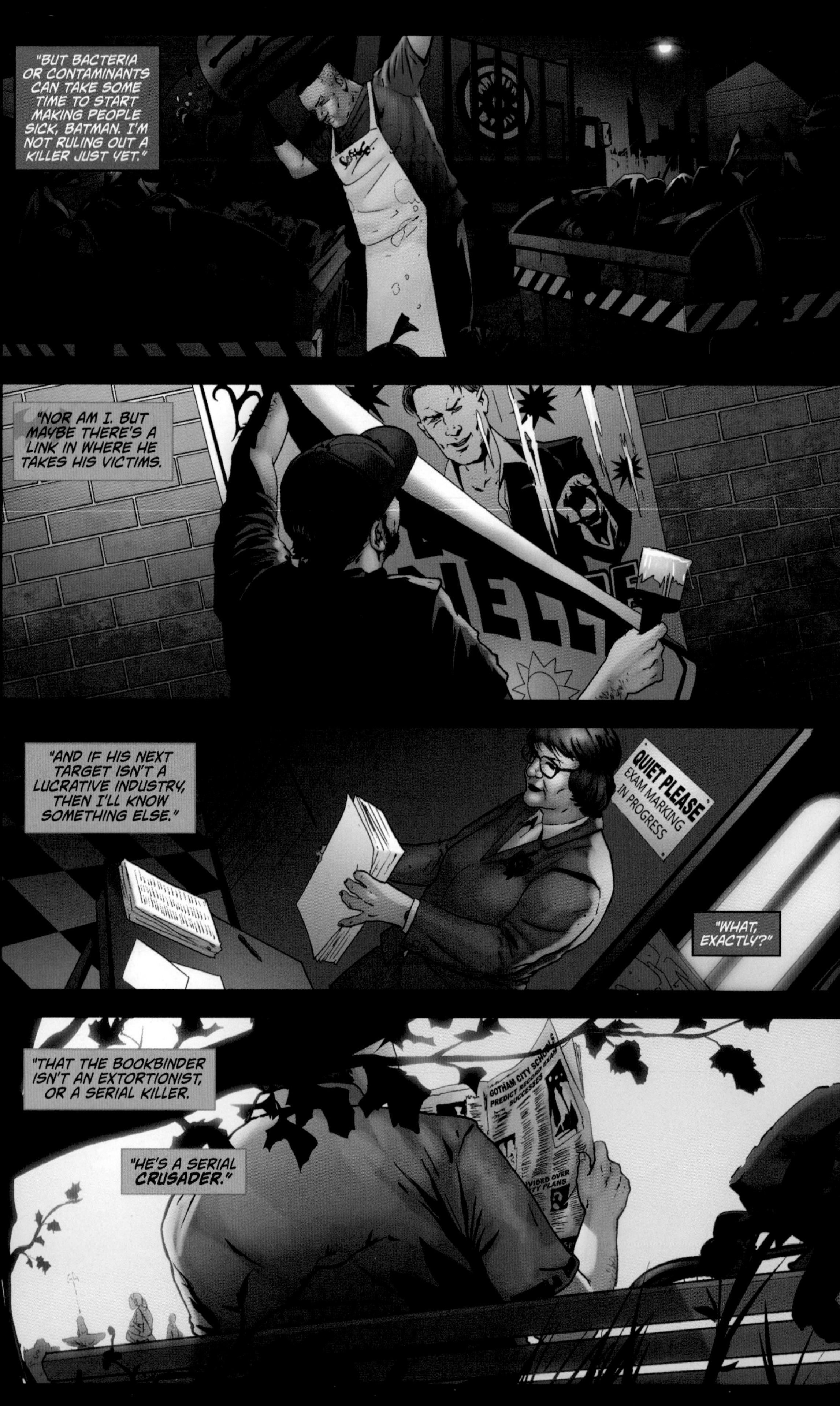
"BUT BACTERIA OR CONTAMINANTS CAN TAKE SOME TIME TO START MAKING PEOPLE SICK, BATMAN. I'M NOT RULING OUT A KILLER JUST YET."
"NOR AM I. BUT MAYBE THERE'S A LINK IN WHERE HE TAKES HIS VICTIMS.
"AND IF HIS NEXT TARGET ISN'T A LUCRATIVE INDUSTRY, THEN I'LL KNOW SOMETHING ELSE."
QUIET PLEASE
EXAM MARKING IN PROGRESS
"WHAT, EXACTLY?"
"THAT THE BOOKBINDER ISN'T AN EXTORTIONIST, OR A SERIAL KILLER.
GOTHAM CITY SCHOOLS
"HE'S A SERIAL CRUSADER."

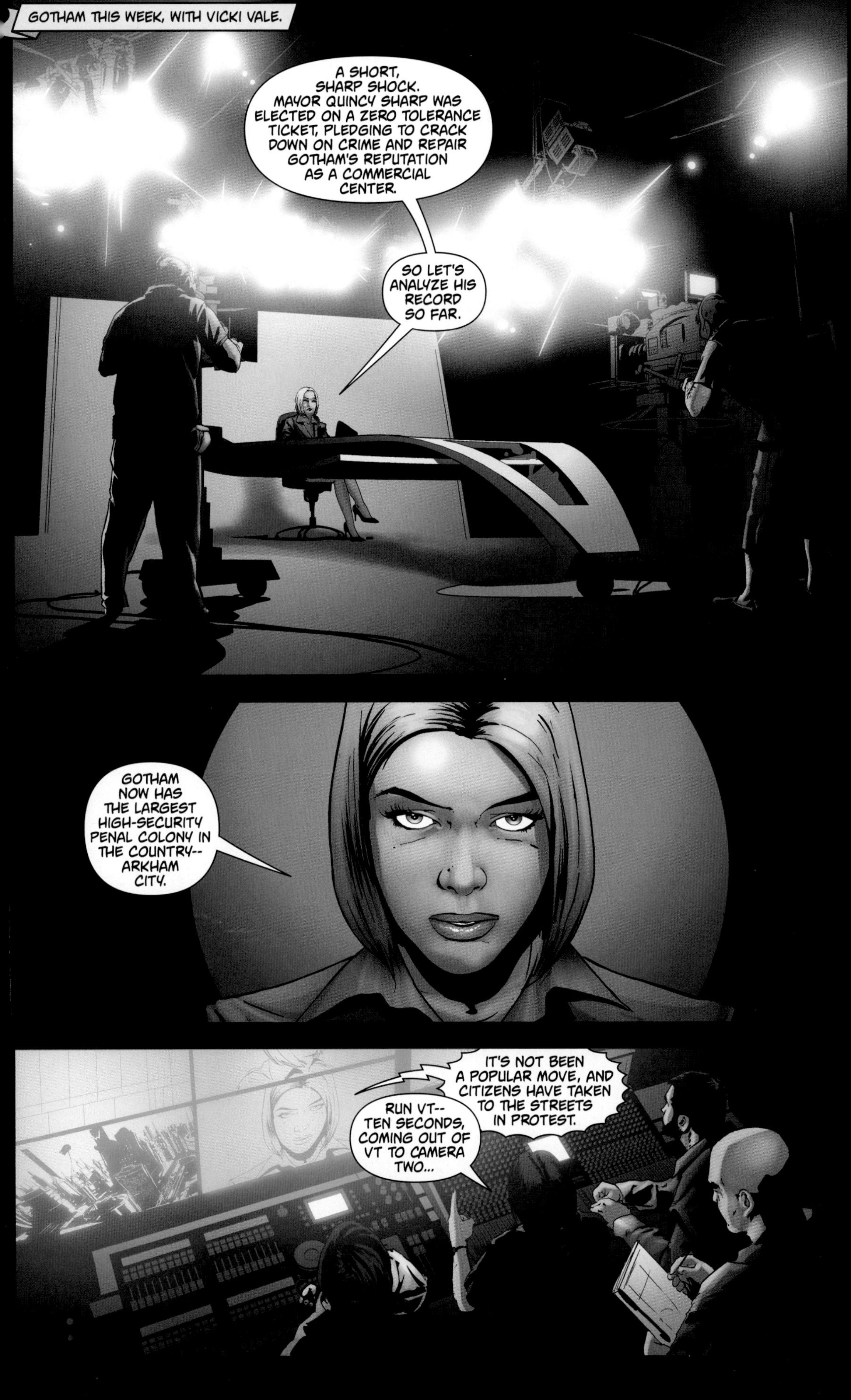
GOTHAM THIS WEEK, WITH VICKI VALE.
A SHORT, SHARP SHOCK. MAYOR QUINCY SHARP WAS ELECTED ON A ZERO TOLERANCE TICKET, PLEDGING TO CRACK DOWN ON CRIME AND REPAIR GOTHAM'S REPUTATION AS A COMMERCIAL CENTER.
SO LET'S ANALYZE HIS RECORD SO FAR.
GOTHAM NOW HAS THE LARGEST HIGH-SECURITY PENAL COLONY IN THE COUNTRY-- ARKHAM CITY.
IT'S NOT BEEN A POPULAR MOVE, AND CITIZENS HAVE TAKEN TO THE STREETS IN PROTEST.
RUN VT-- TEN SECONDS, COMING OUT OF VT TO CAMERA TWO...

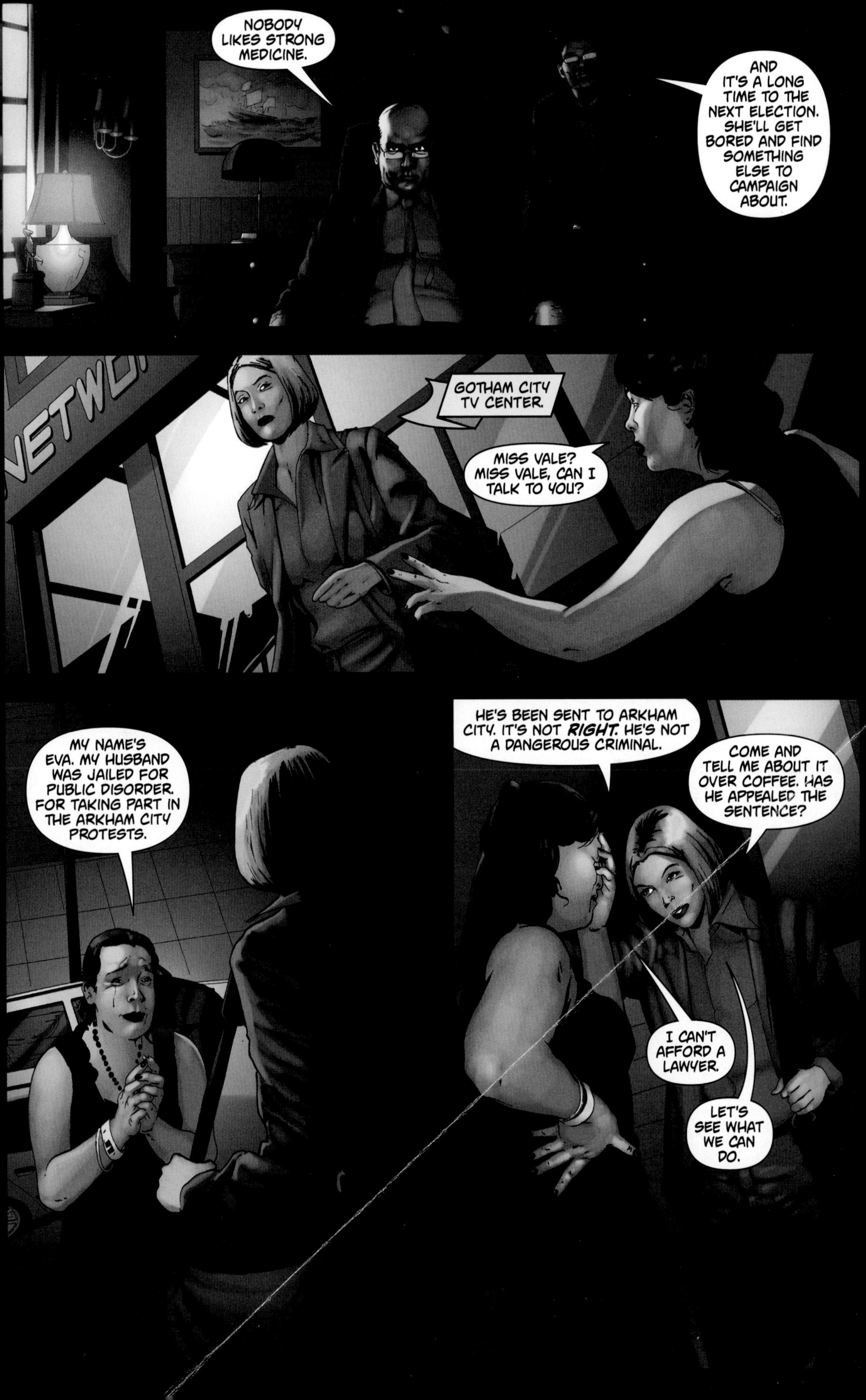
NOBODY LIKES STRONG MEDICINE.
AND IT'S A LONG TIME TO THE NEXT ELECTION. SHE'LL GET BORED AND FIND SOMETHING ELSE TO CAMPAIGN ABOUT.
NETWO
GOTHAM CITY TV CENTER.
MISS VALE? MISS VALE, CAN I TALK TO YOU?
MY NAME'S EVA. MY HUSBAND WAS JAILED FOR PUBLIC DISORDER. FOR TAKING PART IN THE ARKHAM CITY PROTESTS.
HE'S BEEN SENT TO ARKHAM CITY. IT'S NOT ***RIGHT.*** HE'S NOT A DANGEROUS CRIMINAL.
COME AND TELL ME ABOUT IT OVER COFFEE. HAS HE APPEALED THE SENTENCE?
I CAN'T AFFORD A LAWYER.
LET'S SEE WHAT WE CAN DO.

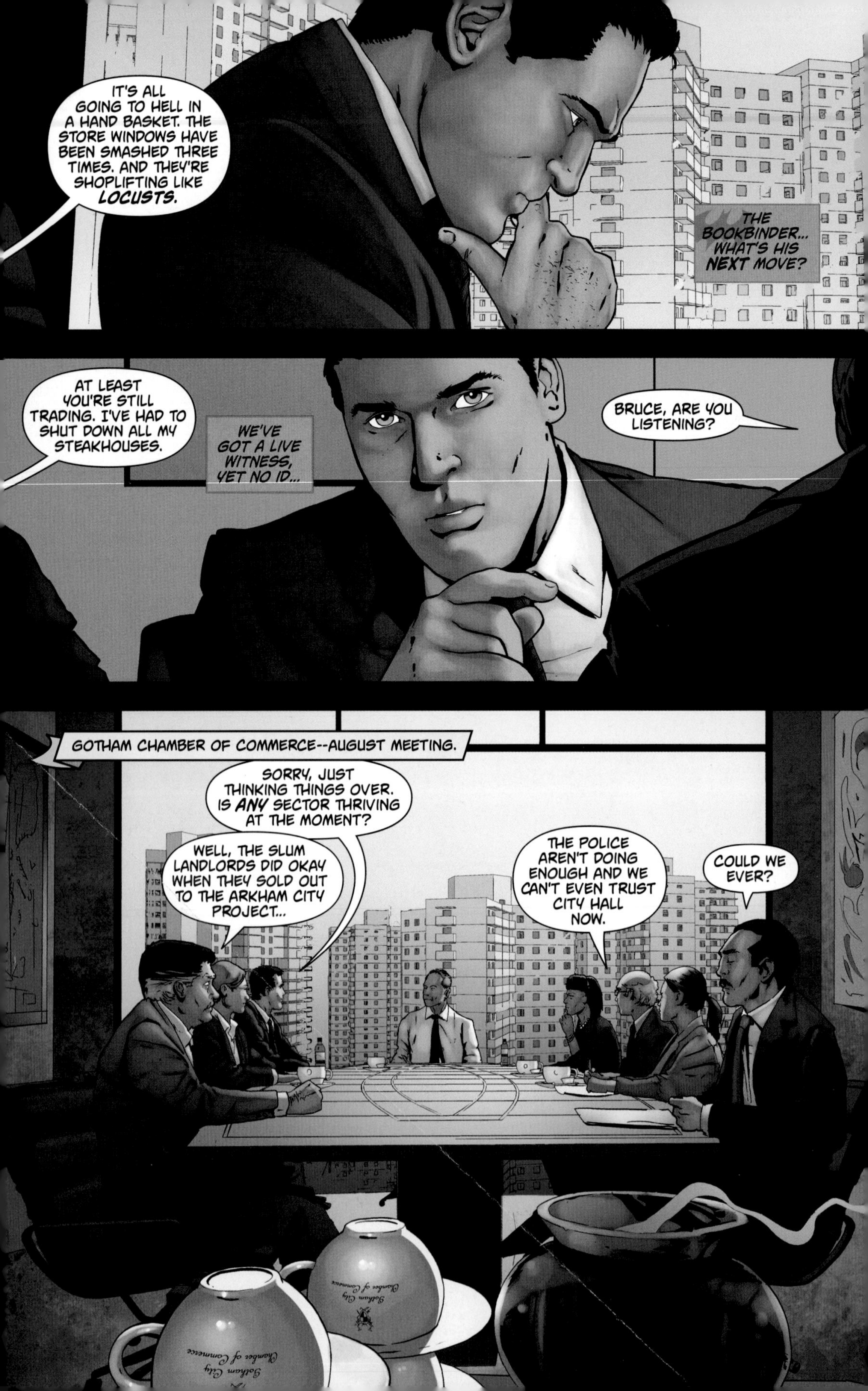
IT'S ALL GOING TO HELL IN A HAND BASKET. THE STORE WINDOWS HAVE BEEN SMASHED THREE TIMES. AND THEY'RE SHOPLIFTING LIKE LOCUSTS.
THE BOOKBINDER... WHAT'S HIS NEXT MOVE?
AT LEAST YOU'RE STILL TRADING. I'VE HAD TO SHUT DOWN ALL MY STEAKHOUSES.
WE'VE GOT A LIVE WITNESS, YET NO ID...
BRUCE, ARE YOU LISTENING?
GOTHAM CHAMBER OF COMMERCE--AUGUST MEETING.
SORRY, JUST THINKING THINGS OVER. IS ANY SECTOR THRIVING AT THE MOMENT?
WELL, THE SLUM LANDLORDS DID OKAY WHEN THEY SOLD OUT TO THE ARKHAM CITY PROJECT...
THE POLICE AREN'T DOING ENOUGH AND WE CAN'T EVEN TRUST CITY HALL NOW.
COULD WE EVER?
Gotham City Chamber of Commerce
Gotham City Chamber of Commerce

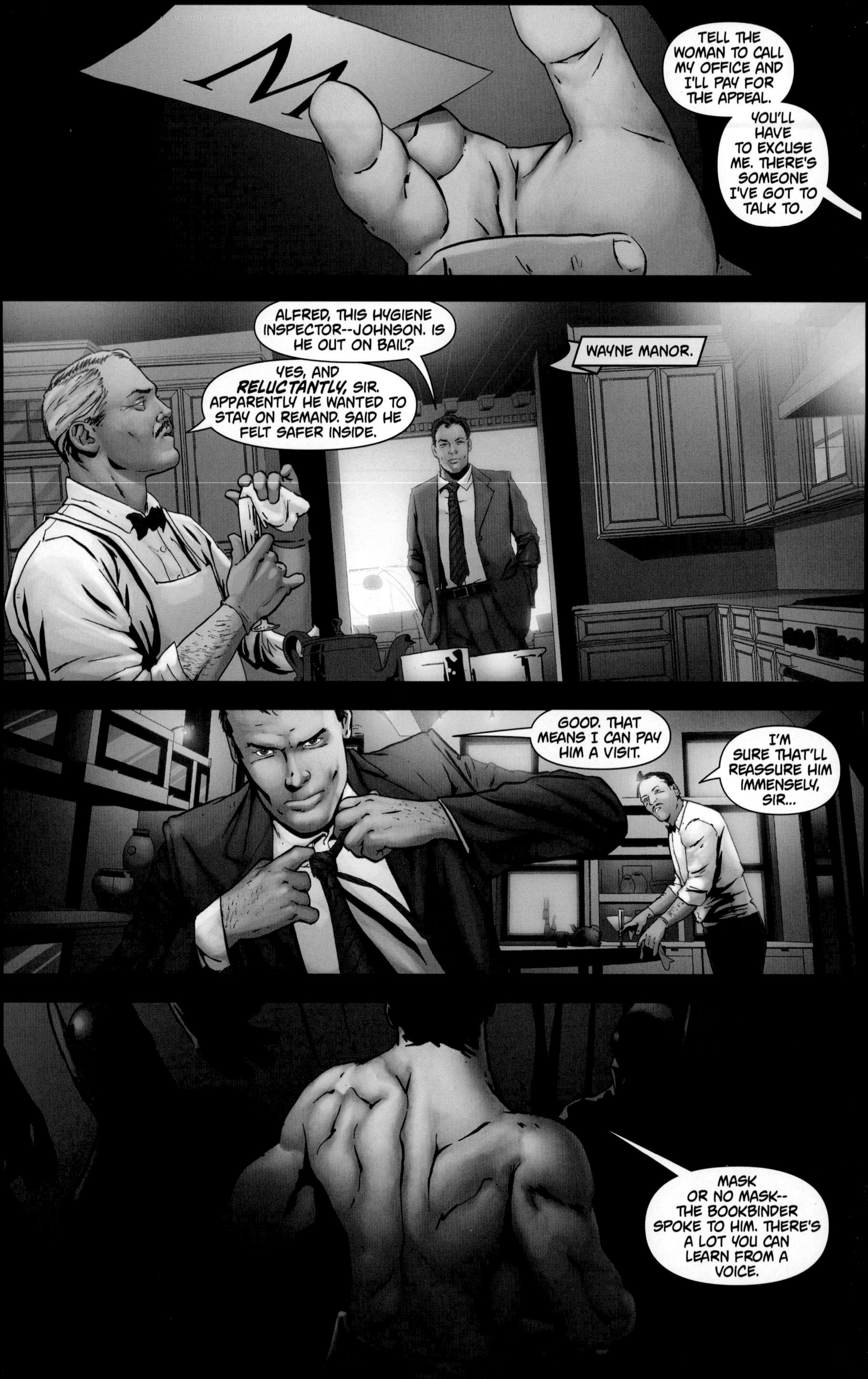
TELL THE WOMAN TO CALL MY OFFICE AND I'LL PAY FOR THE APPEAL.
YOU'LL HAVE TO EXCUSE ME. THERE'S SOMEONE I'VE GOT TO TALK TO.
WAYNE MANOR.
ALFRED, THIS HYGIENE INSPECTOR--JOHNSON. IS HE OUT ON BAIL?
YES, AND *RELUCTANTLY,* SIR. APPARENTLY HE WANTED TO STAY ON REMAND. SAID HE FELT SAFER INSIDE.
GOOD. THAT MEANS I CAN PAY HIM A VISIT.
I'M SURE THAT'LL REASSURE HIM IMMENSELY, SIR...
MASK OR NO MASK-- THE BOOKBINDER SPOKE TO HIM. THERE'S A LOT YOU CAN LEARN FROM A VOICE.

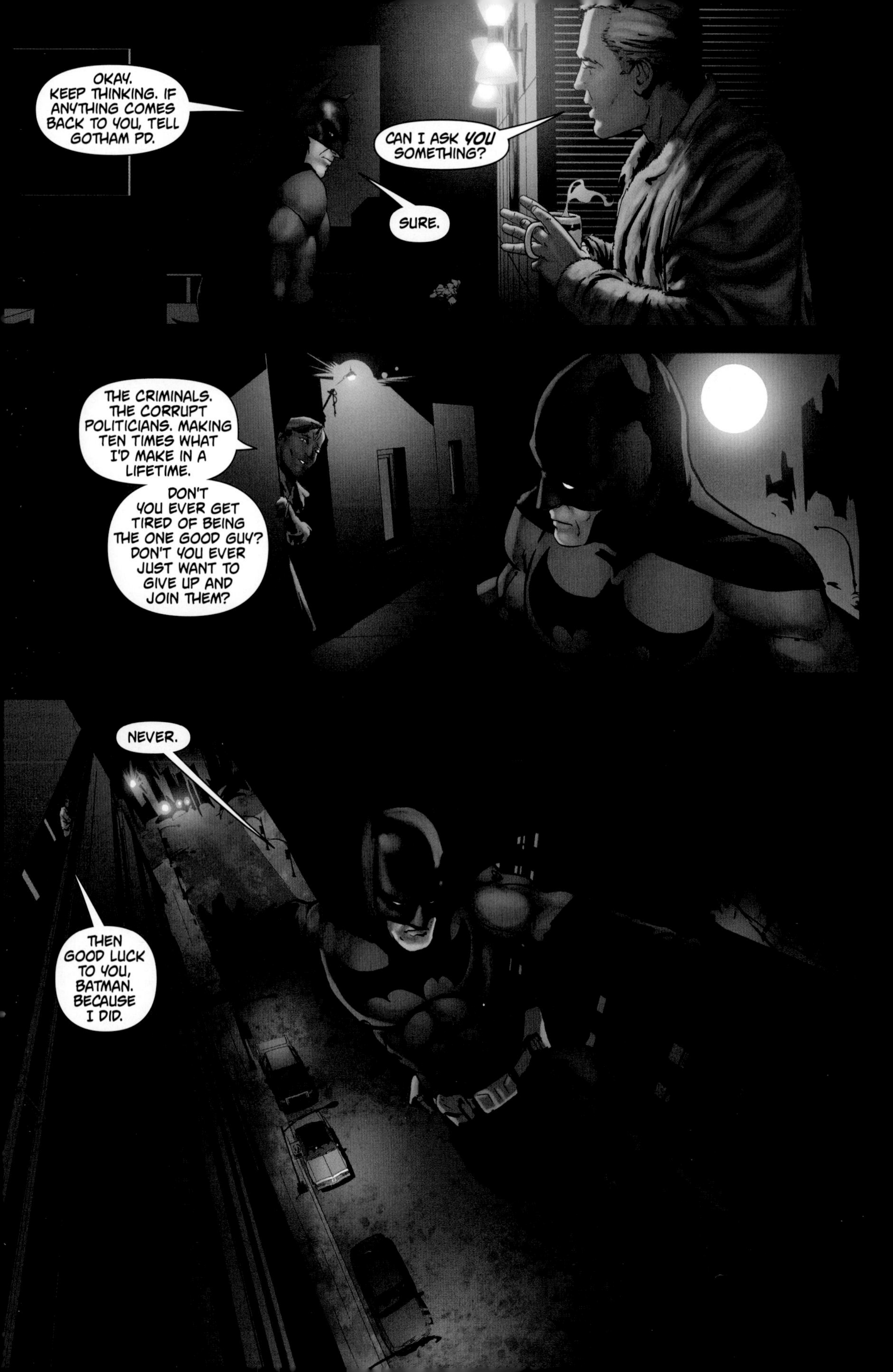
OKAY. KEEP THINKING. IF ANYTHING COMES BACK TO YOU, TELL GOTHAM PD.
CAN I ASK YOU SOMETHING?
SURE.
THE CRIMINALS. THE CORRUPT POLITICIANS. MAKING TEN TIMES WHAT I'D MAKE IN A LIFETIME.
DON'T YOU EVER GET TIRED OF BEING THE ONE GOOD GUY? DON'T YOU EVER JUST WANT TO GIVE UP AND JOIN THEM?
NEVER.
THEN GOOD LUCK TO YOU, BATMAN. BECAUSE I DID.

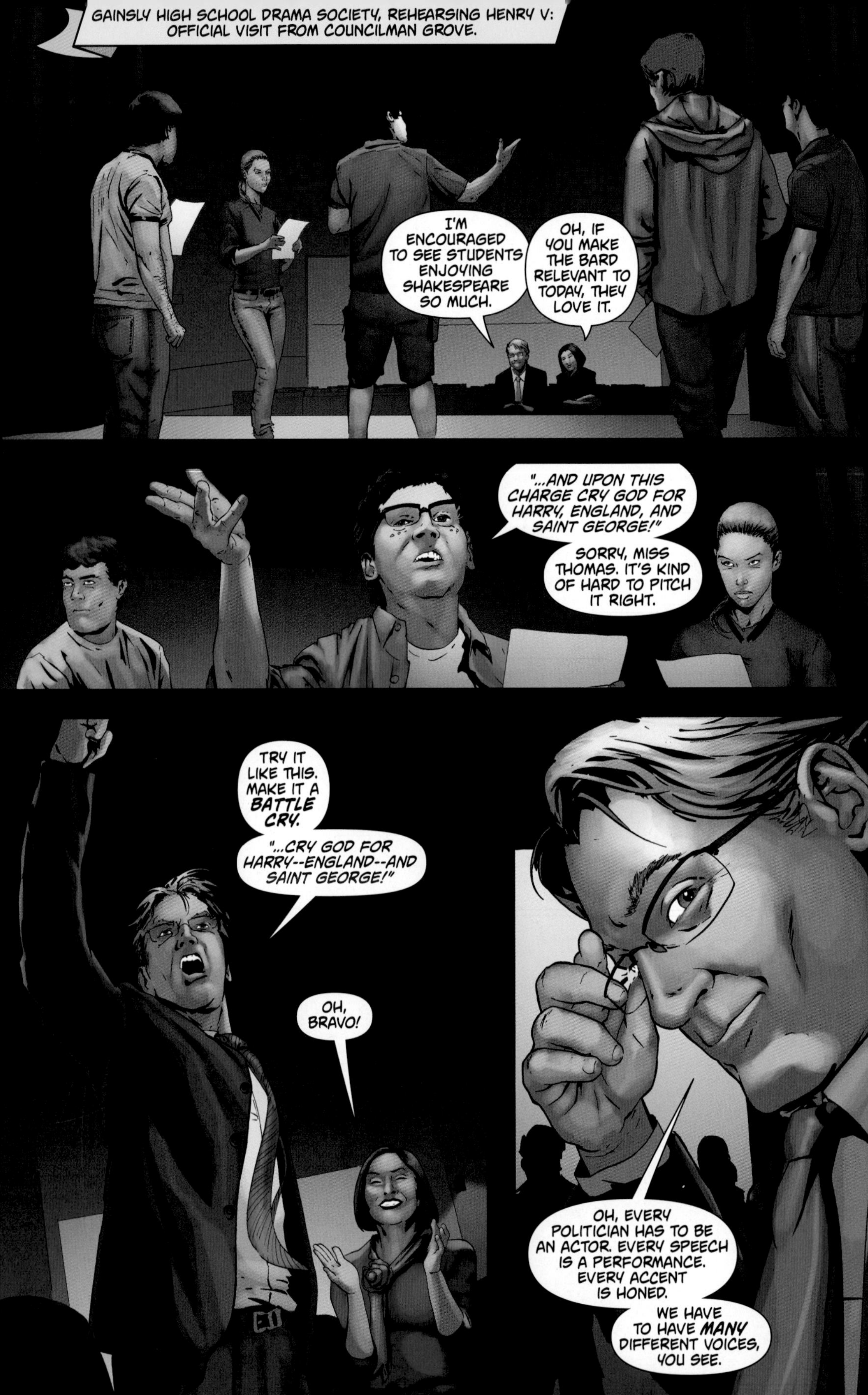
GAINSLY HIGH SCHOOL DRAMA SOCIETY, REHEARSING HENRY V: OFFICIAL VISIT FROM COUNCILMAN GROVE.
I'M ENCOURAGED TO SEE STUDENTS ENJOYING SHAKESPEARE SO MUCH.
OH, IF YOU MAKE THE BARD RELEVANT TO TODAY, THEY LOVE IT.
"...AND UPON THIS CHARGE CRY GOD FOR HARRY, ENGLAND, AND SAINT GEORGE!"
SORRY, MISS THOMAS. IT'S KIND OF HARD TO PITCH IT RIGHT.
TRY IT LIKE THIS. MAKE IT A BATTLE CRY.
"...CRY GOD FOR HARRY--ENGLAND--AND SAINT GEORGE!"
OH, BRAVO!
OH, EVERY POLITICIAN HAS TO BE AN ACTOR. EVERY SPEECH IS A PERFORMANCE. EVERY ACCENT IS HONED.
WE HAVE TO HAVE MANY DIFFERENT VOICES, YOU SEE.

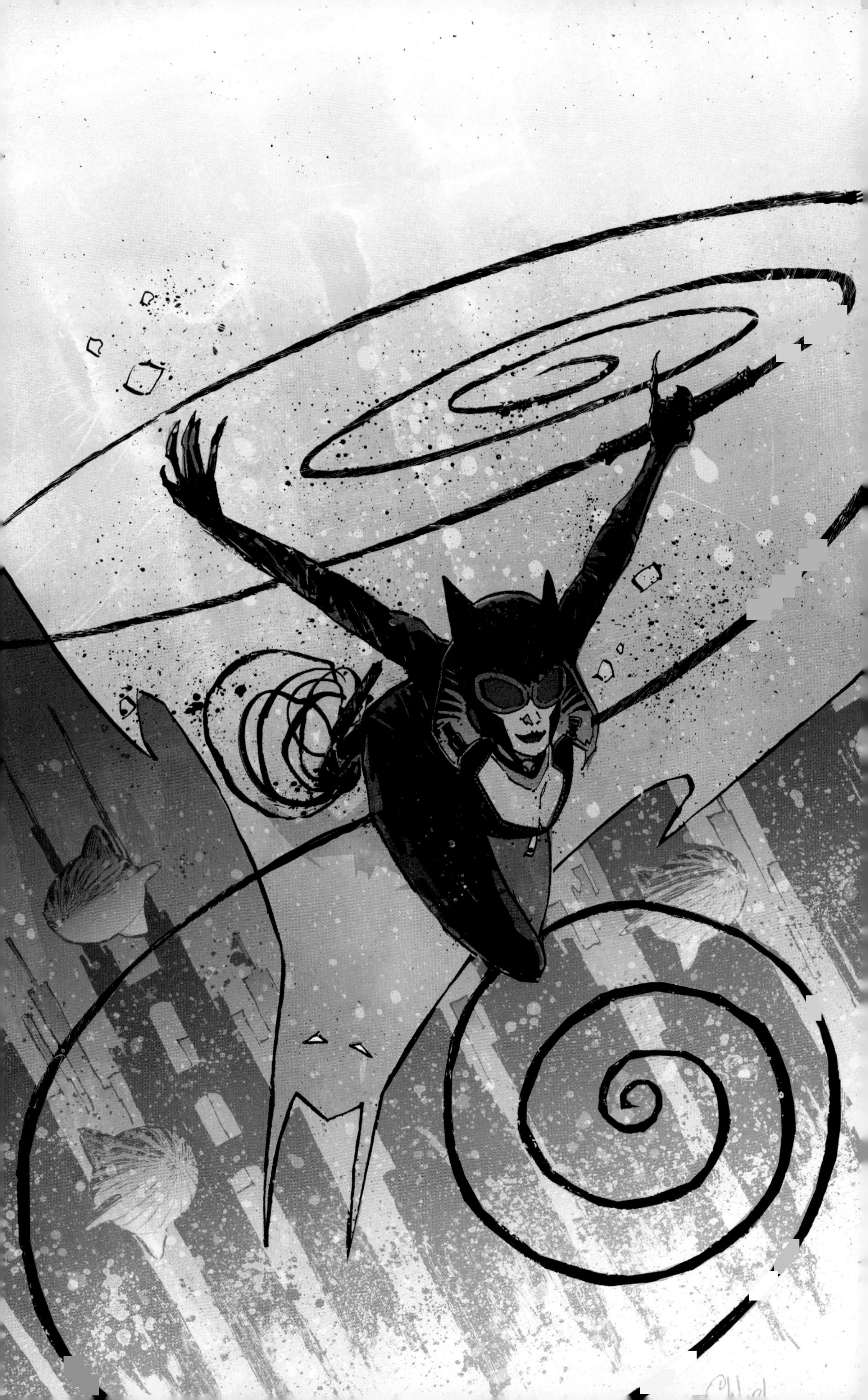

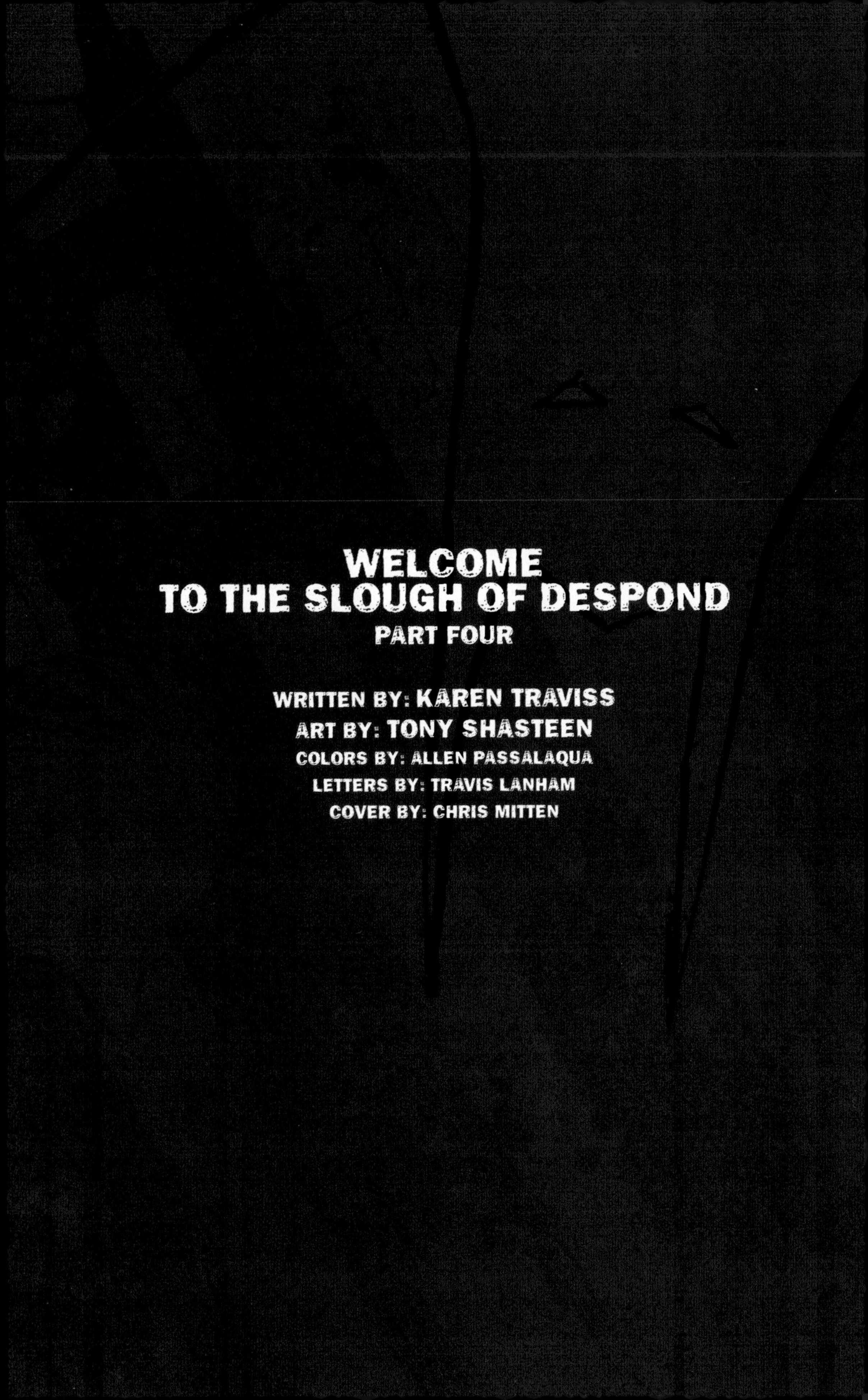

WELCOME
TO THE SLOUGH OF DESPOND
PART FOUR

WRITTEN BY: KAREN TRAVISS
ART BY: TONY SHASTEEN
COLORS BY: ALLEN PASSALAQUA
LETTERS BY: TRAVIS LANHAM
COVER BY: CHRIS MITTEN

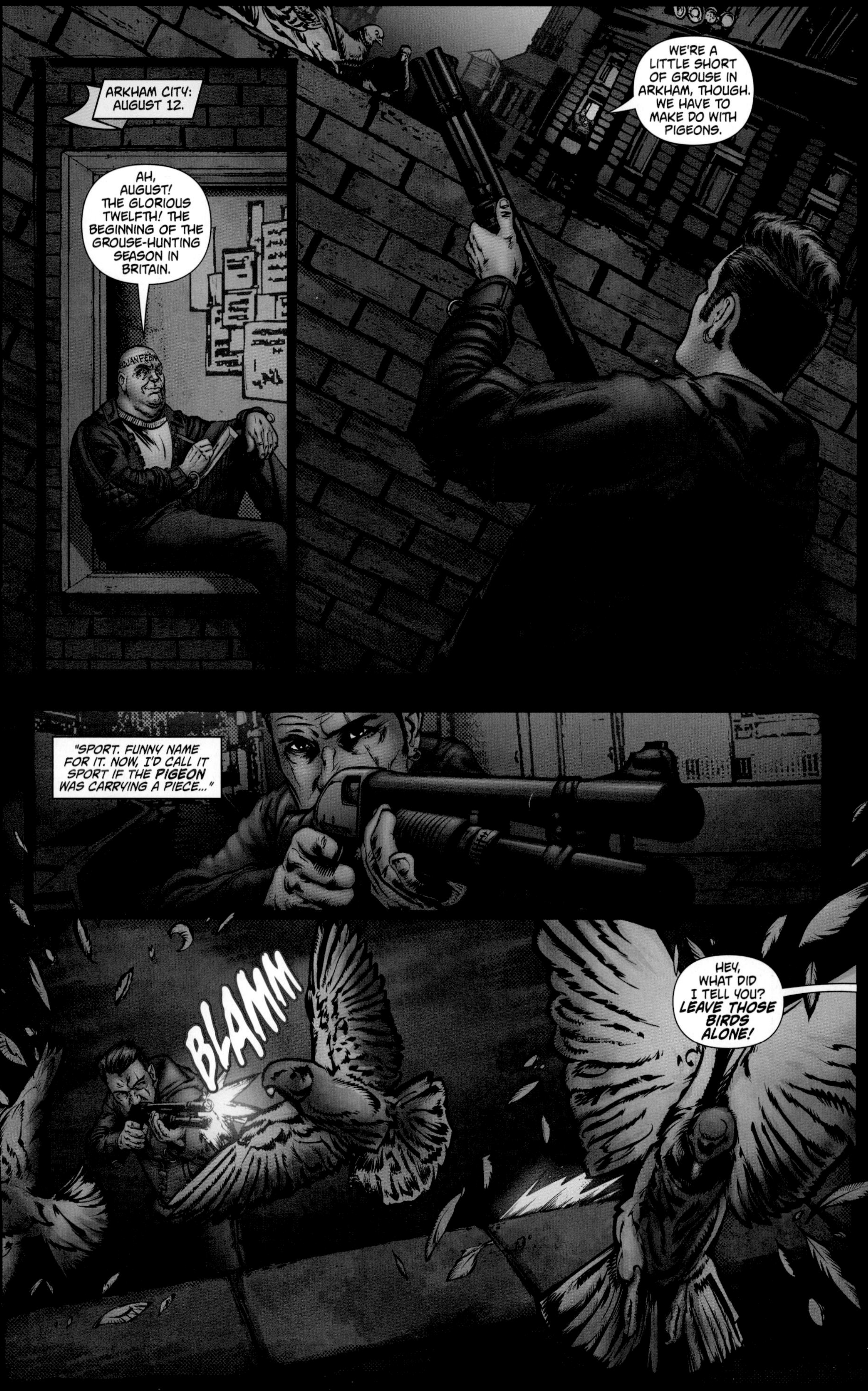

ARKHAM CITY: AUGUST 12.
AH, AUGUST! THE GLORIOUS TWELFTH! THE BEGINNING OF THE GROUSE-HUNTING SEASON IN BRITAIN.
WE'RE A LITTLE SHORT OF GROUSE IN ARKHAM, THOUGH. WE HAVE TO MAKE DO WITH PIGEONS.
"SPORT. FUNNY NAME FOR IT. NOW, I'D CALL IT SPORT IF THE PIGEON WAS CARRYING A PIECE..."
BLAMM
HEY, WHAT DID I TELL YOU? LEAVE THOSE BIRDS ALONE!

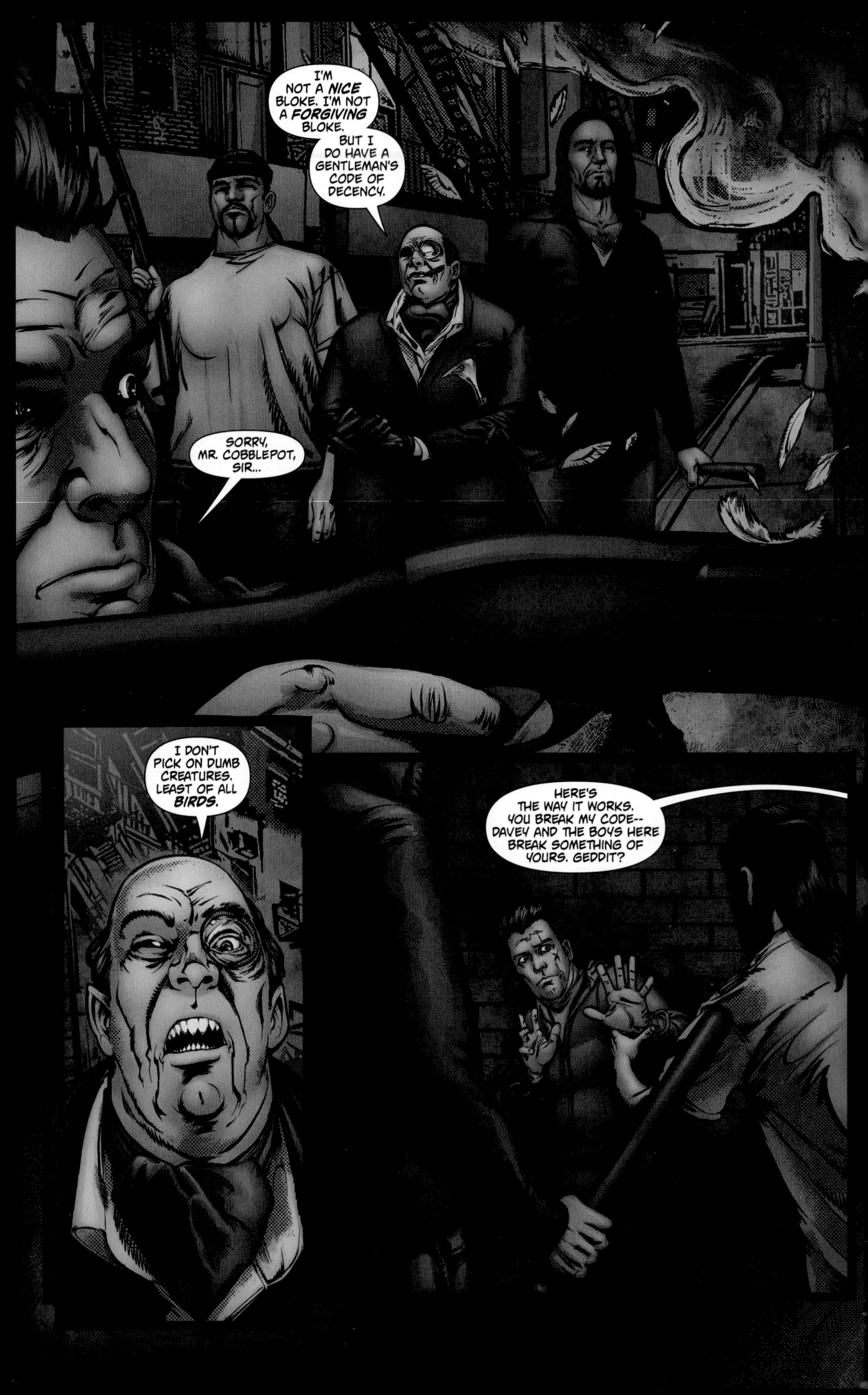

I'M NOT A *NICE* BLOKE. I'M NOT A *FORGIVING* BLOKE.
BUT I DO HAVE A GENTLEMAN'S CODE OF DECENCY.
SORRY, MR. COBBLEPOT, SIR...
I DON'T PICK ON DUMB CREATURES. LEAST OF ALL *BIRDS*.
HERE'S THE WAY IT WORKS. YOU BREAK MY CODE-- DAVEY AND THE BOYS HERE BREAK SOMETHING OF YOURS. GEDDIT?

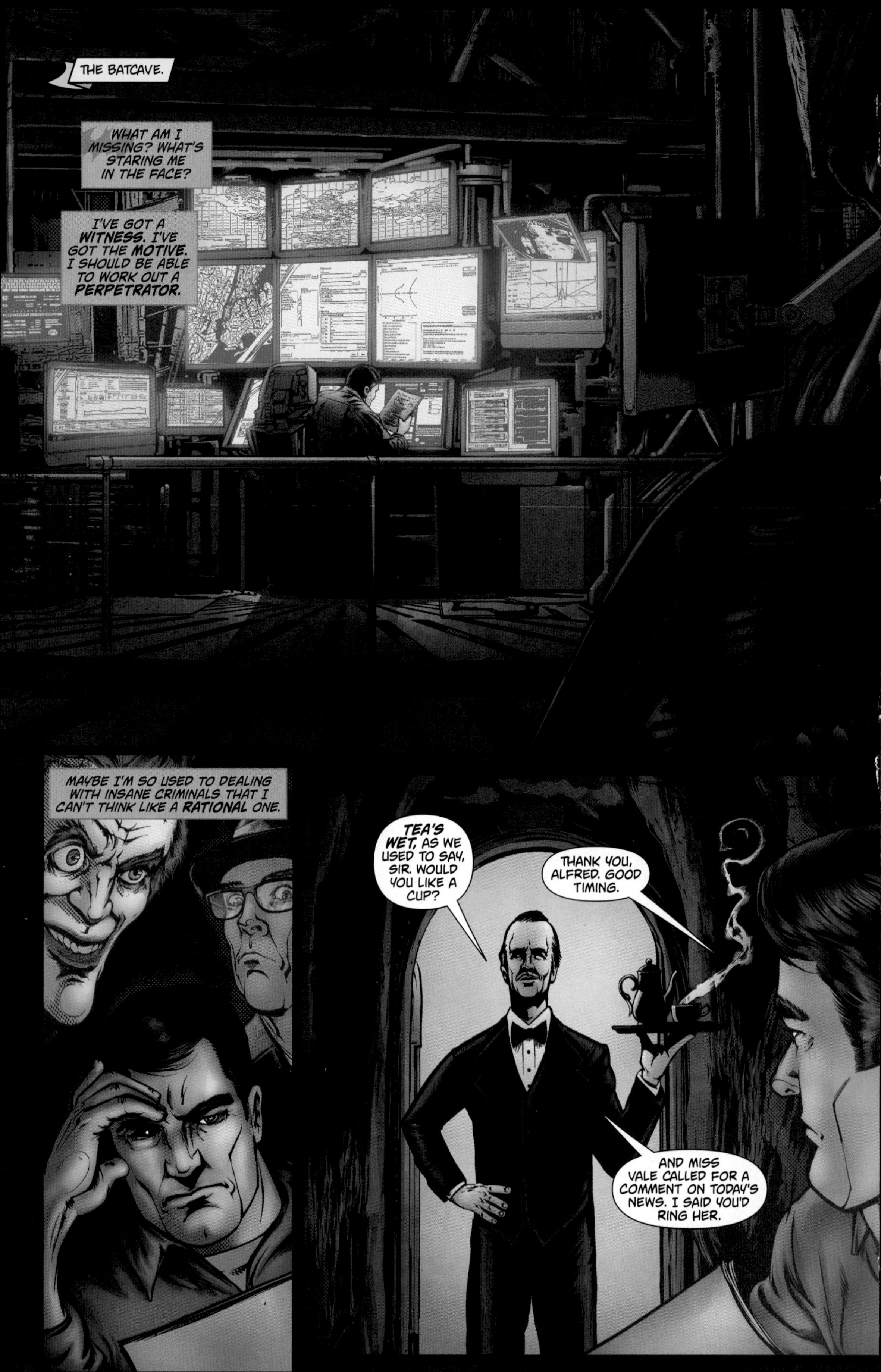
THE BATCAVE.
WHAT AM I MISSING? WHAT'S STARING ME IN THE FACE?
I'VE GOT A WITNESS. I'VE GOT THE MOTIVE. I SHOULD BE ABLE TO WORK OUT A PERPETRATOR.
MAYBE I'M SO USED TO DEALING WITH INSANE CRIMINALS THAT I CAN'T THINK LIKE A RATIONAL ONE.
TEA'S WET, AS WE USED TO SAY, SIR. WOULD YOU LIKE A CUP?
THANK YOU, ALFRED. GOOD TIMING.
AND MISS VALE CALLED FOR A COMMENT ON TODAY'S NEWS. I SAID YOU'D RING HER.

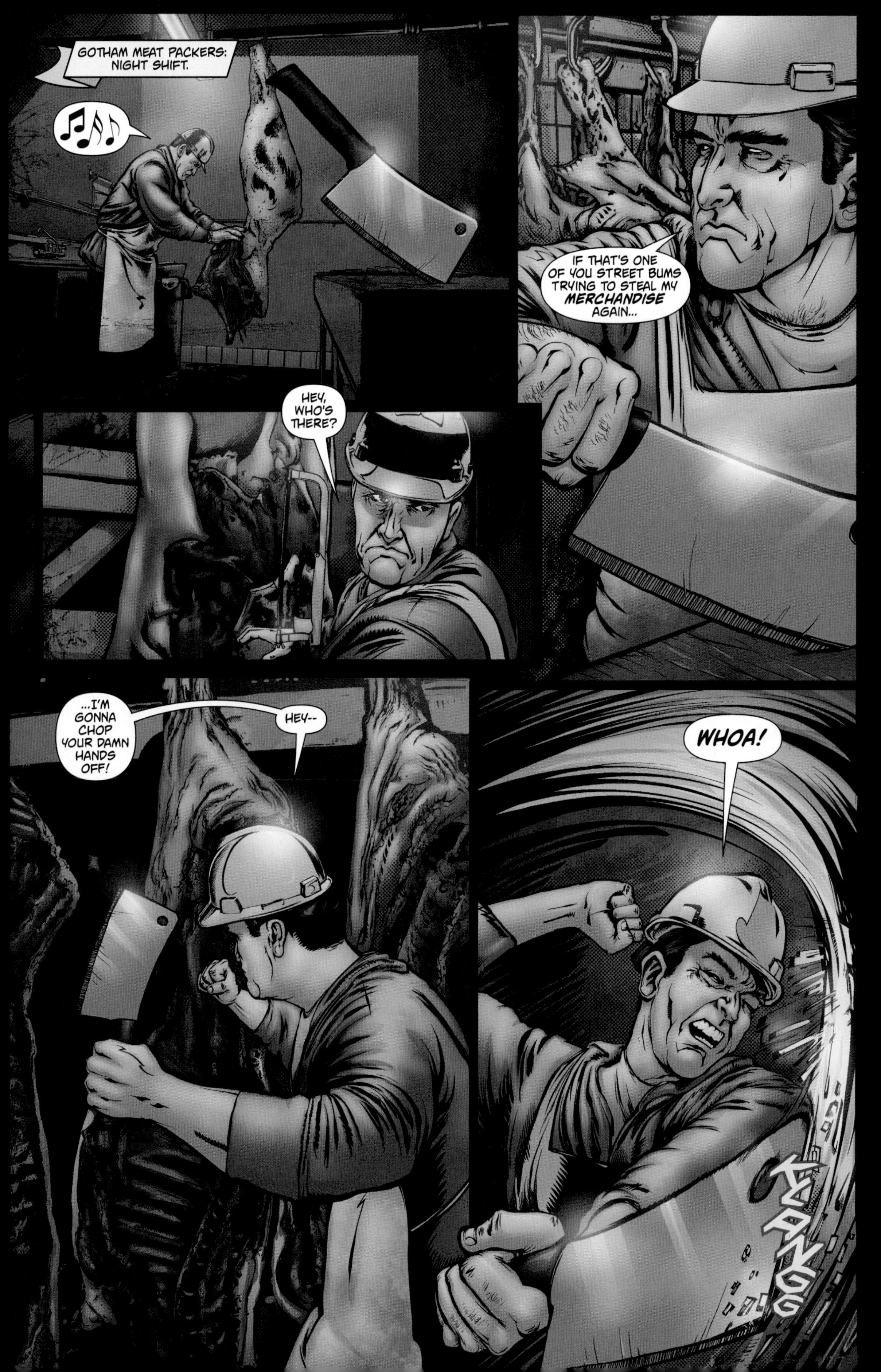
GOTHAM MEAT PACKERS: NIGHT SHIFT.
♫♪♪
IF THAT'S ONE OF YOU STREET BUMS TRYING TO STEAL MY MERCHANDISE AGAIN...
HEY, WHO'S THERE?
...I'M GONNA CHOP YOUR DAMN HANDS OFF!
HEY--
WHOA!
KLANGG

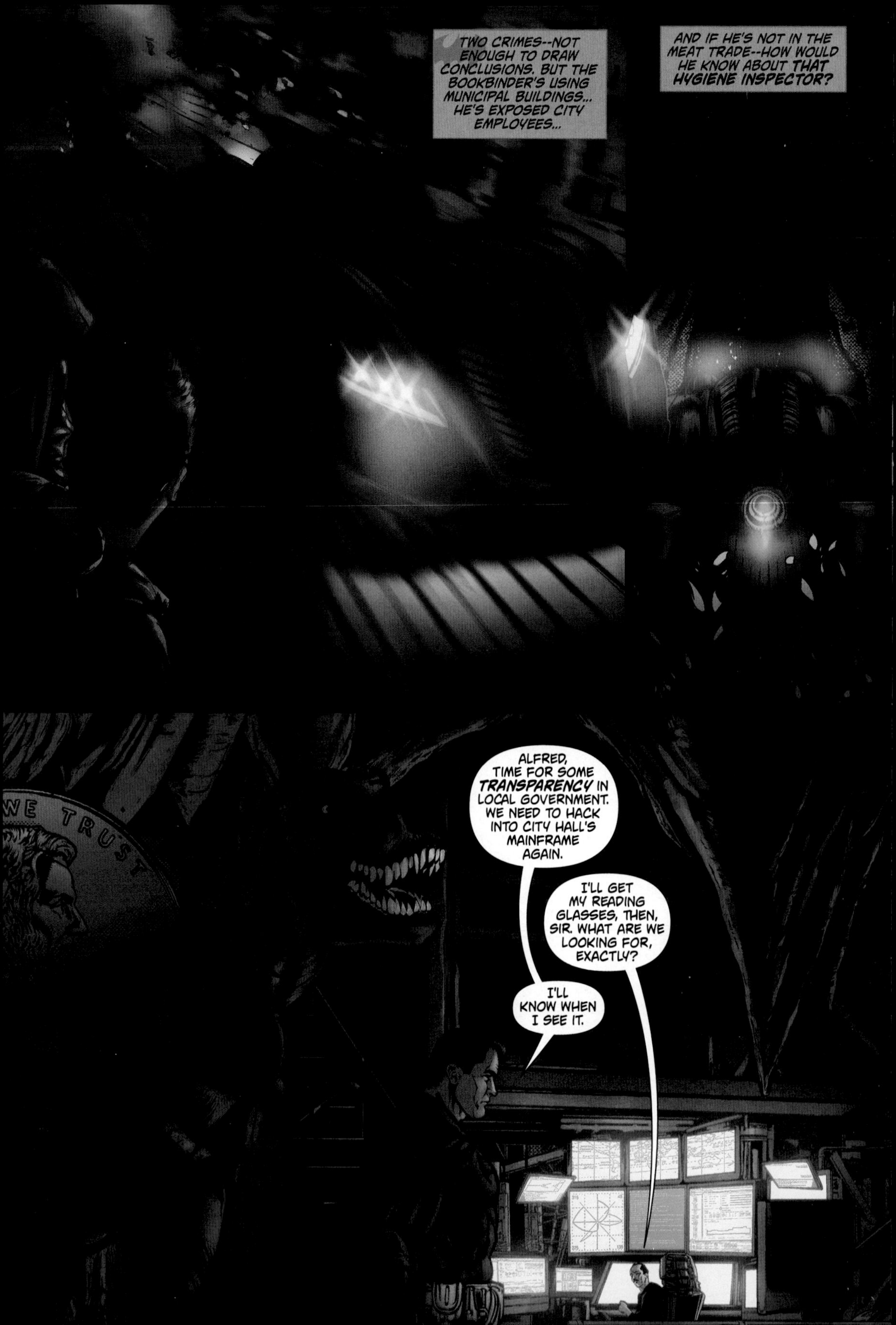
TWO CRIMES--NOT ENOUGH TO DRAW CONCLUSIONS. BUT THE BOOKBINDER'S USING MUNICIPAL BUILDINGS... HE'S EXPOSED CITY EMPLOYEES...
AND IF HE'S NOT IN THE MEAT TRADE--HOW WOULD HE KNOW ABOUT **THAT HYGIENE INSPECTOR?**
WE TRUST
ALFRED, TIME FOR SOME ***TRANSPARENCY*** IN LOCAL GOVERNMENT. WE NEED TO HACK INTO CITY HALL'S MAINFRAME AGAIN.
I'LL GET MY READING GLASSES, THEN, SIR. WHAT ARE WE LOOKING FOR, EXACTLY?
I'LL KNOW WHEN I SEE IT.

"WE FIND FOR MR. MORALES. AND AS HE HAS ALREADY SPENT TWO WEEKS IN CUSTODY, WHICH WOULD HAVE EXCEEDED THE SENTENCE LIKELY TO BE IMPOSED FOR A MINOR BREACH OF THE PEACE, HE IS FREE TO RETURN TO HIS FAMILY."

"AND WHILE SIMILAR DEFENDANTS ARE NOT BEFORE US..."

...WE WOULD URGE THE GOTHAM DISTRICT ATTORNEY AND THE DEPARTMENT OF CORRECTIONS TO RE-EXAMINE THE CASES OF ANYONE CURRENTLY SERVING A SENTENCE IN ARKHAM CITY WHO DOES *NOT* MEET THE CRITERIA FOR DANGEROUS PSYCHIATRIC PRISONERS.

WELL, THE COURT'S RULING IS A MAJOR CHALLENGE TO MAYOR SHARP'S POLICY ON TOUGH JUSTICE. IS HE GOING TO TAKE IT LYING DOWN, JACK?

I THINK HE'S GOING TO HAVE TO TAKE IT ON THE CHIN, VICKI. LOCKING UP GANGSTERS-- FINE. LOCKING UP VOTERS--BAD FOR HIS RATINGS.

AND AFTER RECENT REVELATIONS ABOUT CITY HALL CORRUPTION-- THIS HASN'T BEEN A GOOD MONTH FOR QUINCY SHARP.

GOTHAM

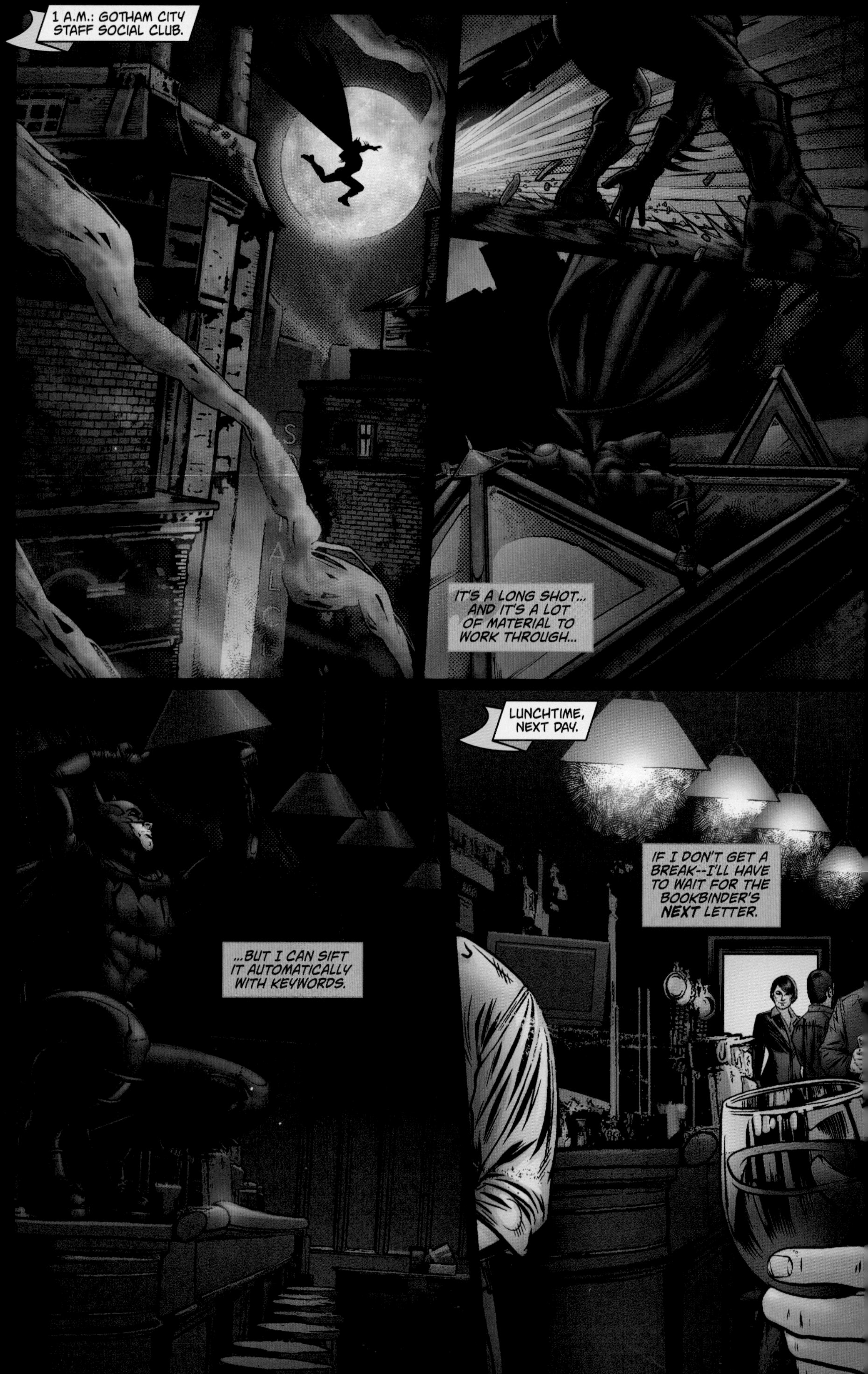
1 A.M.: GOTHAM CITY STAFF SOCIAL CLUB.
IT'S A LONG SHOT... AND IT'S A LOT OF MATERIAL TO WORK THROUGH...
...BUT I CAN SIFT IT AUTOMATICALLY WITH KEYWORDS.
LUNCHTIME, NEXT DAY.
IF I DON'T GET A BREAK--I'LL HAVE TO WAIT FOR THE BOOKBINDER'S NEXT LETTER.

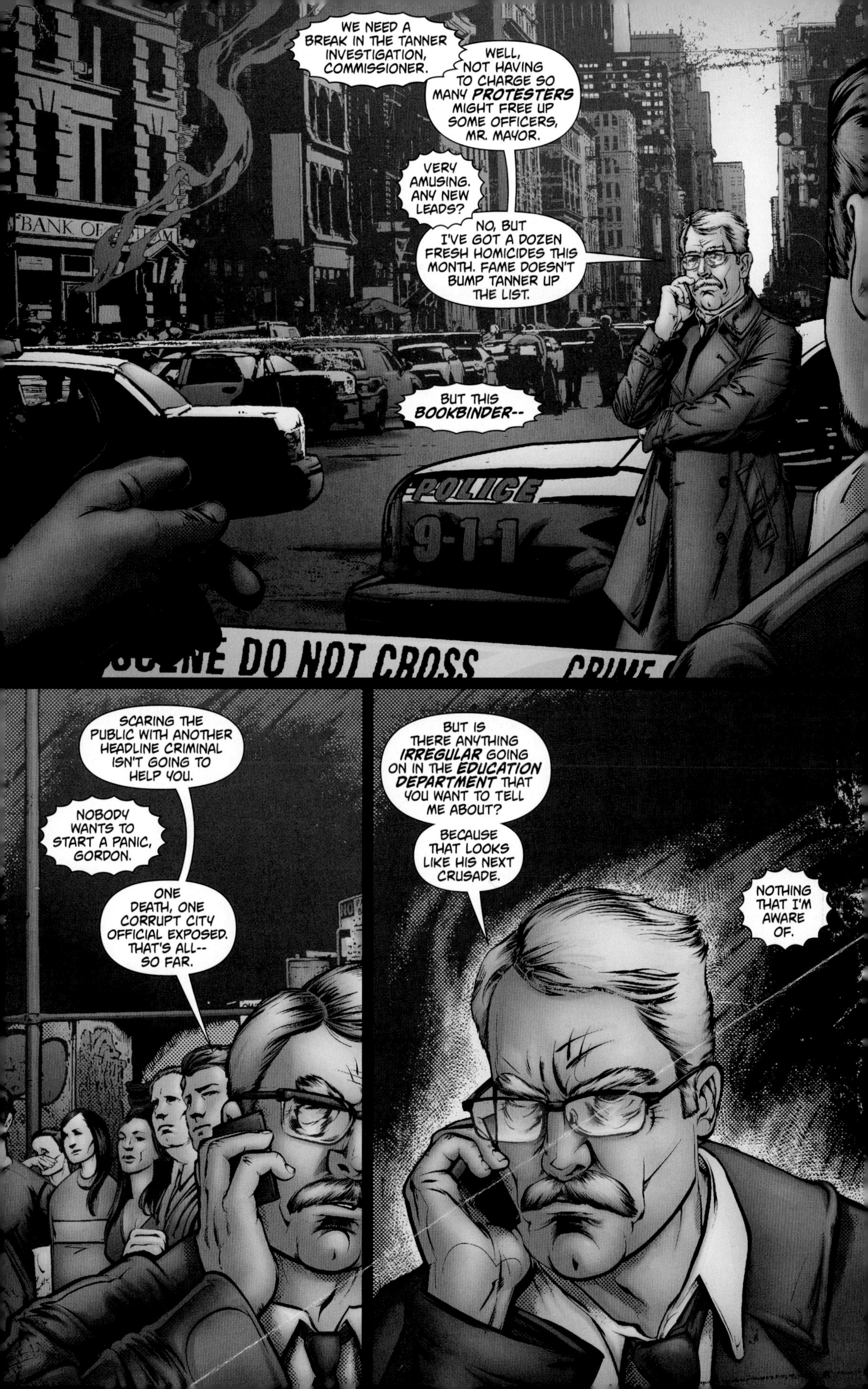
BANK OF G
WE NEED A BREAK IN THE TANNER INVESTIGATION, COMMISSIONER.
WELL, NOT HAVING TO CHARGE SO MANY PROTESTERS MIGHT FREE UP SOME OFFICERS, MR. MAYOR.
VERY AMUSING. ANY NEW LEADS?
NO, BUT I'VE GOT A DOZEN FRESH HOMICIDES THIS MONTH. FAME DOESN'T BUMP TANNER UP THE LIST.
BUT THIS BOOKBINDER--
POLICE
9-1-1
SCENE DO NOT CROSS
CRIME
SCARING THE PUBLIC WITH ANOTHER HEADLINE CRIMINAL ISN'T GOING TO HELP YOU.
NOBODY WANTS TO START A PANIC, GORDON.
ONE DEATH, ONE CORRUPT CITY OFFICIAL EXPOSED. THAT'S ALL-- SO FAR.
BUT IS THERE ANYTHING IRREGULAR GOING ON IN THE EDUCATION DEPARTMENT THAT YOU WANT TO TELL ME ABOUT?
BECAUSE THAT LOOKS LIKE HIS NEXT CRUSADE.
NOTHING THAT I'M AWARE OF.

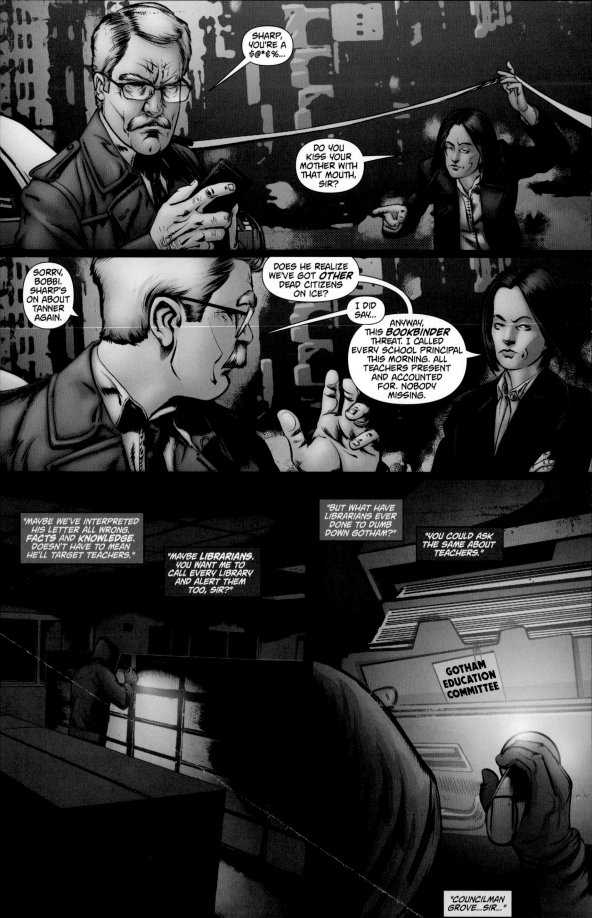

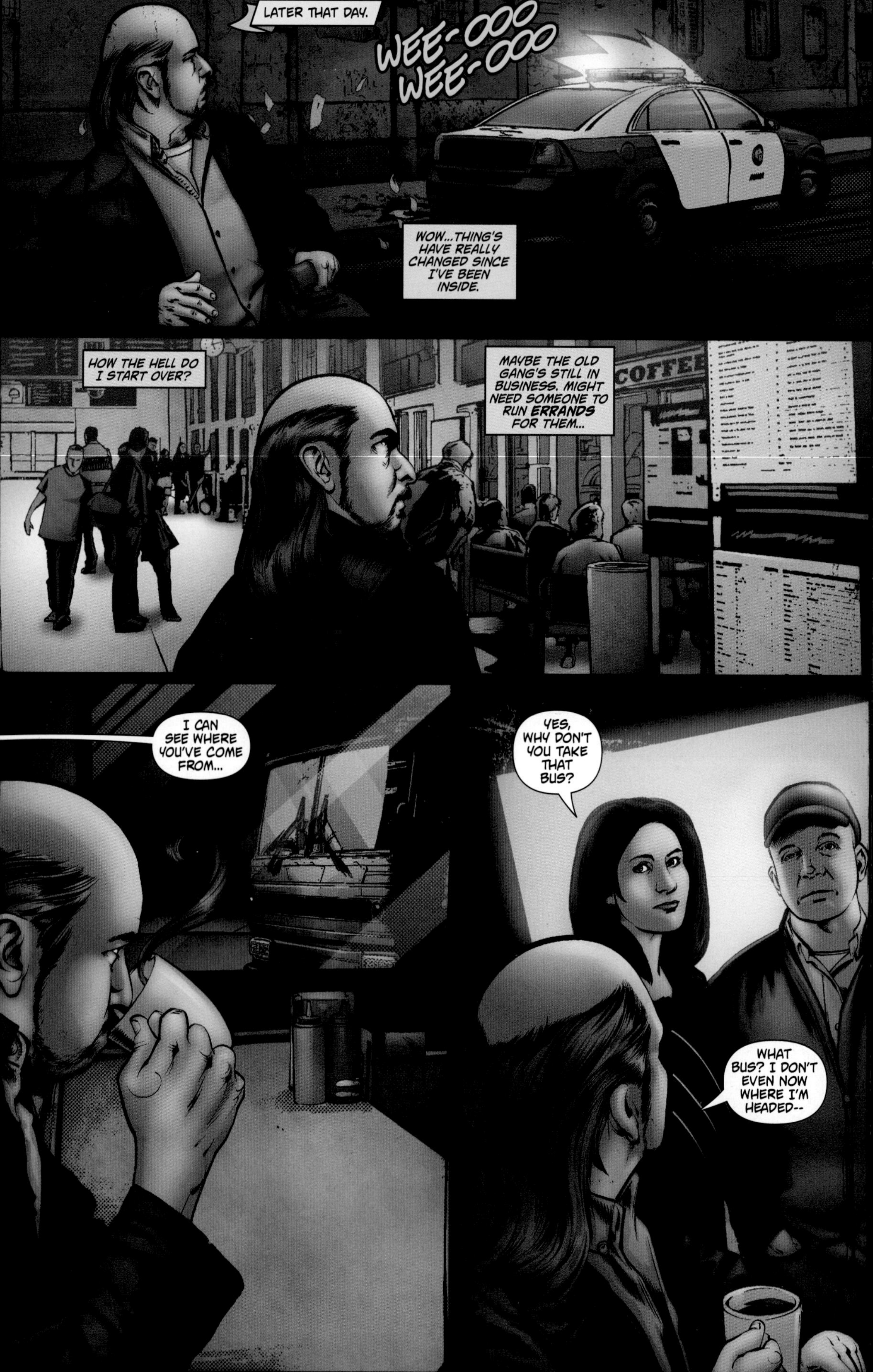
LATER THAT DAY.
WEE-OOO WEE-OOO
WOW...THING'S HAVE REALLY CHANGED SINCE I'VE BEEN INSIDE.
HOW THE HELL DO I START OVER?
MAYBE THE OLD GANG'S STILL IN BUSINESS. MIGHT NEED SOMEONE TO RUN ERRANDS FOR THEM...
COFFEE
I CAN SEE WHERE YOU'VE COME FROM...
YES, WHY DON'T YOU TAKE THAT BUS?
WHAT BUS? I DON'T EVEN NOW WHERE I'M HEADED--

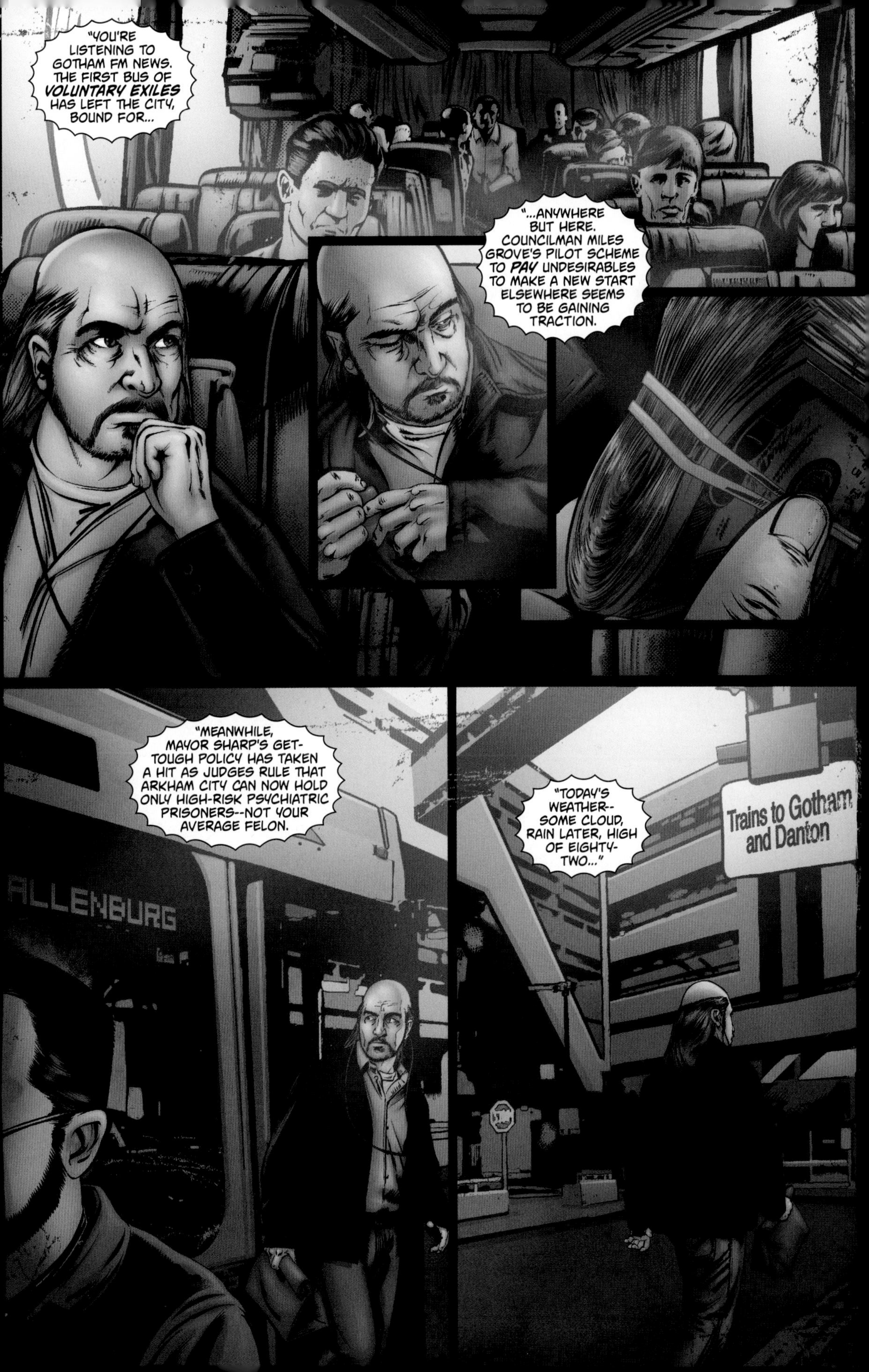
"YOU'RE LISTENING TO GOTHAM FM NEWS. THE FIRST BUS OF VOLUNTARY EXILES HAS LEFT THE CITY, BOUND FOR...
"...ANYWHERE BUT HERE. COUNCILMAN MILES GROVE'S PILOT SCHEME TO PAY UNDESIRABLES TO MAKE A NEW START ELSEWHERE SEEMS TO BE GAINING TRACTION.
"MEANWHILE, MAYOR SHARP'S GET-TOUGH POLICY HAS TAKEN A HIT AS JUDGES RULE THAT ARKHAM CITY CAN NOW HOLD ONLY HIGH-RISK PSYCHIATRIC PRISONERS--NOT YOUR AVERAGE FELON.
ALLENBURG
"TODAY'S WEATHER--SOME CLOUD, RAIN LATER, HIGH OF EIGHTY-TWO..."
Trains to Gotham and Danton

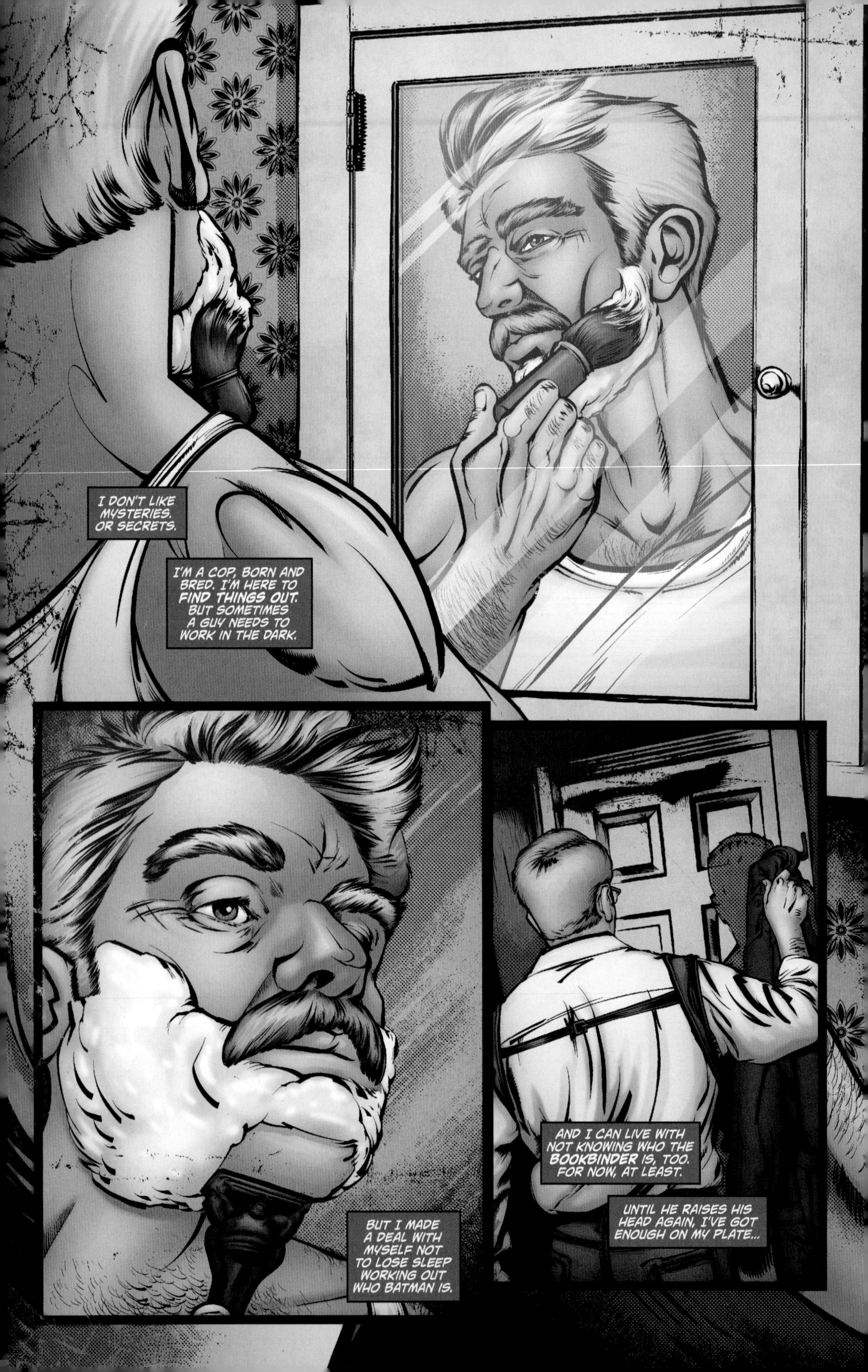
I DON'T LIKE MYSTERIES. OR SECRETS.
I'M A COP, BORN AND BRED. I'M HERE TO FIND THINGS OUT. BUT SOMETIMES A GUY NEEDS TO WORK IN THE DARK.
BUT I MADE A DEAL WITH MYSELF NOT TO LOSE SLEEP WORKING OUT WHO BATMAN IS.
AND I CAN LIVE WITH NOT KNOWING WHO THE BOOKBINDER IS, TOO. FOR NOW, AT LEAST.
UNTIL HE RAISES HIS HEAD AGAIN, I'VE GOT ENOUGH ON MY PLATE...

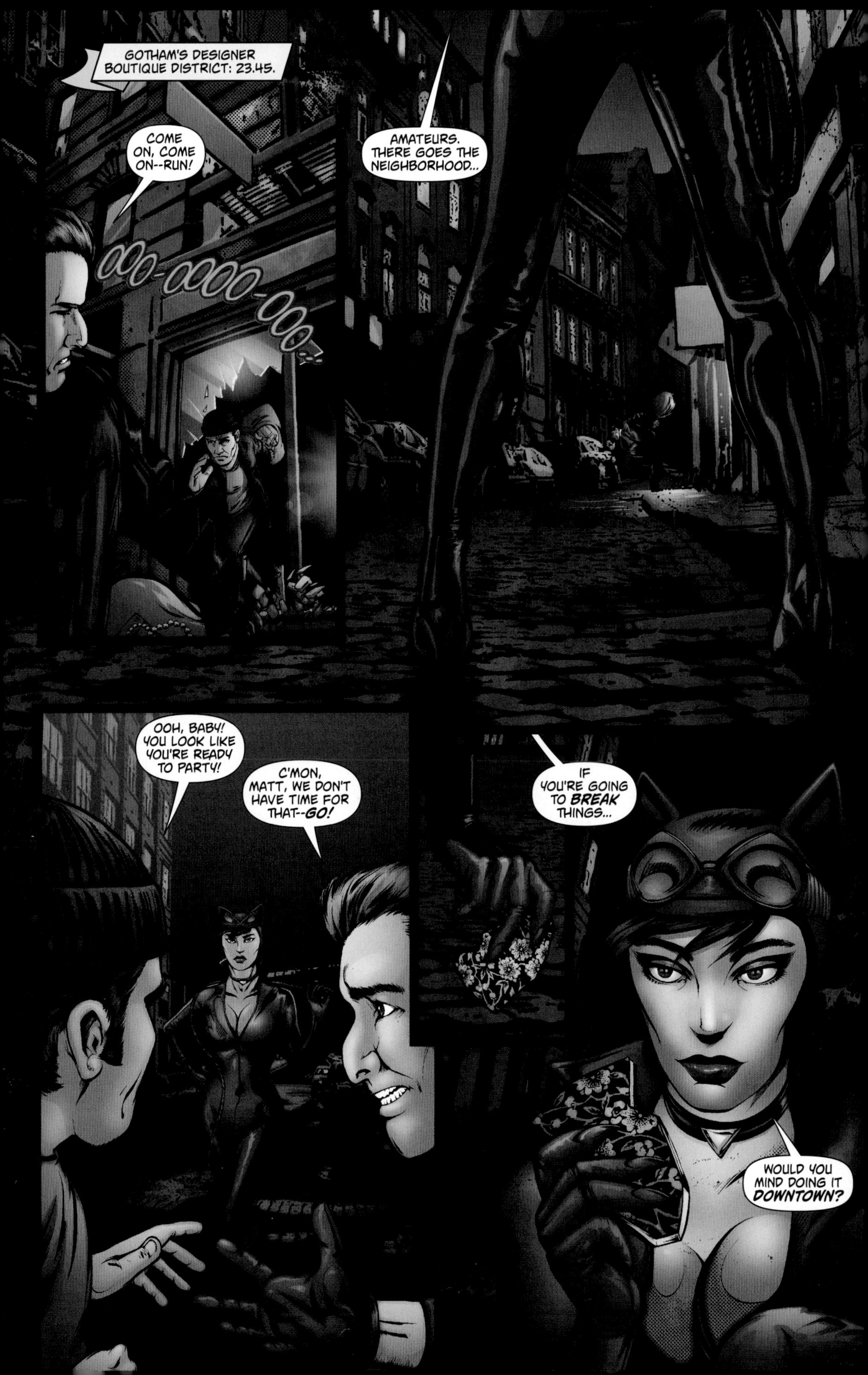
GOTHAM'S DESIGNER BOUTIQUE DISTRICT: 23.45.
COME ON, COME ON--RUN!
OOO-OOOO-OOO-OO
AMATEURS. THERE GOES THE NEIGHBORHOOD...
OOH, BABY! YOU LOOK LIKE YOU'RE READY TO PARTY!
C'MON, MATT, WE DON'T HAVE TIME FOR THAT--GO!
IF YOU'RE GOING TO BREAK THINGS...
WOULD YOU MIND DOING IT DOWNTOWN?

HE'LL ESCALATE EVENTUALLY. IT'LL GET WORSE.
AWW, HE'S INTRIGUED YOU! YOU DO LOVE A CHALLENGE.
IT'S OKAY, I DO TOO. I'LL SEE WHAT I CAN HUNT DOWN...
BUT WHAT'S IN IT FOR ME?
I WON'T TURN YOU IN.
OH, YOU KNOW YOU'LL NEVER DO THAT...
BECAUSE I DON'T KILL PEOPLE.
I JUST BREAK A FEW HEARTS.

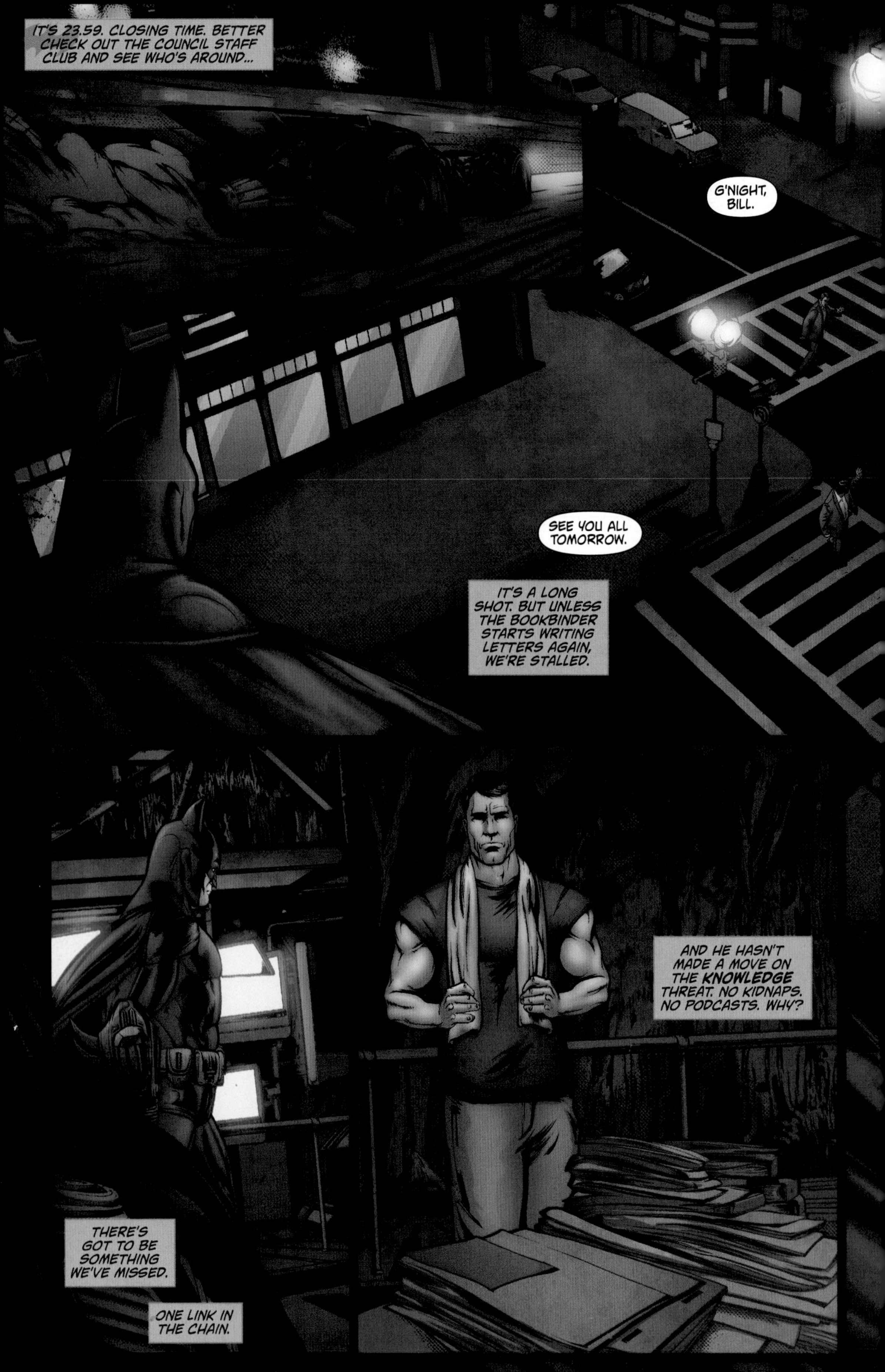
IT'S 23.59. CLOSING TIME. BETTER CHECK OUT THE COUNCIL STAFF CLUB AND SEE WHO'S AROUND...
G'NIGHT, BILL.
SEE YOU ALL TOMORROW.
IT'S A LONG SHOT. BUT UNLESS THE BOOKBINDER STARTS WRITING LETTERS AGAIN, WE'RE STALLED.
AND HE HASN'T MADE A MOVE ON THE KNOWLEDGE THREAT. NO KIDNAPS. NO PODCASTS. WHY?
THERE'S GOT TO BE SOMETHING WE'VE MISSED.
ONE LINK IN THE CHAIN.

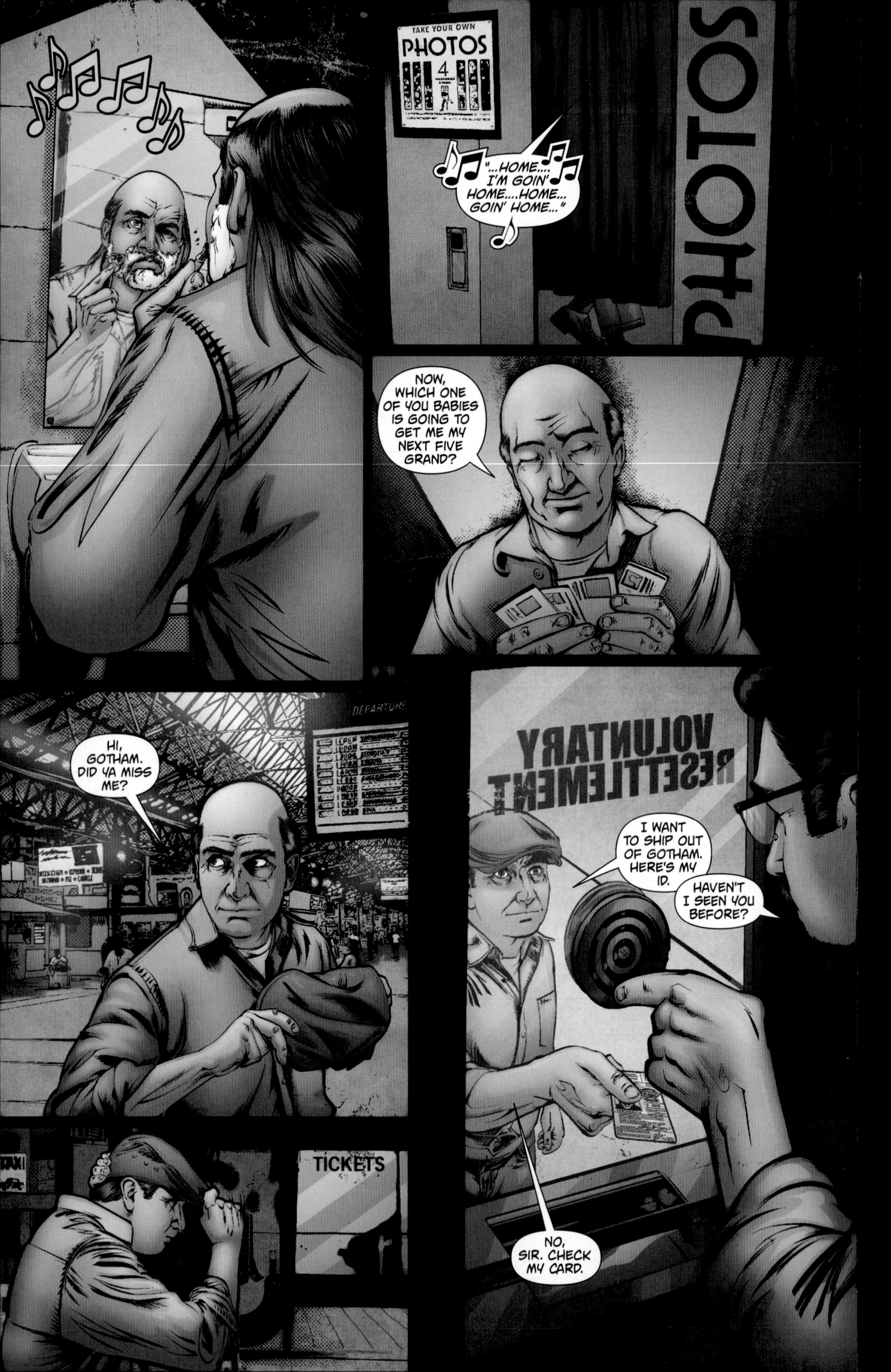
TAKE YOUR OWN
PHOTOS
4
"...HOME.... I'M GOIN' HOME....HOME... GOIN' HOME..."
PHOTOS
NOW, WHICH ONE OF YOU BABIES IS GOING TO GET ME MY NEXT FIVE GRAND?
DEPARTURE
HI, GOTHAM. DID YA MISS ME?
VOLUNTARY RESETTLEMENT
I WANT TO SHIP OUT OF GOTHAM. HERE'S MY ID.
HAVEN'T I SEEN YOU BEFORE?
TAXI
TICKETS
NO, SIR. CHECK MY CARD.

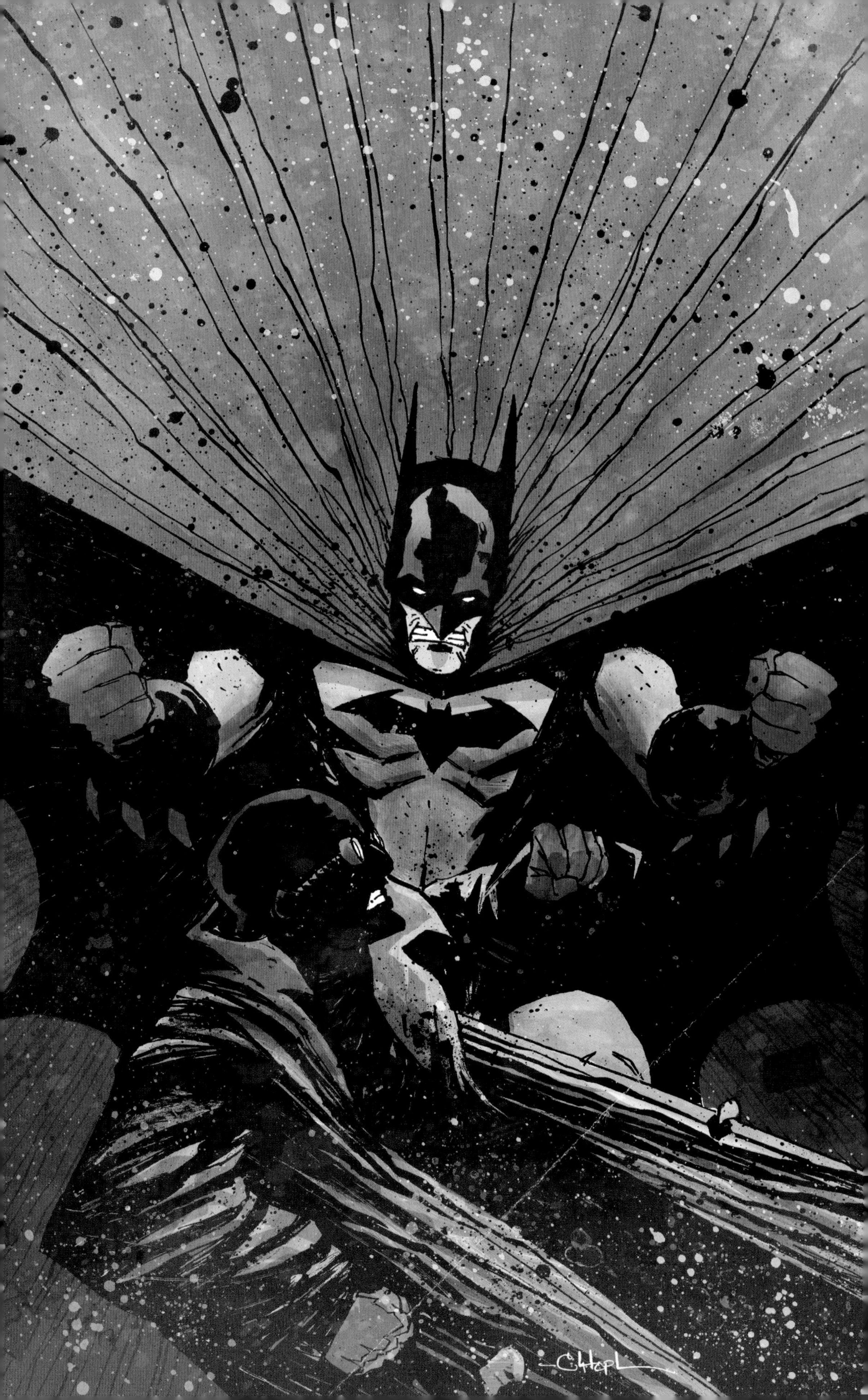

WELCOME
TO THE SLOUGH OF DESPOND
PART FIVE

WRITTEN BY: KAREN TRAVISS
ART BY: CHRISTIAN DUCE (PAGES 1-20)
& BEN LOBEL (PAGES 21-30)
COLORS BY: ALEJANDRO SANCHEZ
LETTERS BY: TRAVIS LANHAM
COVER BY: CHRIS MITTEN

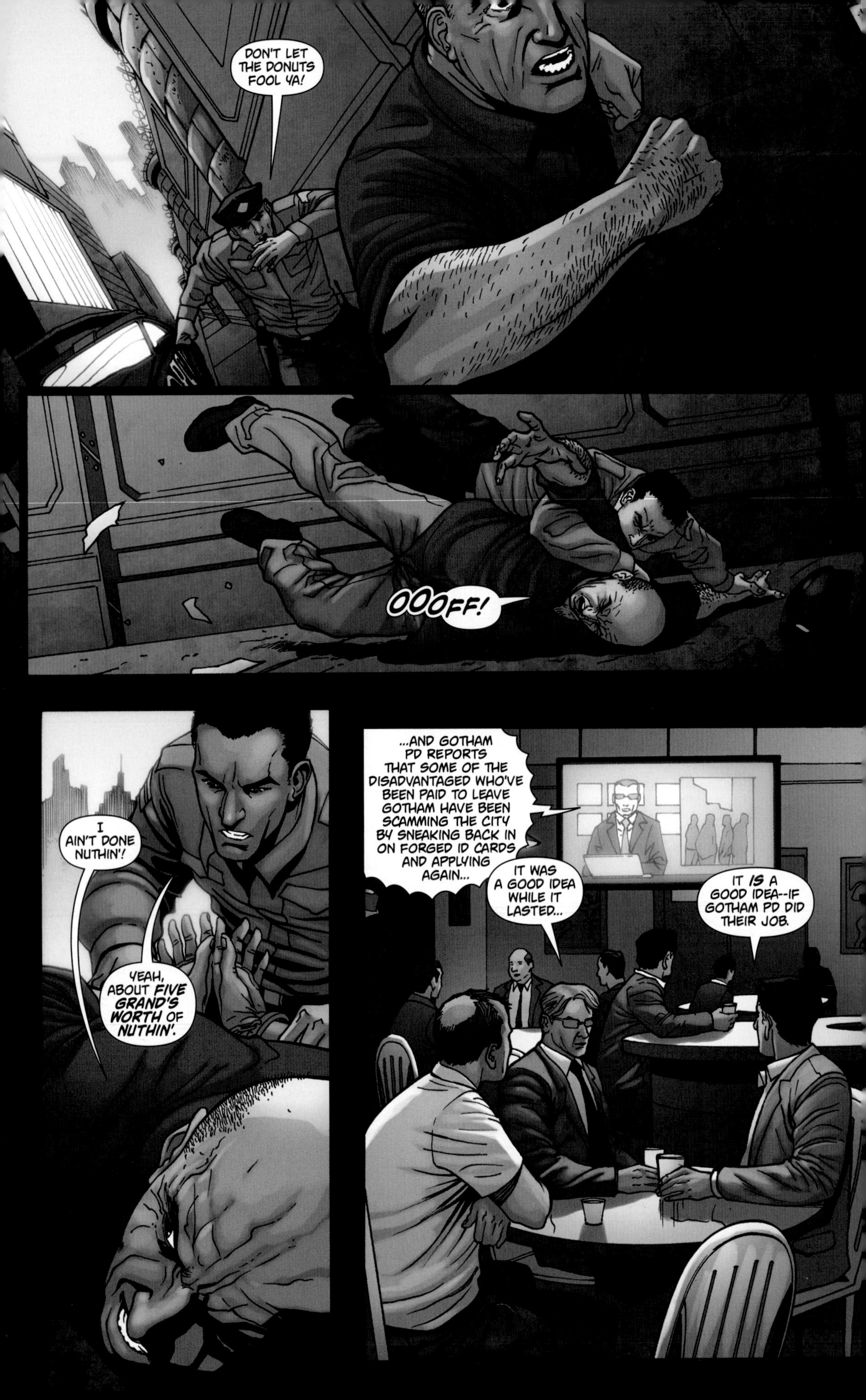
DON'T LET THE DONUTS FOOL YA!
OOOFF!
I AIN'T DONE NUTHIN'!
YEAH, ABOUT FIVE GRAND'S WORTH OF NUTHIN'.
...AND GOTHAM PD REPORTS THAT SOME OF THE DISADVANTAGED WHO'VE BEEN PAID TO LEAVE GOTHAM HAVE BEEN SCAMMING THE CITY BY SNEAKING BACK IN ON FORGED ID CARDS AND APPLYING AGAIN...
IT WAS A GOOD IDEA WHILE IT LASTED...
IT IS A GOOD IDEA--IF GOTHAM PD DID THEIR JOB.

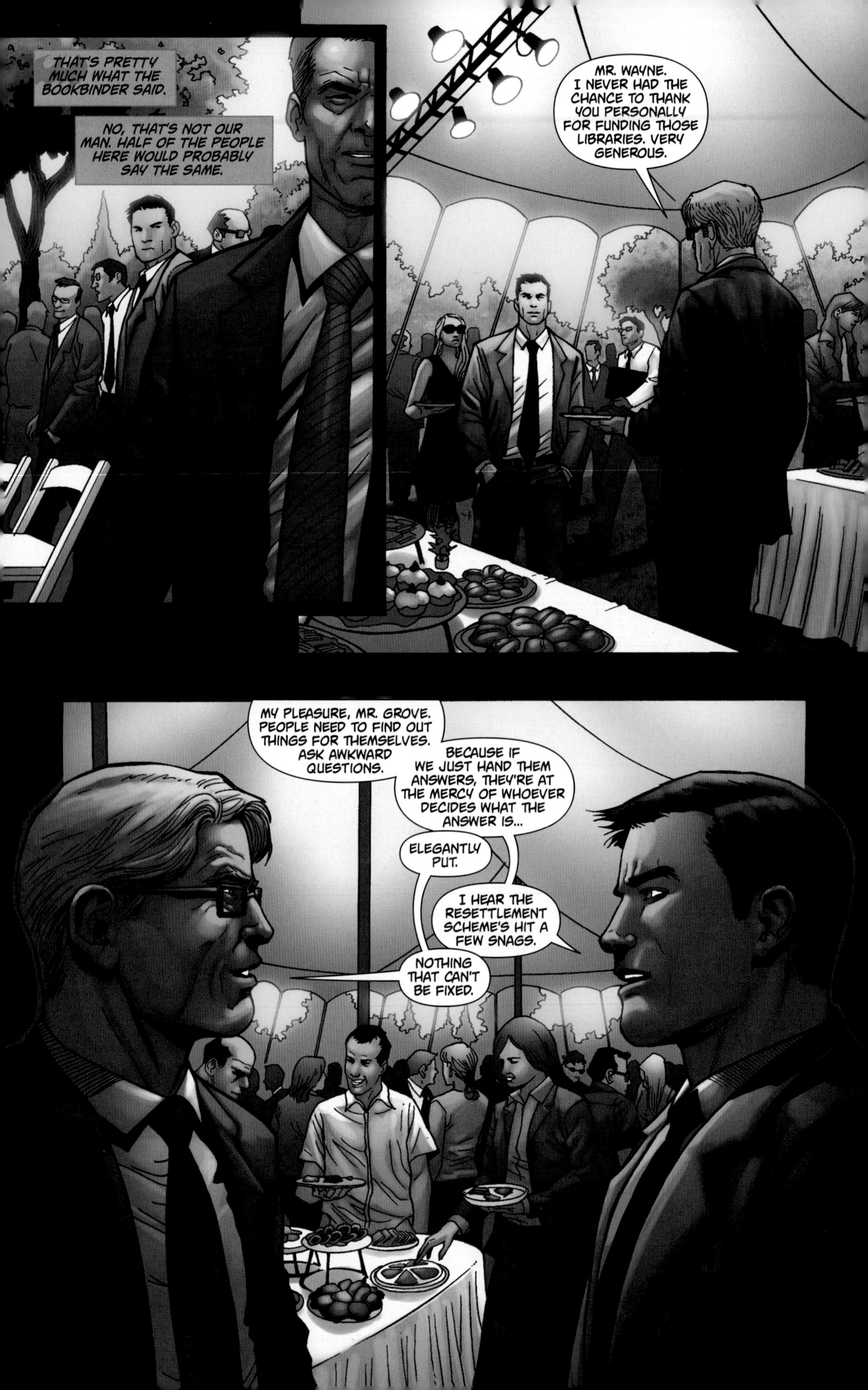
THAT'S PRETTY MUCH WHAT THE BOOKBINDER SAID.
NO, THAT'S NOT OUR MAN. HALF OF THE PEOPLE HERE WOULD PROBABLY SAY THE SAME.
MR. WAYNE. I NEVER HAD THE CHANCE TO THANK YOU PERSONALLY FOR FUNDING THOSE LIBRARIES. VERY GENEROUS.
MY PLEASURE, MR. GROVE. PEOPLE NEED TO FIND OUT THINGS FOR THEMSELVES. ASK AWKWARD QUESTIONS.
BECAUSE IF WE JUST HAND THEM ANSWERS, THEY'RE AT THE MERCY OF WHOEVER DECIDES WHAT THE ANSWER IS...
ELEGANTLY PUT.
I HEAR THE RESETTLEMENT SCHEME'S HIT A FEW SNAGS.
NOTHING THAT CAN'T BE FIXED.

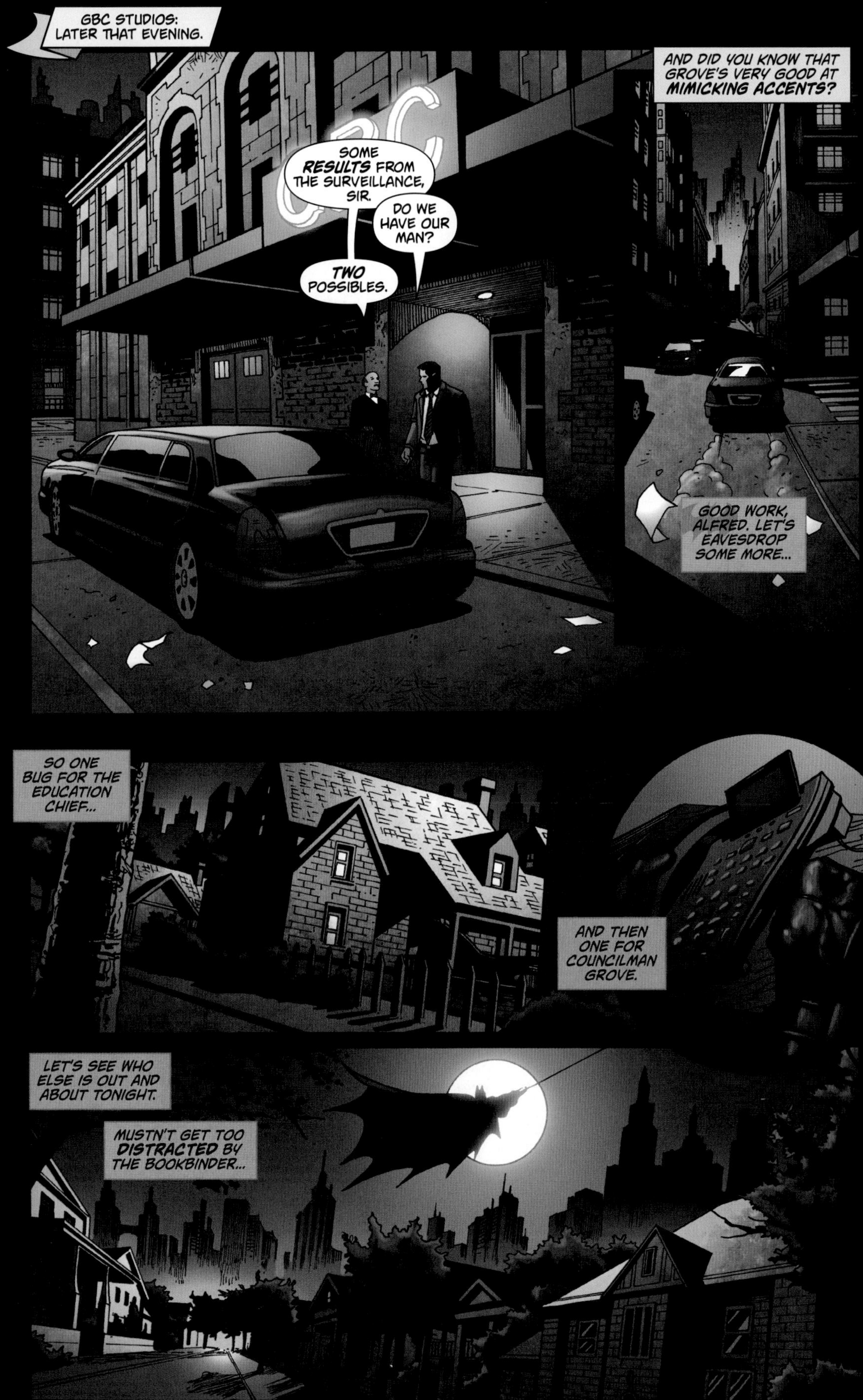
GBC STUDIOS: LATER THAT EVENING.
SOME RESULTS FROM THE SURVEILLANCE, SIR.
DO WE HAVE OUR MAN?
TWO POSSIBLES.
AND DID YOU KNOW THAT GROVE'S VERY GOOD AT MIMICKING ACCENTS?
GOOD WORK, ALFRED. LET'S EAVESDROP SOME MORE...
SO ONE BUG FOR THE EDUCATION CHIEF...
AND THEN ONE FOR COUNCILMAN GROVE.
LET'S SEE WHO ELSE IS OUT AND ABOUT TONIGHT.
MUSTN'T GET TOO DISTRACTED BY THE BOOKBINDER...

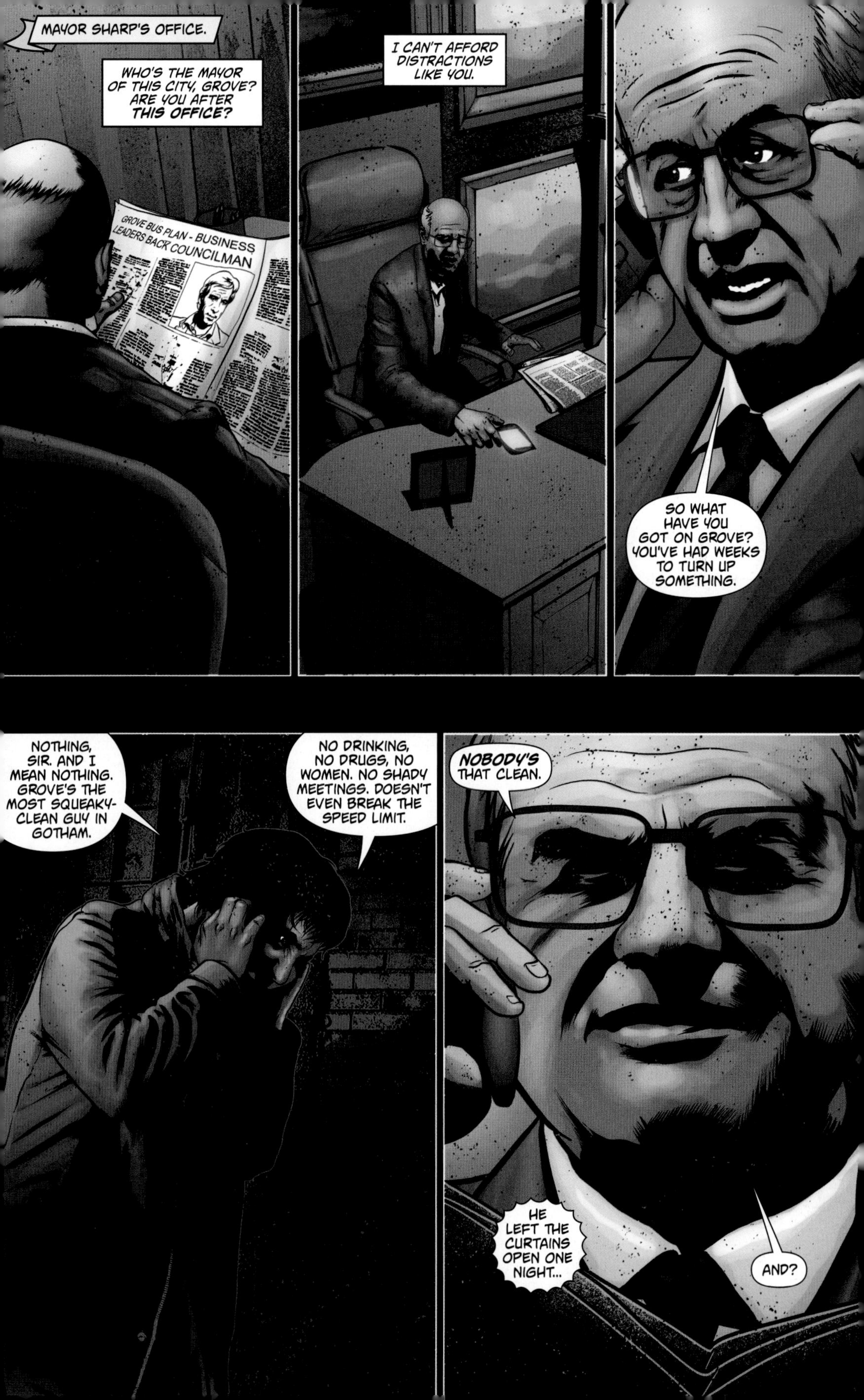
MAYOR SHARP'S OFFICE.
WHO'S THE MAYOR OF THIS CITY, GROVE? ARE YOU AFTER **THIS OFFICE?**
GROVE BUS PLAN - BUSINESS LEADERS BACK COUNCILMAN
I CAN'T AFFORD DISTRACTIONS LIKE YOU.
SO WHAT HAVE YOU GOT ON GROVE? YOU'VE HAD WEEKS TO TURN UP SOMETHING.
NOTHING, SIR. AND I MEAN NOTHING. GROVE'S THE MOST SQUEAKY-CLEAN GUY IN GOTHAM.
NO DRINKING, NO DRUGS, NO WOMEN. NO SHADY MEETINGS. DOESN'T EVEN BREAK THE SPEED LIMIT.
NOBODY'S THAT CLEAN.
HE LEFT THE CURTAINS OPEN ONE NIGHT...
AND?

WELL, I GOT A PICTURE ON THE LONG LENS.

BOOKS. LOTS OF BOOKS. HE *READS* A LOT. AND NEVER LEAVES THE HOUSE AT NIGHT.

COUNCILMAN GROVE'S HOUSE.

STICK WITH HIM.

OKAY, SIR...

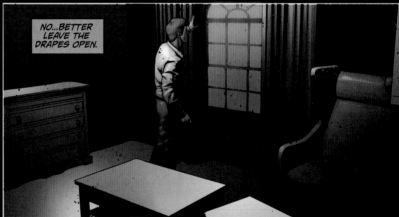

NO...BETTER LEAVE THE DRAPES OPEN.

IF THAT UNFORTUNATE MAN IS GOING TO SPEND ANOTHER NIGHT WATCHING ME...

...I'D BETTER GIVE HIM SOME PICTURES TO TAKE BACK TO SHARP.

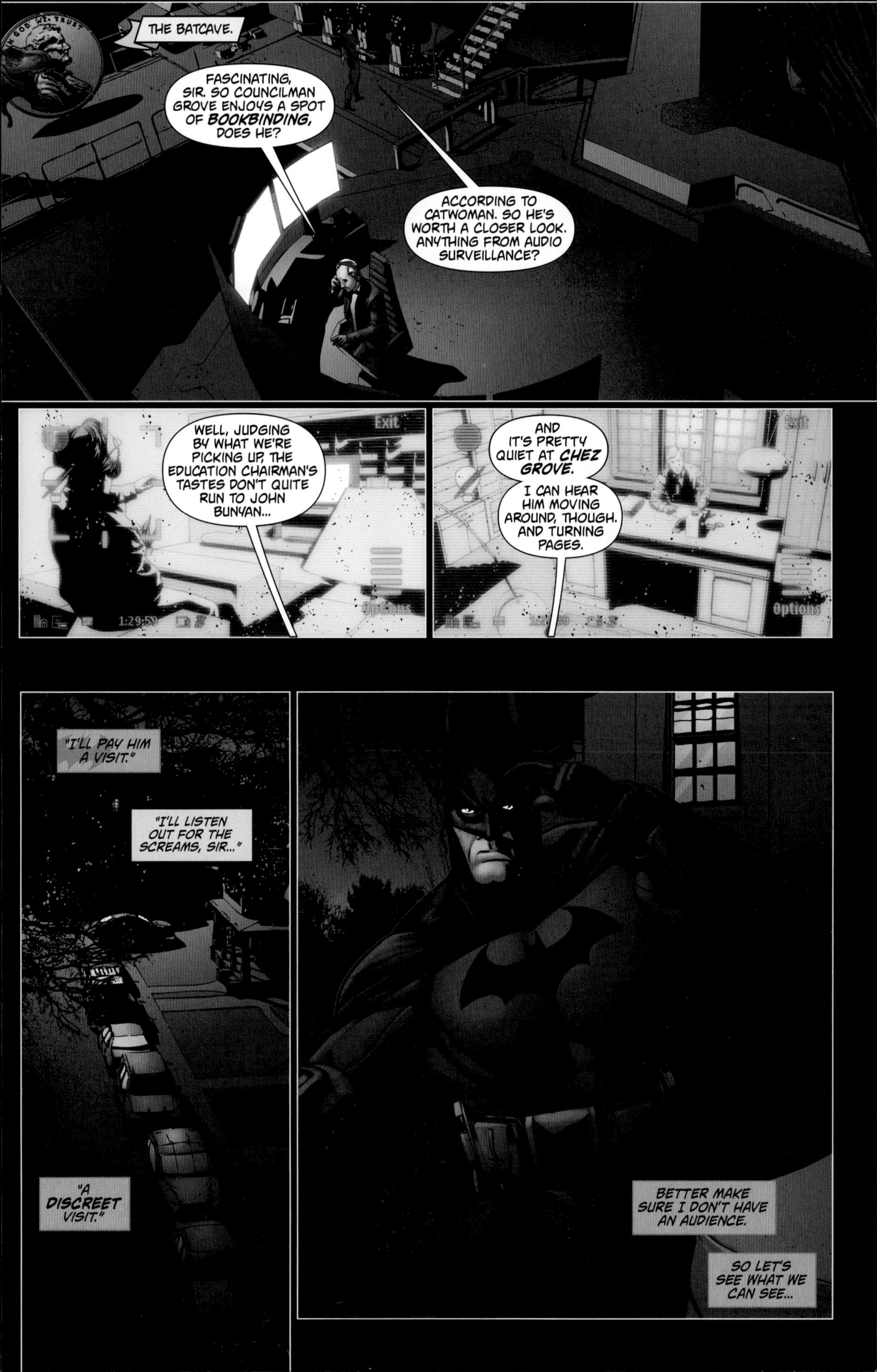

THE BATCAVE.
FASCINATING, SIR. SO COUNCILMAN GROVE ENJOYS A SPOT OF BOOKBINDING, DOES HE?
ACCORDING TO CATWOMAN. SO HE'S WORTH A CLOSER LOOK. ANYTHING FROM AUDIO SURVEILLANCE?
WELL, JUDGING BY WHAT WE'RE PICKING UP, THE EDUCATION CHAIRMAN'S TASTES DON'T QUITE RUN TO JOHN BUNYAN...
Exit
1:29:59
Options
AND IT'S PRETTY QUIET AT CHEZ GROVE.
I CAN HEAR HIM MOVING AROUND, THOUGH. AND TURNING PAGES.
Exit
Options
"I'LL PAY HIM A VISIT."
"I'LL LISTEN OUT FOR THE SCREAMS, SIR..."
"A DISCREET VISIT."
BETTER MAKE SURE I DON'T HAVE AN AUDIENCE.
SO LET'S SEE WHAT WE CAN SEE...

LOOKS LIKE HE'S WATCHING GROVE'S HOUSE.

NOT GOTHAM PD, EITHER.

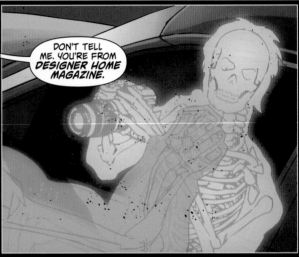

DON'T TELL ME. YOU'RE FROM *DESIGNER HOME MAGAZINE*.

YOU NEED TO USE THE FLASH AT NIGHT, BY THE WAY.

WHAT-- WHAT DO YOU WANT?

WHO, WHY, HOW MUCH...THE USUAL.

UNH-- COUNCILMAN GROVE--

LOOKING FOR DIRT?

CAN'T SAY...

NO NEED. AND *I* WON'T TELL THE MAYOR IF *YOU* DON'T.

NOW GET LOST.

KLIK

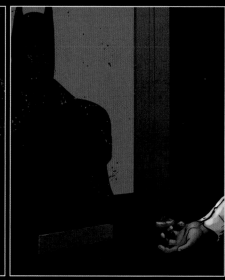

SO--A CELLAR.
DO I SLIP IN NOW,
OR WAIT FOR HIM
TO COME BACK?

30 MINUTES LATER.

MUST BE A VERY BIG CELLAR...

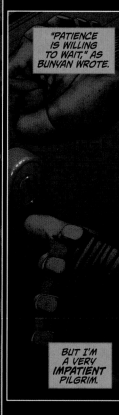

"PATIENCE IS WILLING TO WAIT," AS BUNYAN WROTE.

BUT I'M A VERY IMPATIENT PILGRIM.

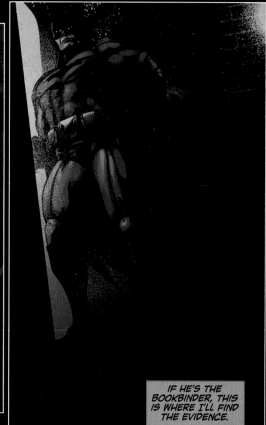

IF HE'S THE BOOKBINDER, THIS IS WHERE I'LL FIND THE EVIDENCE.

WHERE DID HE GO?

CAN'T WAIT TO FIND OUT WHERE THIS LEADS.

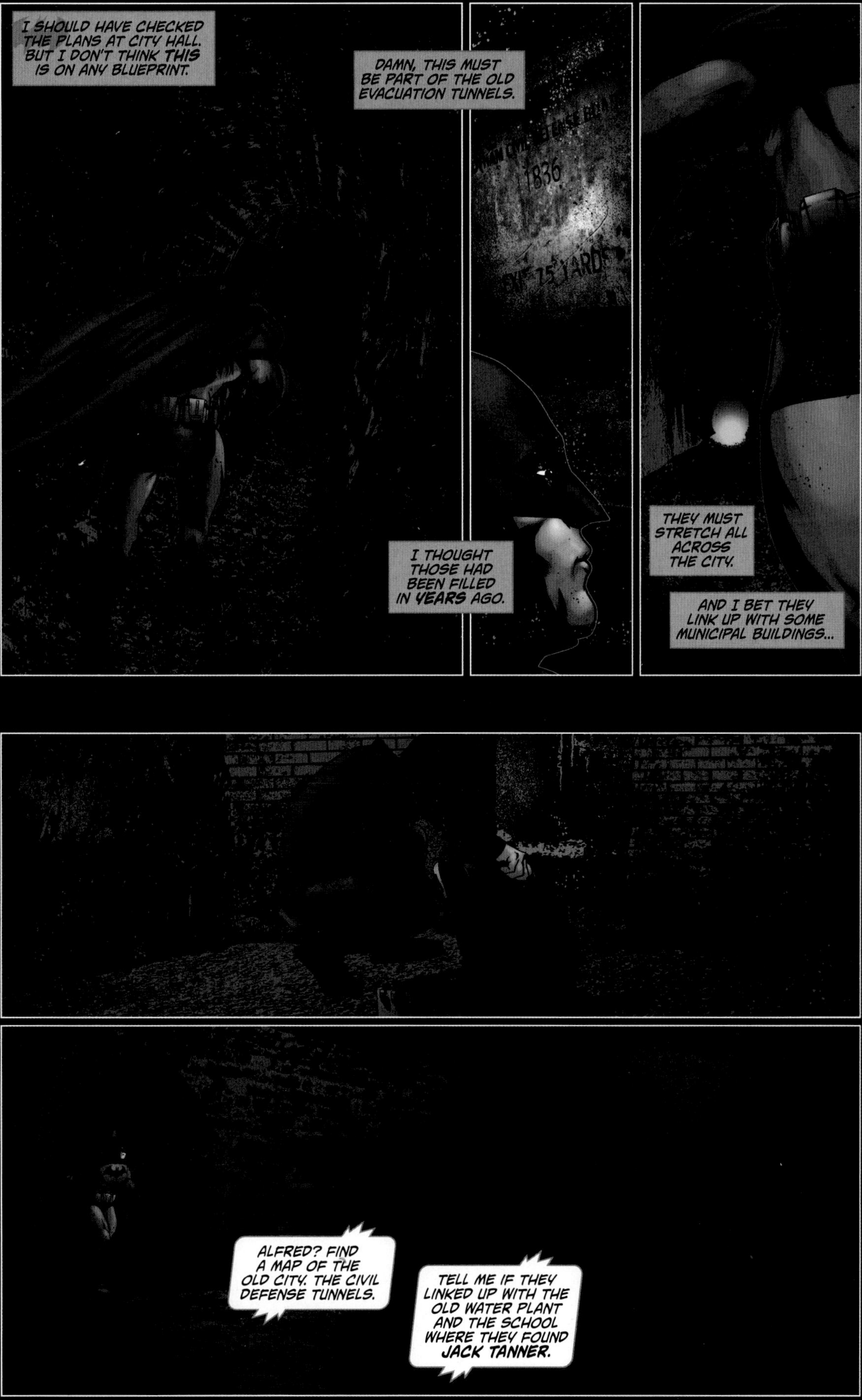
I SHOULD HAVE CHECKED THE PLANS AT CITY HALL. BUT I DON'T THINK THIS IS ON ANY BLUEPRINT.
DAMN, THIS MUST BE PART OF THE OLD EVACUATION TUNNELS.
I THOUGHT THOSE HAD BEEN FILLED IN YEARS AGO.
1836
THEY MUST STRETCH ALL ACROSS THE CITY.
AND I BET THEY LINK UP WITH SOME MUNICIPAL BUILDINGS...
ALFRED? FIND A MAP OF THE OLD CITY. THE CIVIL DEFENSE TUNNELS.
TELL ME IF THEY LINKED UP WITH THE OLD WATER PLANT AND THE SCHOOL WHERE THEY FOUND JACK TANNER.

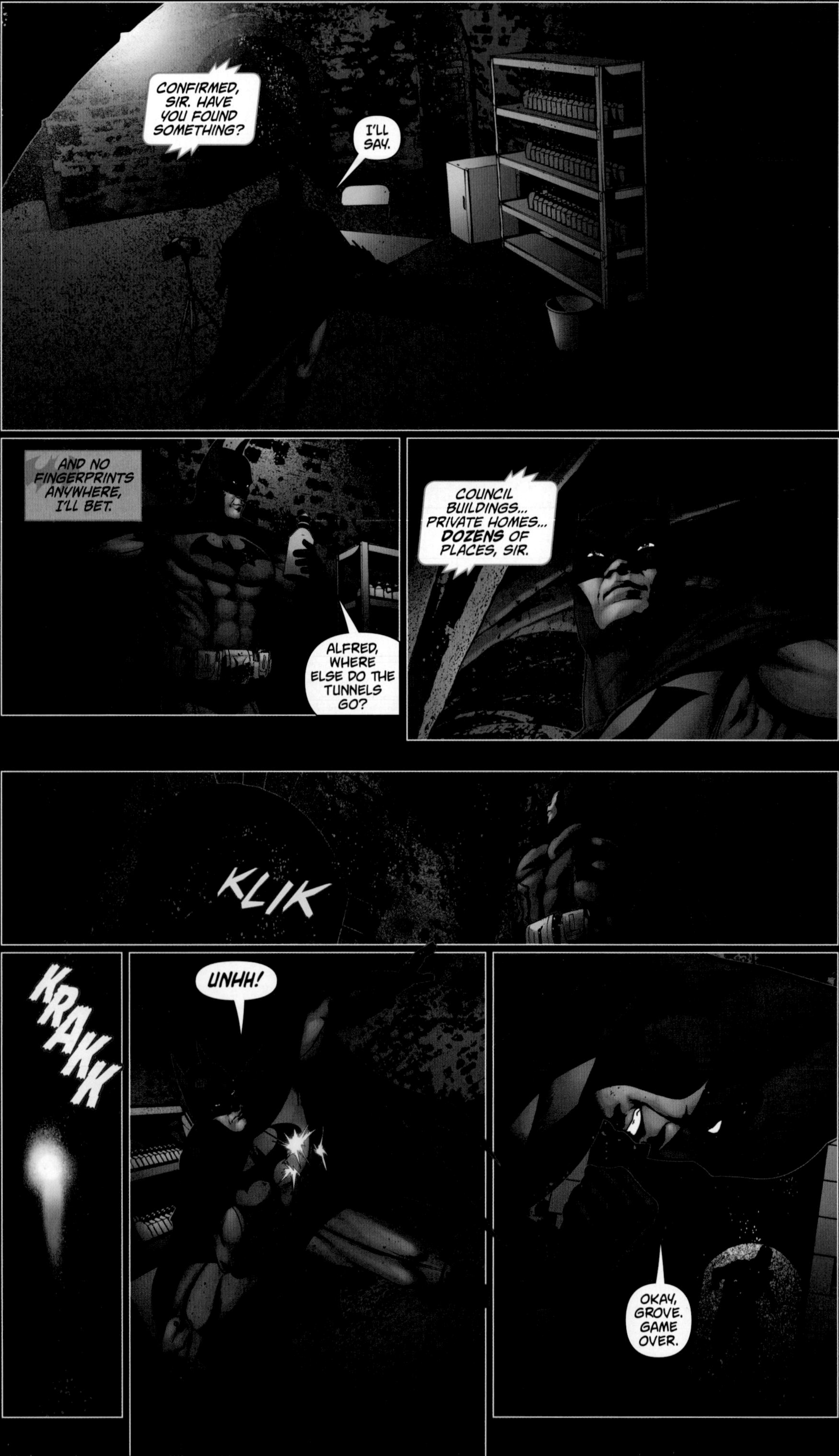

CONFIRMED, SIR. HAVE YOU FOUND SOMETHING?
I'LL SAY.
AND NO FINGERPRINTS ANYWHERE, I'LL BET.
ALFRED, WHERE ELSE DO THE TUNNELS GO?
COUNCIL BUILDINGS... PRIVATE HOMES... DOZENS OF PLACES, SIR.
KLIK
KRAKK
UNHH!
OKAY, GROVE. GAME OVER.

UNH-- **DAMN!**

KRAKK

ARMOR OR NO ARMOR-- THAT **HURTS**.

AND I HAVE NO IDEA WHERE I AM NOW.

HE CAN'T BE THAT FAR AHEAD OF ME.

HE MUST KNOW ANOTHER ROUTE. HOW THE HELL DID HE GET THERE?

GOOD GRIEF. **BATMAN!** THIS IS MOST UNEXPECTED.

I'LL BET. BEEN **RUSHING AROUND?**

AN OCCASIONAL SIN. AT LEAST IT'S HEALTHY.

UNLIKE BURGERS... BOOKBINDER.

BOOKBINDER?

YOU **KNOW** WHAT I'M TALKING ABOUT.

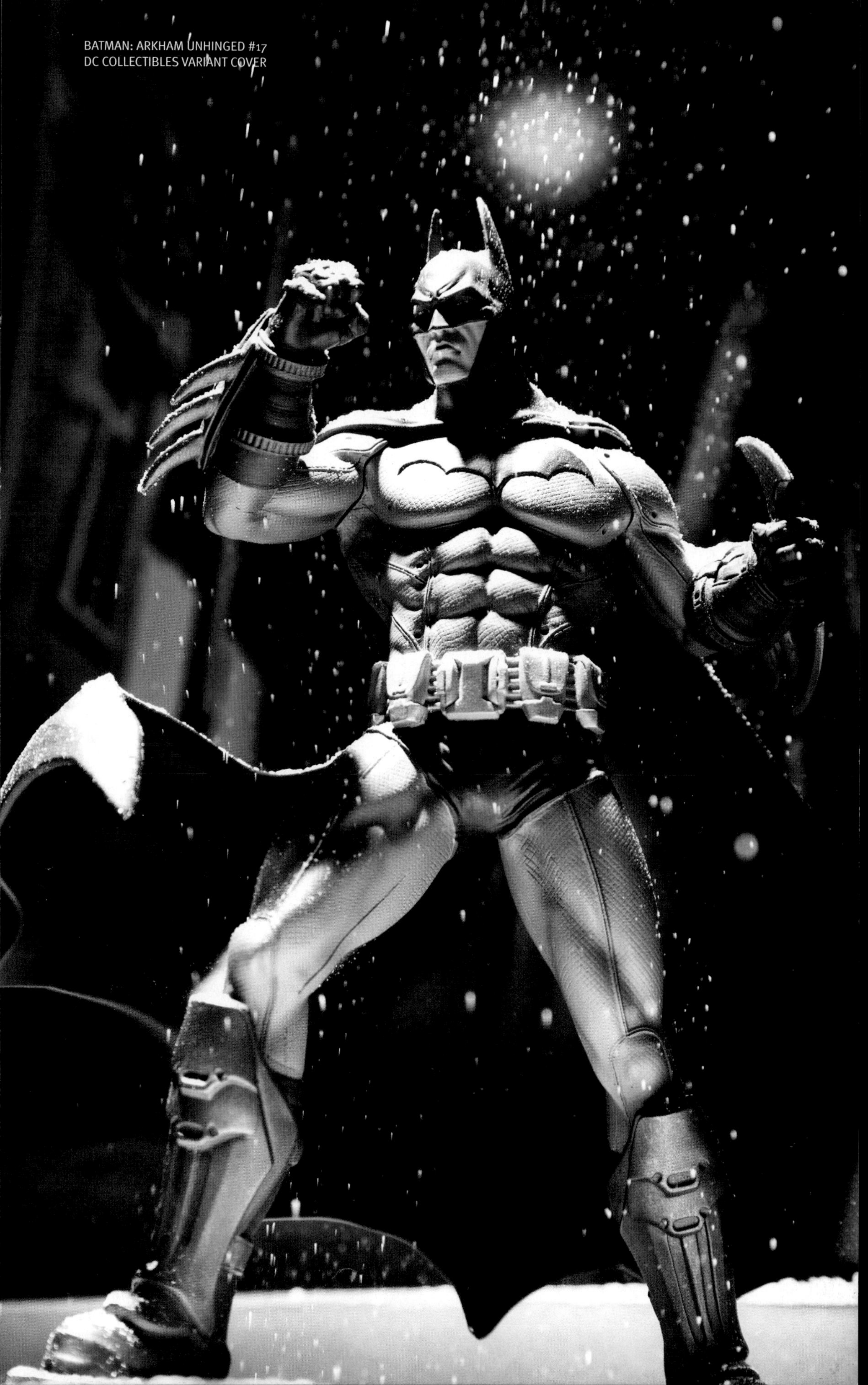

BATMAN: ARKHAM UNHINGED #17
DC COLLECTIBLES VARIANT COVER

BATMAN: ARKHAM UNHINGED #18
DC COLLECTIBLES VARIANT COVER

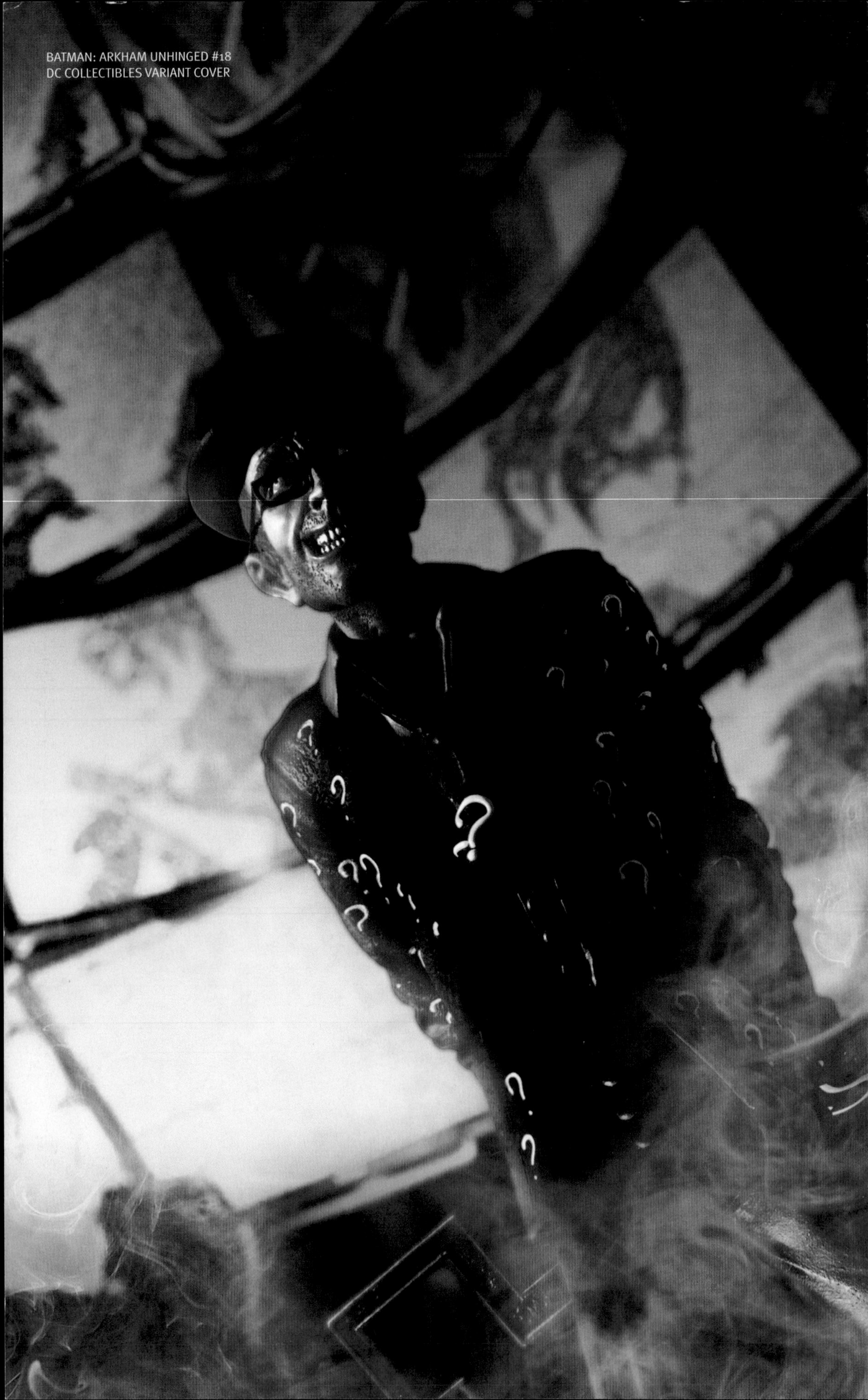